AFRO-CHRISTIAN RELIGION AND HEALING IN SOUTHERN AFRICA

Edited by
G.C. Oosthuizen
S.D. Edwards
W.H. Wessels
I. Hexham

African Studies
Volume 8

The Edwin Mellen Press
Lewiston/Queenston/Lampeter

Library of Congress Cataloging-in-Publication Data

Afro-Christian religion and healing in southern Africa / edited by
    G.C. Oosthuizen ... (et al.).
        p. cm. -- (African studies ; v. 8)
    Bibliography: p.
    ISBN 0-88946-282-8
    1. Spiritual healing--Africa, Southern. 2. Blacks--Africa,
Southern--Religion. 3. Independent churches--Africa, Southern-
-Doctrines. 4. Zionist churches (Africa)--Doctrines. 5. Africa,
Southern--Church history. 6. Blacks--Africa, Southern--Medicine.
I. Oosthuizen, G.C. (Gerhardus Cornelis). II. Series: African
studies (Lewiston, N.Y.) ; v. 8
BT732.5.A34   1988
234' .13--dc19

88-8894
CIP

This is volume 8 in the continuing series
African Studies
Volume 8 ISBN 0-88946-282-8
SGTH Series ISBN 0-88946-175-9

A CIP catalog record for this book
is available from the British Library.

The Edwin Mellen Press
Box 450
Lewiston, NY
USA 14092

The Edwin Mellen Press
Box 67
Queenston, Ontario
CANADA L0S 1L0

The Edwin Mellen Press, Ltd.
Lampeter, Dyfed, Wales,
UNITED KINGDOM SA48 7DY

Printed in the United States of America

TABLE OF CONTENTS

PREFACE   1

INTRODUCTION   5

PART ONE: TRADITIONAL AFRO-CHRISTIAN HOLISTIC   9
       HEALING PROCEDURES IN SOUTHERN
       AFRICA

Introduction   11

1. Traditional and modern medicine in Southern Africa: 13
    some reflective and research considerations.
    S.D. Edwards

2. Religion and healing: the African experience.   25
    M.V. Bührmann

3. A preliminary analysis of student attitudes towards   35
    modern doctors, traditional healers and faith
    healers.
    L.M. Nene

4. The aetiology of spirit in Southern Africa.   43
    W.D. Hammond-Tooke

PART TWO: HEALING IN AFRICAN INDEPENDENT   67
       CHURCHES

Introduction   69

5. Indigenous healing within the context of African   71
    Independent Churches.
    G.C. Oosthuizen

6. Healing practices in African Independent Churches.　　91
   W.H. Wessels

7. A search for abundant life: health, healing and　　109
   wholeness in Zionist Churches.
   D. Dube

8. Baptism & healing in African Independent Churches.　　137
   G.C. Oosthuizen

PART THREE: ZIONIST HEALING AND OTHER　　189
　　　　　　　INDEPENDENT CHURCH PROCEDURES

Introduction　　191

9. The relative influence of participation in　　193
   Zionist church services on the emotional state of
   participants.
   M.B. Motala

10. Amafufunyana Spirit Possession: Treatment and　　207
    Interpretation.
    F.S. Edwards

11. African Independent Churches as healing communities.　　227
    H. Jürgen Becken

12. Music and dance as therapy in African traditional　　241
    societies with special reference to the iBlandla
    lamaNazaretha (the Church of the Nazarites).
    B.N. Mthethwa

PART FOUR: AFRICAN HEALING AND WESTERN THERAPY 257

Introduction   259

13. The iSangoma as psycho-therapist.   261
     I. Mkhwanazi

14. The umthandazi - prayer-healer.   281
     H.B. Mkhize

15. Priests before healers - an appraisal of the   295
     iSangoma or iSanusi in Nguni society.
     J.A. Griffiths & R.W.S. Cheetham

16. The traditional healer/diviner as psychotherapist   305
     and A Schematic Presentation.
     R.W.S. Cheetham & J.A. Griffiths

17. Healers: modern and traditional.   319
     M.V. Gumede

18. Healing: Xhosa perspective.   329
     F.S. Edwards

CONCLUSION   347

19. Healing as a psychosomatic event.   351
     F.B. Welbourn

GLOSSARY   369

BIBLIOGRAPHY   373

CONTRIBUTORS   389

INDEX OF NAMES   391

INDEX OF SUBJECTS   399

INDEX OF AFRICAN TERMS   425

INDEX OF BIBLICAL REFERENCES   431

PREFACE

Books about South Africa are all the rage. At academic meetings publishers fall over themselves to obtain "South African" manuscripts. But there is a catch to all this activity. The manuscripts required must meet certain specific qualifications. They need to "expose the system" and document the political agony of South African Blacks. As a result real academic work is often bypassed for trendy exposes which create a great deal of heat but throw no new light on the situation.

No doubt the current fashion of publishable books on South Africa will change. In the meantime, however, the cause of scholarship is damaged by the sheer weight of frothy information. Instead of aiding the cause of Blacks in South Africa, many contemporary books simply exploit their suffering.

The present work is a rare exception to that trend. It presents the results of interdisciplinary research and field work among Black South Africans. The aim is to inform the reader about African medical practices as they are found among traditional healers and members of the African Independent Churches.

Precisely because the focus is on healing, we also learn how Black South Africans experience their reality and construct their world view. Healing, contextualized by possession cults, traditional practitioners, and African independent churches, is holistic. It makes statements simultaneously about the individual, the kin community, the neighborhood, and the modern industrial world. We learn in this book that the syncretistic aspects of Africanized Christianity and new religions parallel perceived individual and social fragmentation. Using a metaphor from art, one might say that healing within this religiosity mirrors a montage-like reconstruction of self, language, and society.

The appearance of this book thrills us because healing and moya or Holy Spirit theology--however varied in specific contexts --is no longer confined only to Africanized Christianity. Rather, healing and the life-transforming power of the Holy Spirit has also become central to Western and, in South Africa, white-founded, but racially integrated, independent churches which we researched during four months fieldwork in 1977.

But to the Western bystander, what cannot go unnoticed is the meeting of minds--contained though they be in black and white skins--in the sphere of an emergent (black-white) pentecostal theology. Whatever hindrances remain to a new, integrated, and above all, power-sharing South Africa, increasing numbers of its multi-colored population are already tapping the same source of power, namely, that of the Holy Spirit.

In this sense, therefore, neither the authors of the book nor those of the Preface see these findings as the final word on the subject. Far from it, for healing, in the broad sense of the word, remains virgin territory, as does the pentecostal theology that increasingly underpins it.

For the meeting of minds in South Africa, healing as well as pentecostal theology takes on a special meaning. Both are based on narrative and testimony, precisely those areas of cognition and symbolism which most clearly reveal human universals. No matter what the cultural differences, in the narrated testimony the human being is on a pilgrimage: he/she experiences his or her creation, fall, and redemption, and he/she experiences them in the here and now. He/she cannot ignore the similar stages through which fellow human beings pass--not if he/she wishes to be true to others and be healed.

Karla Poewe
Department of Anthropology
University of Lethbridge
Alberta
Canada

and

Irving Hexham
Department of Religious Studies
University of Calgary
Alberta
Canada

INTRODUCTION

Anyone who studies African Independent Churches quickly realizes that their emphasis on healing is one of the main reasons for their phenomenal growth. In Southern Africa, for example, there were 32 such churches in 1913. At the time of the Afrikaner Nationalist election victory, which led to the implementation of the policy of apartheid, in 1948, the number of black Independent Churches had grown to over 800 distinct groups with more than 800,000 adherents.

The growth of Black Independent Church movements continued so that in 1960 there were at least 2,000 separate groups with a membership of 2,313,000. These figures continued to climb to more than 3,500 groups with 5,842,000 followers in 1984. In percentage terms these numbers represent 27.3% of the entire black African population in South Africa (HSRC, 1985, pp.23 and 27).

To put the growth of African Independent Churches in perspective it must be realized that in 1984 among South African Blacks there were 2,419,000 Methodists; 2,022,000 Roman Catholics; 1,300,000 Dutch Reformed; 1,224,000 Anglicans; 948,000 Lutherans; 516,000 Presbyterians; 297,000 Congregationalists; and 141,000 members of the Apostolic Faith Mission. Thus, the percentage of South African Blacks who belonged to mainline denominations associated with traditional missions and churches were: 11.3% Methodist; 9.4% Roman Catholic; 6.1% Dutch Reformed; 5.7% Anglicans; 4.4% Lutherans; 2.4% Presbyterians; 1.4% Congregationalists; and 0.7% Apostolics (HSRC, 1985, pp.20, 22, 23 and 24 cf. Froise, 1986, pp.1-3).

In other words the Independent Churches have more members than the combined strength of the Methodists, Roman Catholics and

Anglicans. Indeed one Independent Church, the Zion Christian Church which in 1984 had over 2,500,000 members was larger than any other Christian Church among Black Africans in South Africa. Since 1984 there are clear indications that African Independent Churches have continued their phenomenal growth with the result that about 40% of all Black Africans are probably members of an Independent Church.

Professor G.C. Oosthuizen began his study of African Independent Churches in the late 1950's and made various attempts to interest anthropologists, psychiatrists, psychologists and theologians with an interest in pastoral theology in the work of the Independent Churches. But, it was not until January 1987 that the South African National Congress of Psychiatrists included a workshop in their bi-annual conference on healing and religious experience. This event followed directly from a symposium at the Natal Medical School in May 1986 which Professor Oosthuizen co-organized with Professor W.H. Wessels to take a formal look at healing practices in both traditional African society and African Independent Churches.

As far as we know these conferences were unique in bringing together academics from a variety of disciplines to examine the question of traditional healing and the way traditional practices have been incorporated into and modified by African Independent Churches. This book brings together papers from both these occasions plus a few other relevant essays.

We believe that the information contained in these papers, even though it is of an introductory nature, offers remarkable insights into the significance of African spiritual realities in the modern world. To us it is clear that the appeal of the vast

African Independent Church movement is based on the indigenous African psychiatric and psychological assistance which African Independent Churches offer their members.

We hope that the publication of this book will stimulate others to undertake intensive investigations of healing practices in African Independent Churches and traditional society generally. Such investigations hold great promise for both the churches and the various healing communities found in modern society.

The co-operation of the various contributors to this book is mentioned with gratitude. Their activity in this field of research are in many ways pioneer works. Some of the contributors have, however, succeeded in making their mark through their studies in this area, and we hope their example will encourage others, especially granting agencies, to pay serious attention to this important subject.

We wish to thank Mrs. Annette Clifford-Vaughan for her work on the original drafts of these papers and Mrs. Avril Dyson for typing the final manuscript and Dr. Irving Hexham for preparing the manuscript for publication in North America. Appreciation is expressed to the Human Sciences Research Council of South Africa for the financial assistance granted to the Research Unit for the Study of New Religious Movements and Indigenous Churches (NERMIC) at the University of Zululand without whose assistance the original symposium would not have been possible. It should also be noted that several contributors strongly expressed their appreciation to Professor Oosthuizen because of his enthusiasm, support and constant prodding. Without his efforts, they frankly admitted, they would never have begun their research or have developed an interest in African society and its healing practices.

Finally, we wish to stress our conviction that the incredible growth of African Independent Churches cannot be fully explained without paying serious attention to their healing practices which take us to the heart of African spiritual reality.

PART ONE: TRADITIONAL AFRO-CHRISTIAN HOLISTIC HEALING
PROCEDURES IN SOUTHERN AFRICA

INTRODUCTION

The four papers in this section introduce the reader to traditional African healing practices and the ways in which they are preserved in contemporary society. The first paper is by Professor S.D. Edward who is head of the Department of Psychology at the University of Zululand. He compares the approach of traditional healers and modern medical personnel emphasizing the human situation in which healing takes place. His paper is stimulating both for its empirical data about contemporary African involvement in traditional health systems and his suggestions about the relationship between traditional and modern health care systems.

Our second paper, by Dr. M.V. Bührmann, a psychiatrist from Cape Town who has done extensive work in the Transkei, looks at the way traditional Africans experience healing and the relationship between healing and religious belief. In the third paper Mr. L.M. Nene, as social psychologist at the University of Zululand, complements Dr. Bührmann's work by analyzing Black African student attitudes to modern medicine and various forms of traditional healing.

Finally, Professor W.D. Hammond-Tooke, head of the Department of Anthropology at the University of the Witwatersand, provides essential background information concerning traditional African beliefs about the spiritual world. He discusses the nature and role of the ancestors and the ways in which Christian beliefs, especially those concerning the Holy Spirit, have been modified by African thought.

All four papers introduce the reader to traditional African beliefs and practices as they continue to exist in Southern

Africa today. Thus, they prepare the way for a discussion of healing within African Independent Churches.

TRADITIONAL AND MODERN SOUTHERN AFRICAN MEDICINE: SOME
REFLECTIVE AND RESEARCH CONSIDERATIONS
by
S.D. Edwards

1. INTRODUCTION

The distinction between traditional and modern medicine is internationally accepted as denoting more regional, indigenous, alternative, functionally strong approaches to medicine as distinguished from modern biomedically orientated structurally dominant systems (NICSSM 1985). The term <u>medicine</u> is used here in its broadest sense as the science and art of healing illness. Problems in Southern African medicine are fundamentally the same as those in any other country. As in other countries, socio-economic, political, legal and other factors all form part of the total healing context. This is not to say, however, that problems in Southern African medicine are not exacerbated by our historical, racial and violent politico-legal and societal divisions, which have tended to maintain regional separation between communities and indigenous and modern approaches to illness and healing.

Phenomenological reflection reveals that the distinction between traditional and modern medicine is essentially an artificial and arbitrary one. Universal components of both approaches are fundamentally far more important than are their relative superficial differences. Consider the universal human event of illness and healing and the possible international population of traditional and modern practitioners, patients and communities within the total context. Overlap between the traditional/modern medicine is considerable. Consider the traditional modern practitioner who combines traditional divination with modern bio-medicine and the modern traditional healer such as the <u>umthandazi</u> or priest.

One fundamental reason for the distinction between traditional and modern medicine is the relative supernatural and natural orientations of traditional and modern practitioners of medicine. Modern medicine is based on the empirical specialized biomedical model of natural science, whereas traditional and alternative approaches to medicine are often both natural and supernaturally orientated.

This distinction can be seen as reflecting the situation of contemporary humanity, living in a technocratic and divided world which is characterized (Toffler 1980; Kruger 1984) by ever-accelerated change and loss of spirituality. Certainly no such distinction exists in the individual world view of many patients, for whom, despite the effectiveness of modern medicine, traditional approaches provide much needed holistic care.

1. RESEARCH FINDINGS
TABLE 1

REACTION TO ILLNESS

	A	B	C
Traditional Medicine	3 (7%)	6 (11%)	11 (13%)
Modern Medicine	30 (73%)	33 (60%)	38 (45%)
Traditional and Modern Medicine	8 (20%)	16 (29%)	35 (42%)

Key:
   A = Non-psychology students at the University of Zululand (N = 41).
   B = Urban residents of Esikhawini Township (N = 55).
   C = Rural residents of Kwa-Dlangezwa/Ngoya (N = 84).

Table 1 refers to a survey conducted by the University of Zululand Psychology Department (Edwards 1985) amongst university students, urban and rural local inhabitants of the Lower Umfolozi area of Kwa-Zulu, Natal. This data was gathered by means of a questionnaire assessing history of and reaction to the respondent's most recent illness. Traditional medicine here included visits to a traditional doctor (inyanga), diviner (iSangoma), faith healer (umthandazi), traditional medicine (muthi) shop and/or religious or ritual ceremony. Modern medicine included modern physician, hospital, clinic or registered pharmacist. It is instructive to note:

a) the apparent urban/rural, modern traditional medicine association,
b) the popularity of modern medicine,
c) the common combinations of traditional and modern medicine.

TABLE 2

HEALERS' AND PSYCHOLOGISTS' INTERVIEW METHODS WITH PSYCHIATRIC PATIENTS (N = 3)

INTERVIEW METHOD	HEALERS				PSYCHOLOGISTS			
	A	B	C	TOTAL	D	E	F	TOTAL
Natural	10	5	4	19	12	10	12	34
Supernatural	2	7	8	17	0	0	0	0

Key: A = Traditional doctor (inyanga).
     B = Traditional diviner (iSangoma).
     C = Zionist faith healer (umthandazi)
     D-F = Clinical psychologists.

Table 2 refers to a research study (Edwards 1985) aimed at comparing the interviewing, assessment and treatment planning procedures used by three indigenous healers--a traditional doctor (inyanga), diviner (iSangoma) and a faith healer (umthandazi) and by three qualified clinical psychologists, when interviewing the same group of psychiatric patients.

Chi-square analysis showed significant differences (p.05) in their interviewing methods. Psychologists used exclusively natural empirical methods, such as psychiatric interviewing, taking a case history, mental status, etc., whereas healers emphasized both natural and supernatural methods, such as divination through bone throwing after invoking ancestral blessings or prayer.

Significant differences were found (p.05) between traditional doctors and both diviners and faith healers in their relative emphasis on natural and supernatural methods respectively.

TABLE 3

HEALERS' AND PSYCHOLOGISTS' DEGREE OF AGREEMENT AS TO DIAGNOSTIC AND TREATMENT METHODS, KENDALLS' COEFFICIENTS OF CONCORDANCE W, (M = 6)

PSYCHIATRIC PATIENT	DIAGNOSTIC METHODS	TREATMENT METHODS
G	0,46 (p.01)	0.68 (p.01)
H	0,67 (p.01)	0,60 (p.01)
I	0,5 (p.01)	0,5 (p.01)

Table 3 shows that the healers and the psychologists (i.e. all six therapists) agree significantly on both diagnostic and treatment methods for each of the three psychiatric patients interviewed, when asked to rank order lists of possible diagnostic and treatment methods for each patient.

TABLE 4

THERAPIST HELPFULNESS

THERAPIST	PATIENT			TOTAL	
	G	H	I		
A	5	3	1	9	
B	4	4	3	11	33
C	6	5	2	13	
D	1	1	4	6	
E	2	2	6	10	30
F	3	6	5	14	

Key:

A   =   Traditional doctor (inyanga).

B   =   Traditional diviner (iSangoma).

C   =   Zionist faith healer (umthandazi).

D-F =   Clinical psychologists.

Table 4 indicates how patients rank ordered the six therapists in terms of helpfulness, with healers (A-B-C) and psychologists (D-F) being viewed as more or less equally helpful.

3. DISCUSSION

The prospects for integrating modern and traditional health systems in various African countries have been a much-debated topic over the past decade. Organizations such as the World

Health Organization (W.H.O.) have suggested retraining of traditional practitioners to serve as primary health care workers. There has been little empirical research on the implications of integration and the problems involved, however. These problems are of more than academic interest in such countries as Nigeria, where the ratio of modern physicians to population is 1:22,000, way below the W.H.O. goal of 1:10,000 for developing countries, and where partial integration of the two health systems has occurred.

In 1974, the South African Medical and Dental Council made official their rejection of indigenous healers in a Health Act which forbade non-registered healers to practice or perform any act pertaining to the medical profession. Registered healers were also forbidden to work in collaboration with non-registered healers. The unofficial view, however, differs from the official one, which was rejected by The South African Medical Journal (1976), the official organ of the Medical Association of South Africa, a professional, non-statutory organization. It suggested that medical professions should attempt to understand the healers' system of operation, should accept healers in certain fields and should help them to recognize those illnesses they are unable to cure (Ferrand 1980). Many modern professions could learn much from medicine. Unfortunately, the attitudes reflected in the legislation have often resulted in many reputable traditional healers being extremely secretive in the practice of their profession.

It should not be construed that healers are unprotected or uncontrolled by law. Provision was made for their practice in the Code of Zulu Law for example. Also, more recently, in the Associated Health Service Professions Act (No.63 or 1982), the

Council of Associated Health Professions, a separate statutory body not affiliated to the Medical and Dental Council, has provided for the registration and control of healers.

Modern mental health medical and paramedical professionals, in particular, have urged for more national integration of the two health systems, with the view that indigenous healers have an important role to play, particularly in the fields of psychology and psychiatry (Rappaport & Rapparport 1981). Various writers have noted, for example, universal components of psychotherapy shared by both indigenous healers and modern professionals (Cheetham & Griffiths 1982).

Shortcomings in the prevailing South African mental health services have been pointed out by various prominent South African psychiatrists and psychologists, who have appealed for greater recognition to be given to and for greater use to be made of the skills of indigenous healers in treating persons who may benefit from their services (Holdstock 1979; and Wessels, 1985).

The relatively widespread patient usage of traditional medicine, alone or in combination with modern medicine, and the research findings mentioned above seem to warrant greater integration of modern and traditional healing systems as has been advocated in neighbouring Swaziland, Zimbabwe and Bophuthatswana. Administratively, this remains a complex issue within the overall South African political, economic, legal and health situation, with its many communities varying in language, modernization, culture and state-allocated health resources. However, in practice, rapprochement and cooperation (if not integration) is effected in many transcultural psychiatric settings throughout the country.

Certainly there are good and bad practitioners in both systems, as in any profession or occupation. Certainly both systems have a lot to offer each other and a lot to learn from each other, as has been the case in the past. Day-to-day practical cooperation is especially in the hands of those primary health care workers who form grass-roots liaison with indigenous healers. Many traditional and modern practitioners and their patients have benefitted by mutual cooperation established in many area of South Africa. Both approaches are currently taught at many South African universities. It is hoped that this process, as well as the more urgently needed building of more hospitals and clinics, will continue.

As mentioned earlier, the roles of the different categories of practitioners are becoming increasingly specialized and differentiated, with the <u>umthandazi</u> or faith healer achieving increasing popularity, particularly in urban areas. It has been noted that patients often regard urban traditional healers as quacks compared to their rural counterparts (Farrand 1985). However, charlatans also exist in rural areas, where some unscrupulous healers have been observed, for example, to utilize public address systems to simulate ancestral voices during patient interviews.

Perhaps the communication explosion and modernized differential perceptions of the relative efficacy, services and different roles of the priest, physician and cultural counsellor, accelerated by increasing urbanization and socio-cultural change,

---

[1] Personal communication with N.W. Sokhela.

in South Africa at least, may soon make the question of integration of traditional and modern medicine redundant.

In the meantime, much can be gained by continuing local health education for and amongst both traditional healers and modern health care workers, with the goal of enlightened communication and the recognition of expertise and limitations in both systems by both systems.

4. CONCLUSIONS

Continuing (perhaps nationally co-ordinated) research into traditional and modern medicine is needed in South Africa, along the lines undertaken in neighbouring Swaziland, Zimbabwe and other African countries with a greater need owing to relative lack of modern medical facilities (Green & Makhula 1984; Chavunduko 1978; and du Toit & Abdalla 1985). Bophuthatswana, for example, has the opportunity (and need) to include all healing practioners in one health act, thus short-circuiting traditional professional exclusiveness. Nationally co-ordinated research should particularly involve those medical, academic and research institutions which already effect practical rapprochement and cooperation between traditional and modern medicine, and which teach both approaches. The following, in particular, are some of the areas that need to be investigated:

a) Research into the effect of modernization, education, economic, socio-cultural and political change on traditional and transitional societies, their related health practices and help-seeking behaviour.

b) Research with large representative groups of patients, traditional healers and modern practitioners to assess the demand for, problems and implications of greater integration of traditional and modern medicine. This research would have to cover definition of terms, variations of traditional belief systems, the cultural integration of illness, the ethical and legal implications of traditional and modern healers working together, the training of traditional and modern healers, etc.

c) Longitudinal follow-up studies on matched groups of patients who have received traditional, modern and combinations of traditional and modern medicine respectively would be valuable.

d) Finally, phenomenologically oriented outcome research is needed to assess the efficacy of traditional/modern medical approaches not only in healing illness but also in providing therapy toward becoming more fully human and healthy.

RELIGION AND HEALING: THE AFRICAN EXPERIENCE
by
M.V. Bührmann

As I do not want to cross swords with the theologians I want to define the concept of religion according to the dictionary and then look at the controversial issue of "Ancestor Worship."

Religion according to Chambers Dictionary is:
"belief in, recognition of, or an awakened sense of, a higher unseen controlling power or powers, with the emotion and morality connected therewith: rites or worship."

Worship according to the New Bible Dictionary is:
"Adoration paid, as to a God: an essential concept is service: in order to offer this worship to God, his servants must prostrate themselves and thus manifest Reverential fear and adoring awe and wonder."

The traditional African approach to health and healing is closely linked to their concept of the ancestors who participate in their day-to-day living. This thinking and the associated rituals and ceremonies are usually called "Ancestor worship." According to the above definition of worship, this is in my thinking a misnomer. The interaction is too natural and even human and there is respect but no adoration.

To understand the relationship between the living and their living-dead kin (ancestors, shades), it is necessary to take cognizance of the spirituality of the people of Africa. If that concept is not understood and accepted it will be difficult to grasp the meaning and rationale of healing procedures in the traditional setting and in the Independent Churches as practiced by prophet priest. Healing and spirituality are intimately linked.

Mbiti is worth consulting in this connection. In his book, The Prayers of African Religion, (1915), he emphasizes this spirituality and the awareness African people have of "other realities." About this collection of prayers he writes that apart from God:

> The spirits are the second category of spiritual realities which emerge in these prayers. There is absolutely no question that African people as a whole are much aware of the reality of spirits, or at least realities, besides God, which fall in the spiritual realm (Mbiti 1975:7).

He continues:
It is remarkable how African people so confidently address spiritual realities in many of their prayers for healing. There is virtually no barrier between the realm of man and the spiritual realm ... This is an outstanding dimension of African spirituality and it should not be carelessly judged, simply as spirit or ancestor worship by people who only betray their ignorance about African religions, feelings and practices (Mbiti 1975:44).

He gives many examples of spiritual realities and states that "God is not always distinguished clearly from the other spiritual realities."

This statement can be difficult for the linear analytical Westerner to accept. The African concept of man in the universe is more synthetic and holistic. Everything has meaning and is related to everything else; there is a constant dynamic interchange and mutual influences.

Instead of African worship of the Ancestors, we should talk about African reverence for and respect of the Ancestors.

This brings one to the indigenous approach to healing. For this, some understanding of the traditional world-view is required. What follows is derived from my work with a particular group of Xhosa healers. They combine the functions of divining and treatment with the performance of rituals and ceremonies-- they are "amaggira."

In the life of African people, concepts about ancestors, witches and sorcerers occupy a central place. Their concept of "illness" is very wide. There is no real distinction between psyche and soma, and in their quest for "health" many apparently unrelated elements are included, such as all kinds of "misfortune" in the family, e.g., deaths which are regarded as unnatural; failure at work, business or studies; difficulty with housing and the authorities, etc.

Basic to this thinking is "If I have a good relationship with the Ancestors, perform the customs regularly, keep them alive and viable by acts of remembrance, they will do their share, that of protecting me and ensuring that I enjoy a good life and have my needs met." It is the idea of a symbolic relationship.

The Ancestors, as appeared from my research, consist of two kinds. The clan-linked deceased forebears and the unrelated Ancestors of the River, and Ancestors of the Forest. The former are experienced as not visible, but very human and living with their kind in and around the homestead. The relationship is natural and usually friendly. They can feel cold, hungry, neglected, annoyed and happy. They are conceived of as being omnipresent and nearly omniscient and they normally function as wise guides and protectors, but when annoyed their roles can be reversed and they may either expose one to the power of witches or themselves ... cause all kinds of illness and misfortune. It is believed that they do this "to remind their children of the error of their ways." They are therefore examples of the other spiritual realities that Mbiti writes about--there is reverence but no awe (Mbiti 1975:3).

The ancestors of the River and Ancestors of the Forest are different. They are not clan-linked, are distant, awesome and so numerous and powerful that it can be dangerous to see or encounter them without having taken special precautions. They can cause serious upheavals, illness, madness and "even death."

These are psychic realities that the African knows, but lives and copes with. An informant told Evans-Pritchard, "The European does not appreciate that the Azande have to take into account mystical forces about which he (the European) knows nothing."

Any illness is therefore ascribed to a disturbance of the balance between man and spiritual or mystical forces, and the aim of health seeking is to restore the equilibrium.

To restore this balance, communication and communion with the Ancestors through the performance of rites, rituals, ceremonies and sacrifices are required. There is a large variety of such rites forming a complicated fabric of behavior, such as purification to protect against evil, ritual dances to stimulate body function and to invoke the participation of the Ancestors in their healing procedures.

These rites are all used to a greater or lesser extent throughout the life of a person or a family, when illness occurs or at times of stress. If the illness or disturbance causes anxiety or stress of more than average intensity, a traditional healer is consulted for divination, advice and treatment--often the performance of rituals is prescribed.

With the spread of Christianity this function of healing has, to varying degrees, been incorporated into the African's system of religious beliefs and practices. It is a corner stone of the Indigenous Churches, of which there are many with a vast following.

According to Martin West (1975), these churches attract members primarily because they promise and provide healing for the physically and mentally ill. They had their origin in the Mission Churches and some remained close to the original church, but others incorporated many traditional beliefs and practices. These churches practicing faith healing believe primarily in the power of God. In the Zionist-type churches, with bishops and prophets, the belief is in the power of God and the guidance of the Ancestors.

Most of the prophets, like their counterparts the indigenous healers, initially suffered an illness, a severe psychological upheaval, in the Nguni culture called thwasa, during which they became acquainted with the Ancestors. On recovery the two belief systems were combined and some of the rituals and ceremonies, with alterations, were incorporated in their services where healing is practiced.

The aspects which are mostly common to the indigenous healers and the practices of the Independent Churches are purification rites, attention to dreams, dancing, singing and clapping with the participation of the family and the community in the case of the former and the congregation in the case of the latter. The dancing, singing and clapping has many similarities to the Xhosa inthlombe and xhantsa which I described as the Healing Dance (Bührmann 1981: 187-201). The inthlombe is performed to purify the blood, to raise the umbelini and open the mind to the messages of the Ancestors. In the church the services, the singing, clapping, dancing and drumming, are used to call the Holy Spirit to descend on the congregation. It is not uncommon for individuals to be possessed by the spirit. For more details see Martin West (West 1975: 91-124).

In urban areas the indigenous healer is hampered by the lack of space and other facilities. His natural "consulting room" and "clinic" are his own homestead and those of his patients and their families.

Apart from the influence of Christianity, environmental factors also influenced the adjustments from rural to urban customs and practices.

Many reasons are given for the phenomenal growth of the Independent Churches:

1. The desire to function independently of the Western-style churches.

2. That the dignitaries in these churches, especially the prophets, understand the complaints and the language in which these are expressed better than do the white doctor or white priest or parson.

3. That they claim to be able to answer the "how" and "why" of the troubled person by divination.

4. Because of the above they can integrate the physical and mental suffering with a myth they and the afflicted believe and thus heal a breach.

5. The faith healers, prophets and sangomas all claim supernatural contact and sanctions.

6. The use of ritual in which the patient, the community and the congregation participate is supportive and highly meaningful.

I think an important factor is usually overlooked--the universality of the need for religion. Depth psychology can make a contribution.

Jung regards religion as a psychological instinct on par with the sex and power instinct. He describes it "as a natural function which existed from the beginning ... (it is an awareness) that the life of the individual is determined largely by a transcendent function" (Jung 1937: 10-653).

Elsewhere he writes how men from earliest times have felt compelled to perform rites for the purpose of securing the cooperation of the gods (the unconscious). In the primitive world one is constantly mindful of the gods, the spirits, fate and the magical qualities of time and space. He concludes man's striving for a spiritual goal is a genuine instinct (Jung 1937:10-656).

The priest healers of the Independent Churches and the indigenous healers all assert that they do not heal through their own powers--they are just the transmitters of a higher power of healing.

It seems that in African healing practices an intuitive integration of religion as a psychic instinct and the acknowledged spiritual realities of the African people take place. Such integration enables healing and union of body and mind and spirit to occur and for the innate recuperative powers of the afflicted person to be set in motion.

A PRELIMINARY ANALYSIS OF STUDENT ATTITUDES TOWARDS MODERN
DOCTORS, TRADITIONAL HEALERS AND FAITH HEALERS

by

L.M. Nene

INTRODUCTION

    This is an analysis of the results of a study, which was prompted through some findings noted in an investigation conducted by Farrand during 1984/1985. Briefly, in that investigation Black psychiatric patients expressed their choices of healers i.e., medical doctors, or medical doctor/izangoma/ inyanga or umprofethi. These were part of many other findings relating to healing generally.

Aim of this study:

    The aim was to make a survey of the choices of people other than psychiatric patients, and to concentrate on what their perceptions are of various healers, what they believe or think about them, and generally how they view different healers. The terms used in this study are: Western medical doctor, izangoma/izinyanga (reflecting traditional healers) and two categories representing faith healers--abaprofethi/abathandazi and abafundisi/abapristi. The "sample" of the study is made up of 160 University of Zululand students of Psychology. For obvious reasons, this "sample" is not representative of the total student population of that institution.

Hypothesis:

    In formulating the hypothesis, the following was taken into consideration: the "sample" comprises university students, who are fairly well educated by African standards and are probably more "Western-oriented" than "traditionally-oriented." THEREFORE: "The general attitude of university students is strongly favorable toward "Western-oriented treatment."

38

Results:

The following analysis of the responses of the sample to specific attitude-scale statements reflects the attitude of the respondents to each type of healer.

THE ATTITUDE TOWARD ABAPROFETHI/ABATHANDAZI (Prophets/Prayer Healers)

The overall attitude towards the services of abaprofethi/athandazi is:

1. Such services are suitable for both males and females;

2. suitable for both urban and rural peoples;

3. suitable for both the literate and illiterate; and

4. suitable for both the superstitious and unsuperstitious, further,

5. Abaprofethi/abathandazi do not cause illness in healthy people, but

6. render a worthwhile service to the sick. They are, however,

7. not as good as Western medical doctors in treating illness, and

8. should not be viewed in the same light as medical doctors.

The responses to statements containing these ideas are statistically significant from the 0,05 level to the 0,001 level.

They are presented in a descending rank order according to percentages of respondents in agreement or disagreement. The percentages range from 90 to 43 percent.

THE ATTITUDE TOWARD ABAFUNDISI/ABAPRISTI Ministers/Priests)

The overall attitude towards the services of abafundisi/abapristi is:

1. Such services are for both superstitious and unsuperstitious peoples;

2. suitable for both males and females;

3. suitable for both urban and rural peoples; and

4. suitable for both the literate and illiterate. The respondents

5. do not look down upon persons who, when sick, consult abafundisi/abapristi. Further, the respondents

6. do not view abafundisi/abapristi as messengers of the devil, but rather

7. as rendering a worthwhile service to the sick.

The response to statements containing these ideas are also statistically significant from the 0,05 to the 0,001 levels. The presentation is once more in descending rank order. The percentages of respondents endorsing an idea range from 91 to 52 percent.

40

THE ATTITUDE TOWARD IZANGOMA/IZINYANGA (Diviner/Herbalist)

The overall attitude towards the services of izangoma/izinyanga is:

1. Such services are for both rural and urban persons. The respondents

2. do not look down upon people who, when ill, consult izangoma/izinyanga.

3. Their services are suitable for both the illiterate and literate;

4. for both urban and rural people. The izangoma/izinyanga

5. do render a worthwhile service to the sick, and

6. are not messengers of the devil. Because of their service to the sick,

7. izangoma/izinyanga should not be viewed in the same light as medical doctors.

The respondents however neither agreed nor disagreed with the idea that:

1. the izangoma/izinyanga do not cause illness in healthy persons; nor that

2. their services are suitable for both males and females; nor that

3.   they are suitable only for superstitious persons.

It therefore appears that the services rendered by all three types of healers, abaprofethi/abathandazi, abafundisi/abapristi, izangoma/izinyanga, are viewed generally suitable for urban/rural people and the literate/illiterate. There are some differences of opinion with regard to their suitability for males/females, and for the superstitious/unsuperstitious. The services are viewed as worthwhile, and the izangoma/izinyanga are not seen as messengers of the devil. However, there is some uncertainty as to whether or not izangoma/izinyanga cause illness in healthy people.

CONCLUSION

The findings, preliminary as they are, have not differed radically from some of those in the Farrand study. It is hoped that this will be an ongoing study project, and that something more concrete will ultimately emerge.

THE AETIOLOGY OF SPIRIT IN SOUTHERN AFRICA
by
W.D. Hammond-Tooke

INTRODUCTION

The problem of syncretism in Southern African Christianity has long engaged the attention of theologians, missionaries and others. There is increasing evidence that, even among African Christians of long standing, there continues to be a lively awareness of the presence and power of the ancestors, even if the specific rituals are no longer performed in their entirety (Pauw 1963:7 West 1975), that much illness and misfortune is still explained in terms of witch beliefs and that in certain communities the last hundred years has seen the increasing spread of new cults centering on possession by alien spirits. In the Christian churches themselves there has been a marked hypertrophy of sects, all of which lay great emphasis on what Sundkler calls the Moya-theology (Sundkler 1961), the life-transforming power of the Holy Spirit.

All this seems decidedly off-centre to mainline Christians. Uncertain how to evaluate the charismatic-like overtones of the Zionist movement, they are disturbed by the frankly nativistic elements of ancestor veneration and witch beliefs, while the drumming and dance-induced trancing of the possession group seem entirely alien to "pure religion and undefiled." Oosthuizen, indeed, has characterized the present religious position among many African Christians as "post-Christianity" (Oosthuizen, 1968).

The present paper seeks an understanding of this phenomenon. It takes its departure from two points of view, one theoretical, one substantive. For purposes of analysis, it is accepted that one of the most important functions of any religious system is to provide meaning to the world and to life, i.e., to fulfill an essentially cognitive function. This is not to underplay other

46

functions, especially the emotional security that religion provides, but it would seem that a primary role of religious doctrine is to state unambiguously that life is not meaningless, that death is not the end and, perhaps most fundamentally, that man is dependent on a power (or powers) that sustain and support him. The way that this occurs has to be conceptualized, and this is done by essentially theoretical systems (Horton, 1967)-- cosmologies or world-views. It is here taken as a datum that the complexities of present-day African theology can best be understood as attempts to come to grips cognitively with certain problems and aspects of existence in late twentieth-century Southern Africa.

The other, substantive, starting point is the fact that the theoretical constructs relevant here are all conceived of as spirits. These are a mixed bag--ancestral spirits, witch familiars, alien spirits, nature spirits, and the Holy Spirit itself, the latter undoubtedly dominant in Zionist Christianity but apparently sharing some of its efficacy with the others. Why this variety? Why is it necessary for so many African Christians to retain indigenous beliefs side-by-side with Christian ones? More particularly, what are the cognitive tasks performed by these constructs? Can this syncretism be explained, and what are its theological implications? What follows is an attempt to share the cognitive field and, if possible, provide tentative answers to these questions. This will involve relating the ideational to the (changing) social structure.

I

The term "spirit" is used here in a broad, common-sense way to refer to the belief in intelligent agencies that are typically invisible and intangible but that have the power to affect the lives of the living. The concept is, of course, part of our own

European, semantic set, which includes such entities as souls, ghosts, devils, demons, fairies, and so on, all of very differing nature. The Oxford Dictionary captures the essence: "Rational or intelligent being not connected with the material body."

The spirits found in South African cosmologies are similarly diverse. They are as follows:

1. Ancestral spirits

Traditionally, the ancestor cult formed the basis of religious worship in all traditional societies. Among Nguni there is a strong agnatic element, involving strict clan exogamy, and this has greatly influenced the nature of the cult, the objects of worship being the patrilineal dead. Literature on the Nguni speaks of the lineage or the lineage segment as the object of worship. Recent work has shown, however, (Hammond-Tooke 1984: 1985) that the commonly-found five or six-generation genealogy (usually taken to define the lineage) does not reflect a functioning social group on the ground. Effective descent groups are small localized groups of kin (agnatic clusters), typically descended from a common grandfather or great grandfather. This is the group that comprises the congregation of the ancestor cult. Among the Cape Nguni a number of these agnatic clusters, linked by a common genealogy, enjoy the offices of a common ritual elder (inkulu), the senior representative of the six-generation genealogy, who must be present to officiate at all sacrifices held by the constituent agnatic clusters. An agnatic cluster, though, does not worship with the other clusters defined by the common genealogy.

Two types of ancestor may be distinguished. At ancestor rituals all the dead of the overarching clan are called to the present. This is done by invoking the name of the clan founder, which has the effect of causing all the (nameless) clan dead to be present on each occasion. But, in addition, rituals may be specifically directed at specific ancestors who have "troubled" their descendants through dreams, illness and other misfortunes and have been diagnosed as doing so by the diviner. These communication ancestors are usually deceased parents, grandparents or, occasionally, great grandparents, often from the mother's side of the family. There is thus a degree of bilaterality in what is essentially an agnatic system. Ancestors thus exist on two levels--the amorphous aggregation of clan ancestors, and specific ancestors, defined by the local agnatic cluster. The five- or six-generation genealogy, so commonly found, thus does not define a functioning social group, nor are its dead singled out for special invocation in worship (Hammond-Tooke 1984: 1985).

The bilaterality referred to above is much more evident in other Bantu-speaking groups such as Venda, Tsonga and Sotho, especially Sotho of the Lowveld (Lobedu, Kgaga). Here there is no question of agnatic lineages and the effective ancestors are drawn equally from both sides of the family, but with a cut-off point at the level of grandparents. All four lines of grandparents are included. Yet in all groups the ancestors (unless singled out for a specific sacrifice) are conceived of as an undifferentiated aggregate, indicated by the fact that the term for them is always expressed in the plural (Hammond-Tooke 1974:7: 328-9).

The importance of ancestors is that they continue to take a lively interest in the affairs of their descendants. But their actions tend to be unpredictable, and this is reflected in the marked ambivalence towards them on the part of their worshipers.

Generally speaking they are benevolent and act as mentors and protectors, particularly against the machinations of witches, but they are liable to complain of neglect, especially neglect of ritual performance. Among Nguni they also complain of being hungry, but this is not general for other groups.

What are we to make of this system in terms of our theoretical approach? What is the explanatory function of the belief in ancestors?

At one level the possibility of ancestral wrath is a post facto explanation of misfortune. Illness and misfortune demand explanation (and action) and the diagnosis by the diviner of ancestral causation allows something to be done about it, typically a ritual killing (Nguni) or a libation of beer (Sotho, Venda, Tsonga). It is significant that ancestor-sent misfortune is never as serious as that sent by witches and, indeed, there is evidence that the theoretical problem (of the "good" ancestor causing evil) is often solved (or side-stepped) by arguing that the evil is allowed, rather than sent, e.g., by the ancestors withdrawing their protection (Kiernan 1982). At another level, the belief in ancestors obviously provides a theory of the human condition, especially as to what happens after death. At the very least, it authoritatively announces the existence of an after-life, although indigenous theory is often unclear as to whether all achieve this state.[1] The concept of spirit also

---

[1]Among Nguni, for example, the ancestors are thought of as all the dead members of the clan, but informants are unsure, if pressed, as to whether this category also includes deceased daughters of the descent group. There is a tendency to assert that a "typical" ancestor is the spirit of a fully-fledged
(Footnote continued)

explains such states as sleep, death, trance and coma, as Tylor pointed out long ago. As such it is a highly potent, and parsimonious, explanatory theory.

But perhaps the main thrust of ancestor belief is its explicit statement of the vital importance of the kinship principle to harmonious social life, especially respect to seniors. It is an undoubted fact that filial piety and respect to seniors is the most important moral injunction in these societies; both the concept of ancestral spirits, and the rituals directed to them, are symbolic statements of this ineluctable fact. The ancestor is a powerful metaphor for the basic principle that underlies and maintains traditional society. This is perhaps the main reason why the belief in ancestors has proved so durable. Despite the great social changes that has disrupted African social life, including a major breakdown in family and inter-generational authority, the moral precepts are still present. Christianity may have had much to say about the individual, and about society at large, but it provides little specific teaching about one's duty towards one's wider kin, a lacuna filled by continuing ancestor beliefs.

But these cognitive ideas also have a social dimension. Belief in the ancestors also provides a charter for important

---

(Footnote continued)
homestead head who has been formally incorporated as a shade by the appropriate ritual (ukubuyisa), but this obviously raises logical problems. If only those accorded the ukubuyisa ritual become ancestors, how is it that all the dead achieve this status? In practice, however, when people speak thus about "all" the ancestors the question as to whether or not every shade has been incorporated just does not arise. There is clearly no indigenous answer to a non-existent indigenous question.

social groupings, especially the extended family, agnatic cluster among Nguni and the family and bilateral kingroup among the others. The ritual provides opportunities for the group to come together and thus express its integration and corporateness.

2.   Witch beliefs

The nature of witch beliefs is too well known to merit extended discussion here. It is accepted that witch beliefs and accusations are both an explanation of misfortune and an index of stresses and strains in social life. What is not so common is the perception of these beliefs as an integral part of the traditional religious system. A strong case can be made out for this. Ancestors, essentially benevolent and sustaining, can hardly be cited as the cause of all evil that befalls man. Somehow the theoretical load must be shared, and this is done by postulating the ability of certain persons to bring about evil. This can be done in two ways. Some people are believed to have an inherent quality that allows them to change shape, go about invisible, and cause death and misfortune, either by themselves or by means of familiars. Some people may use special medicines to kill at a distance. Anthropologists usually call the first type of activity "witchcraft" and the second "sorcery." Witch familiars are typically conceived of as animals, especially the hyena, wildcat, polecat, weasel and civet, but also baboons, owls and certain snakes. They are kept by witches, who often have sexual relations with them and send them out at night to do their evil work. The Cape Nguni are unique in the complexity of their witch beliefs. They have developed a complex system of bizarre familiars which include thikoloshe, a small, mischievous homonculus; the impundulu, or lightning bird; ichanti, a snake that can change shape at will; and mamlambo, a snake that changes into a young girl and demands the sacrifice of a kinsman by its owner. All groups believe in the zombi, a resurrected corpse used by witches to do their bidding.

But are witches and their familiars truly to be considered spirits? Information is conflicting, but there seems no doubt that familiars are not believed to be real animals, especially as they are invisible to those not specially doctored to see them. But have they the intelligence and autonomy usually associated with our concept of spirit? On the face of it, they appear to be merely agents of their owners, but there is some evidence of their having freedom of action.[2] Witches are also difficult to classify. On the one hand they are human beings, but their status is equivocal in that they inherit their evil disposition and its associated power, while their ability to change shape and become invisible makes them highly ambiguous.

One has to be careful here to avoid too formal a classification. There is no indigenous word for "spirit" in the

---

[2]Hunter, for instance, records for Mpondo familiars: "Some say that the ichanti works sometimes by itself, others that it is always controlled by a witch" (Hunter 1936: 286): "That iguana is the servant of ichanti and Thikoloshe, fetching firewood for them, smearing their huts, and clapping for them when they wish to dance" (p.287): "Thikoloshe has a mind of his own, and occasionally disobeys the orders of its owner. Sometimes Thikoloshe feels sorry for you and loosens the enchantment of izulu (impundulu)" (p.277). Thikoloshe live in dongas and on river banks and children are said to play with them, frequently being sent by them to steal their father's poultry. They are believed to cause poltergeist activities. It thus seems that there are "wild" Thikoloshe who are caught by witches and trained to become familiars. Lobedu familiars are animals tamed by their owners. How the witch tames these animals is unknown, but "they become so intimate that they come at night and ask for food and call the witch their mother" (Krige and Krige 1943: 251).

Bantu languages of South Africa. Specific types of spirit are specifically named. The word moya (lit. "wind") has been used to translate the term Holy Spirit, and is sometimes also used to include the (modern) idea of a ghost, but ancestral spirits are badimo, amathongo, amadlozi, not meya (plural). In Zulu the familiar are referred to as izilwane (little animals) or, in Sotho, as dithuri or dithongwa. Witches and their familiars should perhaps be seen together as a unitary "spiritual" force.

The question as to why witch beliefs exist has been answered in terms of their explanation of evil in society. This evil is clearly shown in the metaphors used to conceptualize witchcraft. Evil in Southern Africa can be categorized either as evil incarnate (the witch) or evil inherent in matter (sorcery) (Berglund 1976: 236-66), and it is quite explicitly associated with negative emotions of envy, jealousy and anger. Evil refers to the essentially antisocial attitudes and actions that threaten the very basis of social life. The respect and loyalty due to genealogical seniors is extended to all senior consociates, whether related or not (Hammond-Tooke 1974: 360) and the social field in which this injunction operates is thus wider than the descent group and includes neighbors. The terrible thing about a witch is that it attacks its nearest and dearest, people who should be respected and cherished. Unlike the ancestors, who can follow one wherever one goes (even to town), the effective range of witchcraft is limited to the little community. The metaphors used to picture witches also vividly reflect the malignant inversion of normal life that is its main feature. Mpondo witches ride backwards on baboons and approach their victims backwards; they and their familiars work at night, when normal people are asleep; they indulge in cannibalism; they are terrifyingly ambiguous. But, worst of all, they attack the very pillars of healthy social life: they are the enemy within the gates. Witch beliefs also act, in a way, as an indigenous psychological theory, making profound statements about human personality and motivation.

3. Spirits of affliction

Ancestral spirits and witches comprise what may be termed the "mainline" religion of the South African peoples. However, the implacable processes of social change have seen the introduction of new theodetical entities in spirit form notably what have been called "spirits of affliction," as well as the Christian concept of the Holy Spirit, the third Person of the Trinity. Unlike the "traditional" spirits, who remain external to man, these spirit manifestations are believed to actually possess the individual, by entering into his very body.

Spirits of affliction are associated with possession cults that have appeared over the last eighty years or so, mainly in the Transvaal, Natal and Mozambique. They have been explicitly recorded for Tsonga, Ndau, Venda, Pedi, Lobedu, Kgaga and Zulu.

All the evidence points to a locus of origin in Zimbabwe, as all manifestations of the cult show obvious similarities with the shave cult of Shona and Zambian Tonga, described by Bourdillon (1976), Bucher (1980), Colson (1969) and others. Colson (p. 94) believes that the cult was originally Shona, for the Tonga term masabe is obviously a derivative and Jesuit missionaries reported the introduction of the cult into Zambia as late as 1918. It is clear that the cult in South Africa also derives from Zimbabwe. The earliest Southern reference is by Junod (1927, 2:479), who describes it as a new cult among the Tsonga, introduced "in the last fifty years": (i.e., c. 1870's) while Lee dates the appearance of the similar Zulu form (amandiki, amandawe) at about

1910 (Lee 1969: 130). Other estimated dates of introduction are Lobedu, c. 1900 (Krige and Krige 1943: 241) and Venda, 1914, (Stayt 1931: 302). Possession cults of this type do not seem to occur among Cape Nguni or South Sotho. Rather, the latter have adopted, in part, Nguni-type divination, with its emphasis on mediumistic trance (the so-called iSangoma syndrome), in addition to their traditional divining dice. In passing, it should be stated that Nguni divination is an example of what Firth (1969: xvii) terms "spirit mediumship," rather than "spirit possession" --an important distinction as spirit mediumship is an integral part of Nguni mainline religion, while true possession cults tend to be peripheral and, of course, recent.

The crucial point about these possession cults is that they typically concern possession by an alive, not ancestral, spirit although there is evidence in some groups that a long-deceased ancestor can also possess a person.[3] Thus Tsonga spirits are

---

[3]Thus Lee (1969: 131) states that some Zulu informants claim that some amandiki spirits are ancestors, but Asmus (1939) states categorically that they are different from the amadlozi. Sundkler, perhaps uncritically, classifies the amandiki/amandawe cult as "a modern form of ancestor-possession" (Sundkler 1966: 23), but the clearest comment on the Zulu is by Ngubane:

> An indiki is believed to be the spirit of a deceased person, a spirit that was never given the necessary sacrifice of integration with the body of other spirits. The people of countries further north who come to work on the mines of South Africa often die at the place of work, and their families, not hearing of their death, perform none of the rituals.... Such spirits wander about in desperation and become a nuisance to the local people, taking possession of them and causing illness.
> Indiki is therefore a male spirit (usually only

(Footnote continued)

believed to be those of Zulu and Ngoni warriors that raided into Mozambique under Gugunyane, and the (much feared) Ndau spirits who followed them (Junod 1927, 2:479). Venda spirits speak Karanga (Stayt 1931: 302), Kgaga cult members are frequently possessed by Tsonga spirits (Hammond-Tooke 1984) while Zulu amandiki or amandawe (Ndau) express themselves in so-called "Indian" or "Thonga" languages (Sundkler 1961: 23). The cult is believed to have originated in Swaziland or Tongaland.

(Footnote continued)
one) who enters a person and resides in the chest. The patient then becomes deranged ... crying in a deep bellowing voice and speaking a foreign tongue, usually identified as one of the languages spoken ... in the north. (Ngubane 1977: 143)

Ngubane states that the aim of the ritual is to replace the alien spirit with one of a male ancestor but her treatment of this raises conceptual problems. The Kriges, on the other hand, state that the Lovedu lelopa spirit is always an ancestor, but then refer to cases of possession caused by contact with "certain localities or people associated with possession" (e.g., the Sekhwashe or Mozambique) Krige and Krige 1954: 242). Among Venda the spirit (tshilombo) is "usually" the spirit of some offended ancestor, "sometimes obviously remote," but occasionally it has no genealogical connection with the person it enters (Stayt 1931: 302). Obviously the (new) phenomenon of possession does not yet enjoy a well-defined doctrine: what is clear is that this type of possession is by individual spirits and that in most groups they are typically defined as alien or non-kinsmen. It is significant that, in the probable region of their origin, the shave spirits are often animals or natural/artificial objects. "Mashave include the spirits of neighboring peoples, of white people, of certain animals (especially baboons) and occasionally of other objects such as aeroplanes. But usually little is known about the person or animal during its life, and these spirits normally come out as complete strangers to the communities of their mediums" (Bourdillon 1976/82: 232; see also Stayt 1931: 303).

Recruitment to the possession cult is through illness, usually of psychosomatic origin and diagnosed as alien possession by the diviner. The patient attaches herself to a cult leader (môkhoma) S. gobela TS) who has herself experienced possession, and seances are arranged at which drumming and dancing play an important role (as is often the case in Zionist groups). The drumming induces trance, during which the novice mimes the indwelling spirit, which is believed to be "pressing her down," and often the same patient may be possessed by a number of spirits seriatum. Therapy appears to involve a form of exorcism, as the spirit is enjoined to manifest itself and "come out," but more research is needed on this point. Each cult leader has a following, and these groups (or "schools") resemble somewhat the small Zionist congregations.

The most striking thing about these cult groups is that they are composed almost entirely of women, a fact that has led Lewis to typify them as "an oblique protest strategy against husbands and menfolk" (Lewis 1971: 88). Although the primary emphasis is on the exorcism of the intrusive spirit, possession tends to recur so that "what is eventually achieved is often more in the nature of an accommodation between the chronically possessed patient and her familiar" (op.cit). As can be imagined, this can be used (perhaps unconsciously) by women to enhance their power and importance in a society in which they are otherwise dominated and peripheral. Individualistic behavior, frowned on by the men, can be justified as being due to the promptings of the spirit, and there is little that men can do about it. As Lewis says: "Consequently, we have a feminist sub-culture, with an ecstatic religion restricted to women and protected from male attack through its representation as a therapy for illness" (op.cit. p. 89). Cults of affliction can thus be looked on as a response to fundamental social change in these African societies, in this case confined to its most helpless class. Female revolt against the "system" cannot easily be rationalized through the use of traditional cosmological ideas--ancestors uphold patrilineal and male interests, and witchcraft is unacceptably immoral--so new spirit entities are created to symbolize and facilitate new attitudes and behavior patterns. What more appropriate a metaphor for this than the image of the alien spirit?

4. The Holy Spirit

All the evidence is that indigenous ideas of a Supreme Being were relatively undeveloped. The poverty of the very few creation myths is striking and there were no rituals directed to the Supreme Being. Sometimes an event was explained as being caused by him, but this was more in the nature of an expression of ignorance of the true cause--rather like our idea of luck or chance, or as in the exasperated expression, "God only knows!" It is difficult to know why there should be this lack of conceptual elaboration. Horton (1975) has suggested that this phenomenon, fairly common in Africa, is associated with an emphasis on a microcosmic social structure, in which trade and other inter-community relations are not highly developed and where the vision and interests of the individual are confined to parochial matters of descent group and neighborhood. Theological theories thus do not have to cope with widescale theological problems. The idea of a Supreme Being, it is argued, only becomes theologically necessary in handling the problems of the wider macrocosm. The concept of the world has expanded, necessitating an expanded cognitive universe.

Be this as it may, when missionaries first came into contact with South African societies, it was this underdeveloped construct that they found. In many respects its vagueness was a blessing, as it was an empty container into which the rich complexities of Trinitarian doctrine could be poured. The traditional names were retained, however, the Unkulunkulu (Zulu), Qamata (Xhosa) and Modimo (Sotho) were equated with the Christian God. Later a name of Khoi origin, Thixo, came to replace the Nguni variants and was specialized to this usage. Among Nguni the break with tradition was thus complete: today many non-Christians accept the reality of a universal God and may occasionally pray to him directly (Pauw 1974: 431). In terms of the approach taken in this paper, one can see the adoption of the Christian God as an attempt to cope intellectually with the realities of an increasingly complex society, into which traditional communities were progressively incorporated and for which descent-based ancestor beliefs were quite unable to provide adequate understanding. One might almost say that if the Christian God had not been introduced an indigenous substitute would have had to be created.

The early African Christians became members of white-dominated mission churches, and the Christianity they received was essentially orthodox and mainstream. The earliest missionaries were Protestant and Evangelical--the London Missionary Society, Methodist, Presbyterian (Glasgow Missionary Society), Moravian, Lutheran and Congregational, most established between 1820 and 1835. Anglicans entered the field somewhat later, followed by the Roman Catholic Church (Pauw 1974: 416). But, for the particular interests of this paper, the most significant development was the introduction, from 1914 onwards, of pentecostal teaching stimulated by the USA-based Christian Catholic Apostolic Church of Zion and the Apostolic Faith Mission, with its emphasis on healing, adult baptism, and, especially, baptism by the Holy Spirit. It is in these so-called

Zionist churches that syncretism is most clearly revealed (Pauw 1974: 431).

The latter development is suggestive. Two factors are associated historically with pentecostal-type religious movements in the West. On the one hand, they possess a simplistic, but powerful, theology with a marked emphasis on this world, paradoxically associated with apocalyptic teaching: on the other, they tend to attract people marginal to the establishment (Niebuhr 1929). These two factors are related.

To take the theology first. It would seem that the doctrine of the trinity, with its tripartite structure of three Persons in the Godhead, is in practice psychologically difficult to maintain in balanced equilibrium. There is a tendency for one or other of the Persons, perhaps unintentionally, to be awarded greater emphasis. Thus God as Father is prominent in Calvinist theology as expressed recently in a sermon by the reverend Ian Paisley calling on God to punish the British Prime Minister, Jesus Christ in mainline Evangelical and Catholic Christianity (the devotion to Mary in the latter Church is a further complexity) and the Holy Spirit in forms of pentecostalism. (Greek Orthodoxy tries desperately to prevent this tendency by forbidding the invocation of the Father in liturgy without also mention of the Son of the Paraclete). One could speculate at length on the reasons for this phenomenon: in this paper I wish to concentrate on the implications of the salience of the Holy Spirit in pentecostalism.

If the main emphasis on the paternal metaphor is protection, guidance, compassion, love--but also (ultimate) authority, justice and, in some cases, punishment, the position of the Son is much less clear in the "practical religion" of the layman.

Accepted as equal to the Father, and saviour of mankind, there seems to be uncertainty in picturing his exact role in everyday religion. In a sense he is a brother (both men and Jesus are sons of God) but this dimension of the metaphor does not appear to be typically emphasized. Rather is he a companion, a concerned mediator between mankind and the Father, and perhaps most important, an exemplary for Christian living. For many Christians it is his role of saviour that is to the fore, rather than any clear picture of an ongoing functional relationship. This, of course, is a vast generalization, and does not represent the experience of all believers: it is based on conversations with an unrepresentative sample of what would be called in some circles "nominal Christians," who are perhaps, unfortunately, the great majority. It would seem that the metaphors of Father and Son both emphasize dependence, the essential incapacity of man to live a fulfilled, meaningful and moral life without the assistance and concern of the Holy Family.

The person of the Holy Spirit, on the other hand, is rather more ambiguous. Theologically, of course, he is the Comforter, the Enabler--the "agent" on earth which makes it possible for man to approach the Godhead. But the aspect that springs to mind when thinking about the Paraclete is power, a power that can work miracles and move mountains. Now, the problem with power is that it has overtones of autonomy. Although theologically the power of the Holy Spirit works ex definitione in the interests of the Godhead, there is the danger, in practice, that it can be used for other purposes. The history of the Church is full of examples of fission due to individual interpretations of the scriptures and of the mind of God, justified as being due to the "working" of the Holy Spirit.

Without denying the possibility of divine guidance, in some case, at least, these interpretations have their roots in such secular aspects as individual psychopathology, ethnic and racial preoccupations, social and political interests, and so on. This ambiguity in power is reflected in a discernible ambivalence in the mainline Christian Church to the doctrine of the Holy Spirit. As a doctrine it is extraordinarily undeveloped, especially when compared with the intellectual effort spent on the other two Persons of the Trinity.

Now the concept "power" resonates strongly with traditional African conceptions. It is the (unanalyzed) essence inherent in all medicines and in the symbols of "magical" ritual. It is also the characteristic par excellence of the ancestors, witches and alien spirits. The external manifestation of this power, apart from its effects on people and things, is typically seen in ecstatic behavior, the bursting of the bonds of personal constraints and of normal reality, often expressed in trance, glossalalia, visions and healing. Much of this is also part of traditional religion, and Sundkler (1961) has pointed out the marked parallelisms between the Moya-theology of the Zionist churches and the Zulu diviner. They are indeed striking.

But there is another reason for the salience of Spirit in African Independent Churches. The only thing that can be said about the position of blacks in South Africa is precisely their powerlessness. Not only are they socially and economically marginal to the total society, but they have no political control over their destinies and their perception of their position must be that of impotence. It is surely here that one must look for the great emphasis on the work of the Holy Spirit: the concept provides a potent counterbalance to the realities of the existential situation. But, paradoxically, it does this in a

microcosmic mode. One of the striking features of African
Zionism is that it does not provide a recipe for transforming
society as a whole. In this sense it is pietistic. What it does
do, though, is to localize the macrocosmic power of the Holy
Spirit in effective local groups--the small Zionist bands so ably
described by Kiernan and others. These tiny congregations (the
enormous structures of Shembe and Lekganyane are exceptions)
create pockets of believers--communities of the saved--that seal
themselves off from the wider community so that they attain a
kind of introverted integrity. It is almost as if the Spirit is
refracted, in Evans-Pritchard's term, to become identified
specifically with such small units. At the same time the very
marginality that these groups experience is transformed into a
benefit. Their theology explains and justifies their marginal
position in terms both of salvation and of meaningfulness in the
here-and-now. It is precisely their marginality to the centers
of secular power that provides the true power that comes from on
high.

5. The logic of syncretism

We are left with a final problem. Why the syncretism? Why
is it African Christians find it necessary to operate with a
religious world-view that includes four disparate elements--
ancestors, witches, alien spirits and the Holy Spirit?

The answer, it is suggested, lies in the fact that each of
these constructs "handles" different aspects of the cognitive
problems that confront blacks in Southern Africa today, on the
one hand, and express (and maintain) important social groups, on
the other. The core of the argument is briefly charted in the
following diagram.

Figure 1

THE TOPOGRAPHY OF SPIRIT

Social Field	Spirit	Explanatory Function	Social Function
descent group	ancestor	justifies kinship authority and amity: explains after-life, death, and some types of misfortune	expresses in ritual kinship authority: provides occasions for descent group inter-action: sanctions custom.
neighborhood (kin/ neighbors)	witch/ familiar	explains illness, misfortune and evil in terms of envy and conflict: theodicy.	objectifies conflict and provides means for elimination.
possession cult-group	alien spirits	explains female diseases	deflects female resentment/ protest into non-disrup-tive channels.
Zionist band	Holy Spirit	justifies poverty and marginality	localizes macrocosmic power in effective local group (ensures survival)

It appears from the above that the main reason for the hybrid nature of the religious world-view of some twentieth-century black Christians is the need (perhaps unconscious) to cope cognitively with the practical and moral dilemmas that face them in a fast-changing and highly unstructured society. Put simply, their experience of their life-in-the-world is one of dislocation, anomie and general lack of integration: small wonder, then, that their cosmology also exhibits this characteristic. Black Christians live in a world in which descent group loyalty is still an important moral precept, in which close interaction in an open social situation is still an important life experience, both in rural and urban contexts (There is little opportunity for an encapsulated withdrawal into middle-class seclusion in elite suburbs), women are undergoing vast modifications in their relative position vis-à-vis men (the old patrilineal chauvinism is becoming less and less appropriate in the modern world) and, until recently, the rigid structures of apartheid doomed most to powerlessness and poverty. It will be noted that each of these conditions is handled theoretically by the acceptance of an appropriate construct, conceptualized as spirit, which allows the problem to be thought about, and manipulated--not, significantly, in terms of human powers (which are manifestly inadequate) but in terms of external superhuman intelligences.

PART TWO: HEALING IN AFRICAN INDEPENDENT CHURCHES

INTRODUCTION

This section, which introduces the healing practices of African Independent Churches, starts and ends with very stimulating and provocative papers by Professor Oosthuizen. In his first paper he places indigenous healing practices within the context of African Independent Churches and shows how the office of prophet and of healer overlap and supplement each other. He also discusses the role of traditional African beliefs such as witchcraft and sorcery as a necessary background for understanding the development of an emphasis upon healing within the Independent Churches.

The second paper examines the results of an investigation conducted by Professor W.H. Wessels into the practices of traditional healers in the Durban area. He then discusses his findings in light of his own training as a psychiatrist. The result is a highly informative and original essay which provokes many questions for future research and analysis.

The next paper, by Mr. Dube, discusses various rituals found in Zionist churches and their relationship to healing. He demonstrates the intricate relationship between the traditional African world-view and the beliefs and practices of Zionist type churches. The result is an intriguing paper which makes the reader aware of the communal context within which the symbols, beliefs and practices of Zionist churches find their meaning. It also demonstrates how and why Zionist healing techniques appeal to many Africans because of the ways in which they establish rapport with the patient in ways that Western medicine does not.

Finally, Professor Oosthuizen provides a detailed discussion of baptism within both the historic Christian tradition and African Independent Churches. To most people "baptism" implies a rite of membership whereby an individual joins a particular church. But, in African Independent Churches baptism is a far more versatile and multifaceted ritual. Rather than having one baptism for membership the Independent Churches have many baptisms for a whole range of needs. Baptism is a rite of initiation, but it is also a rite of purification, healing and repentance. Understanding the full range of baptismal acts within African religious experience helps us reflect on the theology of baptism and what appears to be the reductionism of Western Christianity.

INDIGENOUS HEALING WITHIN THE CONTEXT OF THE
AFRICAN INDEPENDENT CHURCHES
by
G.C. Oosthuizen

The healing ministry of the church has been neglected in the so-called historic or "mainline" church. It has become central in African Independent Church. The largest group of the African Independent Church, base their healing activities on charismatic and indigenous procedures, in which the prophet and/or prayer healer plays a most significant role.

The office of prophet and prayer healer are not always interchangeable. Some African Independent Churches make a distinction between the two. Nevertheless they play a vital role with regard to those diseases which are associated with witchcraft, spirit possession and sorcery. In other words, those diseases which are seen in terms of a specific African cosmology.

Of the three main groups that constitute the African Independent Churches movement, namely, the Ethiopian (Amatopi) the Zionist (AmaZioni) and the African Apostolic Churches (Abapostoli), the later two most emphasize healing in a cosmological context.

About 80% of African Independent Churches are Zionist. This movement was started by the Christian Catholic church in Zion, which originated from Zion City, Illinois, USA, in 1896. In 1987 the emphasis of this church, namely healing by faith of physical and mental ills, plus a rejection of medicine, alcohol and tobacco, were brought to Blacks in South Africa. African Independent Churches became one of the most dynamic church movements on the African continent, in fact, in the contemporary world. In 1913, there were 32 denominations, supported by not more than 2% of the African population. In 1912 the Ethiopian churches leadership played a leading role in the founding of the African National Native Congress, which became the African National Congress (ANC) in 1925. In 1948, there were 800 denominations with 800,000 adherents or 9% of the African population. By 1960, this had grown to 2,000 denominations with 2,100,000 adherents or 18% of the African population; and in 1980, 3,270 denominations were supported by just under 6 million adherents or 29.3% of the African population. This, the fastest growing church movement in Southern Africa, will most probably have doubled by the end of the century.

Although healing is also effected by those who have ministerial offices, the prophet/prayer healer in general has become a central figure in these activities. In the historic Western churches the role of prophet disappeared as a church office in the 3rd century AD. But it reappeared strongly in the Zionist churches in Southern Africa. The office acts as a replacement for the diviner--the seer, reconciler, problem solver, healer--within the traditional African context.

In the New Testament, Jesus is also referred to by the designation "prophet"--although He never said He was a prophet-- and he is sometimes compared with the Old Testament prophets. He had visions, auditions and even ecstatic experiences; he had prophetic knowledge and saw through human plans; he could read the thoughts of people. He knew the future. In the early, also sometimes referred to as the "primitive," church of the first and second century, the prophet was the inspired charismatic proclaimer though whom God's plan of salvation with the world and the congregation became known to the individual person. The main task was proclamation.

Although he held in high esteem, prophecy was seen by the apostle Paul as passing away (1 Cor. 13:8f, 12). Since, eventually, the congregation would not be dependent upon prophecy, it would have no need for prophets. The office of prophet disappeared for several reasons. False prophets were a major problem. According to some of the early church fathers, such as Hermas, he sees the true prophet as gentle, calm, keeping himself away from evil desire, while the false prophet is arrogant, lying, seeking his own honor, unashamed ... not waiting upon what is revealed but acting as if he knows everything. Such prophets are accused of being only interested in remuneration for false acts.

The need for contextual healing

The office of prophet/prayer healer in the African Independent Churches fulfils a much felt need because of the traditional society's age-old role of the diviner and herbalist, for which the missionary or pastor in Christianity had no substitute. Sin in the historic churches is seen from the individual perspective, while in the African context it is seen from the social context. Sin in these churches is basically seen as a wrong relationship with God, for which the individual should make amends without further considerations. In the African context, based on the traditional African world-view, diseases are due to malicious external factors or the victim's own doings. The main causes for such diseases are sorcery, witchcraft, spirit possession, pollution, neglect of or disobedience to the ancestors, relatives, community and environment. Restoring social relationships implies healing--both physical and psychical. To restore a person's equilibrium, a holistic approach is necessary, and herein the supernatural forces play a vital role. The bad and negative influences have to be detected and removed from the situation and from the person, and only then can normal health be restored.

Sorcery, witchcraft and spirit possession are realities for many Christians in the established churches and the African

Independent Churches. In this context, the Western medical profession, as well as the churches established and directed by Western missionaries, have little to say. In the past, it was even taboo in many cases to mention such diseases in the presence of a missionary. Yet, there are churches which acknowledge the effectiveness of the rituals utilized in the indigenous healing of typical African types of diseases and consider that they should receive sympathetic attention rather than mere short-sighted condemnation.

The problem is that the world-view from which missionaries started was not the one with which Africa initially concerned itself. Thus, no serious attention was given to the realities of Africa, where indigenous healing of diseases related to the African cosmology, which includes such issues as witchcraft, sorcery and spirit possession, and places primary emphasis on restoration of relationships, on purification and on cleansing. The only way to be relevant and meaningful in the existential context, is to take these forces seriously. This is what happens in the African Independent Churches and is the main reason why they attract people by the thousands--not because they offer an easy way out but because they provide help. They acknowledge that bewitching, sorcery, spirit possession are realities; that sickness and disturbed social relationships are bound together; and that restoration of relationships has a healing effect. The diviner is the restorer of relationships in the traditional society; in the indigenous churches this role is accorded to the prophet.

Evil spirits are considered to be responsible for the type of illness which Western trained medical practitioners fail to detect. Such illness includes that type of physical, mental and psychical discomfort which is seldom related to insanity. Spirit possession may increase when tension intensifies as a result of transition from the traditional to the modern way of life and its different world-view. Hence Sunday after Sunday, one observes groups of the African Independent Churches at pools, rivers, dams and beaches, seeking personal purification through immersion. Such "baptism" has largely become a purification rite and a healing procedure in the African Independent Churches since it is quite natural to interpret the hardship experienced in transitions from the traditional to the modern, in the socio-economic and political context in this country, in the context of spirit possession, witchcraft or sorcery. Here lies one of the main reasons for the exceptional growth of the African Independent Churches movement in Southern Africa although one must also take into account the efforts of transition out of the microcosmic into the macrocosmic world, from an ontocratic into a secularizing world-view.

Nothing, however, is more responsible for the rapid growth of African Independent Churches than the fact that they take the negative forces of the African cosmology seriously and that the problems they see as real concern witchcraft, sorcery, demons and evil spirits. Evil spirits are considered to be the main obstacles to development and progress. They symbolize the reaction to change as well as the vicissitudes of the new situation, which force them to question the traditional way of life and beliefs. The ensuing deep psychological tensions are often hypostatised in foreign spirits. (Cf. Hammond-Tooke: 1986).

The ideological approach of missionaries to the forces in the African traditional cosmology has kept them away from the specific problems of Africa. Equally, Christian and Western orientated hospitals seem to have failed to reveal any understanding of the role of the African metaphysical world on matters concerning illness and health. As a result, one still awaits a dynamic therapy for treatment in this connection. Fortunately, one does begin to observe signs of change. Knowledge is power in understanding the forces that reign in the African context.

In a society where harmony in social relationships is vital, the antisocial effects of sorcery and witchcraft should be taken seriously. Disharmony affects the very health and well-being of people. Reconciliation with one another and with the metaphysical forces is thus a vital issue. The ancestors who sanction customs, rituals and taboos are neglected in a modernizing situation. Thus, relationships are disturbed, leading to sickness, misfortune, bad luck, attacks by various types of evil forces and even death. Merely to pray to God will not solve conflicts--relationships have to be rectified.

In African Independent Churches especially the Zionists, the real adversary is the sorcerer, who is an antagonistic human being. Kiernan indicates that because of the looming presence of the evil forces, Satan, a spiritual being, is pushed into the background. While Satan attacks the group and tempts people directly to do what is morally wrong, such as committing violent acts which disturb the peace of the group, the sorcerer attacks the individual (Cf. Kiernan: 1985). Thus, complaints of sorcery call for a realistic functional approach, since they indicate a deep seated psychic element which needs serious attention. Less problematic to the prophets in the African Independent Churches is witchcraft, although sorcery is regularly referred to by them as witchcraft. Most "witches" are women.

In the indigenous churches the adversary is always confronted but never really overcome. The scapegoat mentality which projects destructive instincts on to an individual now projects them on the adversary which continuously confronts the group. This unifies the group against the common enemy. The same approach lies behind hell-fire preaching in certain churches. Such groups possess a corporate personality and members are protected and fortified against their adversaries through the ritual acts they observe and the sacred objects they use and wear, such as uniforms, cords, medals, photos of leaders, holy sticks and holy water prayed over. These acts and objects fortify them against their enemies, for traditional fetishes and amulets cannot be erased with the stroke of a pen or with Bible texts. Furthermore, the churches have their own protecting objects--as seen even in the pious reference to Bible texts, which could perform the same function as do fetishes and amulets.

While historic churches in general have no rituals to counteract the effects of witchcraft and sorcery, the African Independent Churches give specific attention to these issues. It is clear that African cosmology cannot be erased overnight in the mind of those nurtured in it. If their deepest needs are not meaningfully addressed, many revert to the traditional securities. Life, health and wholeness are vital issues within the African context, and the adverse forces need to be taken seriously, as do the various symbolic acts and signs. Theological problems often arise when the impression is created that these rituals take place in the traditional rather than the Christian context.

Exorcism is high on the list of African Independent church activities and takes place at every healing ceremony. Hitting the spirit-possessed person with staves and with the hands, especially on the shoulders and arms, "drives out" the evil forces. Although the African historic churches tend to look at this as outmoded superstition, many of their members go to the African Independent Churches sessions for such help. The Bible takes these issues seriously, as is seen in the attitude of Jesus to demon possession. Spirit-possessed people need serious attention, and a church which ignores this in the African context is in this respect culturally unrelated to Africa.

Apart from its negative associations, belief in bewitchment, sorcery and spirit possession is functional as it assists a person to deal with any personality crisis that arises as a result of social control. As someone of worth, the victim is "allowed" to mistrust the environment, and such issues as bewitchment are related to a process of identify formation to a network of psychological dynamics.

It also helps to put into motion the symbolic acting out of inner guilt feelings. Ancestor presence and the influence of evil spirits are so strong that a person could hardly be responsible for specific actions and could hardly feel guilty about them. Yet a deep sense of guilt can develop and often only the performance of a traditional ritual can take this guilt feeling away. (Cf. Masamba ma Mpolo: 1984, 152; and Lagerwerf: 1985, 1-62). The historic churches reject such acts as "pagan." Yet although they may not be "Christian," they are realities which need close attention.

Prophet/diviner activities

Africa's first- and second-century Christianity has not completely alienated itself from traditional spirituality since healing is still basically a religious and holistic activity.

A sociological survey which indicated clearly that the role of the prophet is of vital significance in most African Independent Churches where the office of prophet/prayer healer is a substitute for the office of diviner in the traditional society. The survey showed that none of the prophets in the Durban area was first treated by a diviner before the "Christian power" could function. Yet, in the Rand area, especially Soweto, thirty percent of the prophets received subsequent treatment from a diviner after being treated unsuccessfully by a prophet. Thirty percent of the Rand prophets emphatically stated that traditional medicines are not acceptable, while the rest admitted that they utilize these medicines for their healing procedures.

The prophets have a very encompassing task in diagnosing illnesses, utilising methods to heal them, establishing causes of misfortune, settling conflicts, "predictions" future events, warning clients about brooding problems, praying for them, etc. They work either under the guidance of an ancestor(s), or under "the Spirit." An Ancestor(s) could be a mediator(s) between the person and "the Spirit." Some see the prophet in a sense as a modernized diviner.

There are a number of parallels between the calling and activities of a diviner and a prophet. The diviner reinstates the importance of the ancestral spirits in the lives of many; so do a large number of prophets. Like the diviner, most prophets have an ukuthwasa experience, when "the Spirit" and/or ancestral spirit approaches them to become a prophet and they become ill. The prophet also goes through a period of apprenticeship, like the diviner. During this time, inter alia, sacrifices are usually made to the ancestral spirits, purification rites are observed, and both learn how to interpret dreams, how to receive visions, how to diagnose, predict and heal.

As in the case of diviners, most of the prophets are assisted by ancestral spirits in the diagnosis and treatment of illnesses. The ancestor informs the prophet what disease affects the victim, how a patient should be treated, the types of medicines to be used, the color of the vestments to be worn and often the type of sacrifice to be made, especially in crisis situations. The designation "victim" refers to people against whom sorcery has been practiced, who feel bewitched, or who are spirit possessed. In the traditional context they are patients who have to be healed. This accounts for the combined designation of victim/patient.

Why the combination of traditional and scriptural approach?

The Zionist prophet uses his/her healing powers against witchcraft and sorcery. Socio-economic, cultural and political tensions, especially in the urban areas, are due to factors pertaining both to the traditional and the secular world. The combined adverse forces are experienced so strongly that Bible study and prayer are considered to be inadequate. "Much more" is needed than what is offered by either the Biblical or Western approaches. Rituals have to be performed. These rituals often follow the traditional lines of divining but are streamlined in order to be effective in the modern context, as has been observed by other researchers (Cf. Sundkler: 1948, 255; Schlosser: 1958, 205-6; and West: 1975, 97). The rituals, the ingredients used, the procedures observed and the various symbols employed have a miraculous effect when correctly utilized. Prophets are considered to have supernatural power which comes from that world. One very seldom hears among the prophets/prayer healers that Jesus Christ gave them their various gifts or that there is any involvement from his side in healing procedures. This is probably due to what they see as neglect of healing procedures in the so called historic churches, where the name of Jesus is limited to "salvation," a word which means in the original language healing.

Much emphasis is put on "the Spirit of power" and/or "the spirits," which could either be the Holy Spirit or the ancestors. These metaphysical contacts give the prophet a specific position as he/she is considered to understand the victim's/patient's problem much better than any Western doctor and better even than the diviners. The prophets' supernatural contact with "the Spirit" and/or ancestral spirit(s) gives them special insights into the nature and cause of illnesses, according to their own testimony and those whom they treat. Prophets are thus considered to be more convincing in their diagnosis and procedures than is the Western trained doctor.

A variety of remedies are given, a variety of techniques are utilized and the healing process is in the hands of a robed person, who has supernatural contact and thus supernatural power --a combination of traditional and Christian forces. The ritual impresses with its fervent prayer (word therapy), its use of candles, cords, holy water, staves, drumming, singing, and rhythmic movements as well as its employment of various traditional types of medicines and rituals. When the patient/victim is before the prophet, he/she, usually receives instant information on the type of illness and how it should be cured. Sometimes, before the victim/patient arrives, the prophet has dreams in which the ancestors and/or "the Spirit" reveal the illness. Not many questions are put to the patient, contrary to the practice of the Western trained doctor and to the diviner's vumisa technique of asking leading questions. A few do utilise this procedure, during which "Amens" are loudly expressed by the bystanders. In the traditional context, bystanders used to express their agreement when the diviner in his leading questions approached what they thought was the correct diagnosis.

Some observe a sooth-saying or divining ceremony, which is referred to as prophecy. Hidden sins are "seen" in the individual and in the church members thorough such prophecy; in other words, it is made known to them by "the Spirit" and/or ancestral spirits. Vilakazi emphasized the centrality of the ancestral spirits in cases of illness or misfortune in the traditional Zulu society. He states "I cannot remember a single instance when I heard a prayer by a traditionalist offered to uMvelingqangi.... In diagnosing the cause of the disease or misfortune, the diviner discovers the cause either in witchcraft and sorcery and/or in the anger of the spirits, not of uMvelingqangi" (i.e., God)--(Cf. Vilakazi: 1962, 89). "The Spirit" and/or ancestral spirits are central in the healing procedures--only for a few are the Bible and prayer "mighty weapons" against the adverse forces. The traditional "power house" against adversaries has to be brought into play and only then will the way be opened to the future. Sundkler states that "the actual belief in witchcraft is vital in the Zionist church. Both Zionist prophesying and Zionist healing are based on such a belief. No healing is complete until the prophet has found and removed from the patient's hut some horn or bottle, supposed to contain ubuthakathi poison" (i.e., bewitched poison). (Sundkler: 1948, 264). Divination is used even against those who refuse to join a specific church.

Preference for the prophet as contextualiser

Leaders of the Zionist type of churches put much emphasis on having prophets within their churches. For them it is important that they get the right person with special gifts. Their visions and predictions are a great asset to the church and they are consulted on most of the important matters pertaining to the church. They decide on the colors of the uniforms of new members; they assess candidates for leadership positions in the church; they indicate the sins and adversaries of the congregation; they express the wishes of "the Spirit" and/or ancestor spirits and they "predict" the future development of the church. The prophet is consulted on all important issues in most indigenous churches where this office exists. Of the three ways of healing, namely by immersion in the sea, river, pool or dam; by drumming, singing and laying on of hands; or by consulting a prophet/prayer healer, the latter takes a significant position.

There is a strong desire among many females to become prayer healers and prophets. In most of the Zionist churches, as indicated earlier, a distinction is made between prayer women and prophets. The former are sometimes referred to as "half prophets" or "healing assistants" and are given holy staves for healing purposes. They receive the authority to visit and pray for the sick and to follow healing procedures with them. (Cf. West: 1975, 98). Most prophets receive training while most of the prayer women do not. The life history of the prophet is in many respects parallel to that of the diviner--they are also called (often through the mediatorship of an ancestor); they too, go through a period of illness which is only successfully treated by a senior prophet; they are purified, trained (i.e. to "see" illnesses and causes for mal-relationships, etc.,) and initiated as prophets. As in the case of the diviner, the calling includes illness, (ukuthwasa in Zulu), nervousness and ancestors informing the future prophet to go to a specific person to be trained. As in the case of the diviners the initiation procedure includes learning how to interpret dreams and how to act on visions, singing and rhythmic movements (dancing in a circle). White ash mixed with water is also used both during the initiation of a diviner and the training of a prophet.

The diviner's hair remains uncut as does that of the prophet, who refers to Judges 13:5 and 1 Samuel 1:11 in this connection. Both use vestments and cords (with symbolic colors), which are attached in both cases around the neck, wrists, ankles, waist and cross-wise over the shoulders. The diviner uses a "holy" stick to which often the tail end of a beast is attached, while the prophet uses a rod or staff based on Exodus 7:9-12 which says: "And the Lord said to Moses and Aaron when Pharaoh says to you, 'Prove yourself by working a miracle' then you shall say to Aaron, 'Take your rod and cast it down before Pharaoh, that it may become a serpent' ... and it became a serpent ... the wise men and the sorcerers ... the magicians of Egypt, did the same by their secret arts ... every man cast down his rod, and they became serpents. But Aaron's rod swallowed up all their rods." With the prophet's staff miracles are performed and evil spirits are kept away or driven out. Through it, the power of "the Spirit" is transferred to the sick person, thus strengthening him/her to overcome the weakness which sickness brings. The staff is one of the main objects used in exorcism. It is regularly purified and thus ritually strengthened in running water, in water mixed with ash and in the sea. Sometimes all the staves of those who are allowed to have them are bundled together and put into the sea--a purification rite which also symbolizes the unity of the group.

There are other parallels between diviners and prophets in their behavior and activity after initiation. They both work under the injunctions of the metaphysical world: ancestor(s) in the case of the diviners; "the Spirit" and/or ancestor(s) in the case of the prophets. Dreams and visions play a significant role for both diviners and prophets. Much of their work is based on dreams and visions, and both have the ability to "predict," referred to sometimes as fortune telling.

Although the work of diviners and prophets varies in detail, there is "considerable uniformity," as West has also observed (West: 1975, 104). Greatly appreciated is the reintegrative work of both their warmth, empathy and integrity. The traditional-orientated world-view of the patient/victim is not foreign to the diviner, nor to the prophet. What is an enigma to the patient/victim becomes clarified and his world-view becomes meaningful. Inner turmoil is replaced with understanding; a meaningful relationship is created between patient/victim and healer, which is important for effective treatment. Within the context of the Christian approach but in association with the indigenous world-view, such treatment does not involve the traumatic break that hospitalization brings. The emphasis is on togetherness, on reintegration; not on hospitalization, which means individualization in distress. Just as the diviner treats the patient/victim in the context of his family, so the prophet's activities are supplemented by a genuine interest and the support of the church group. The group is essential for shared experience. Group therapy plays a significant role, not only in physical and mental healing processes but also in removing tensions brought about by adaptation to the urban environment. Explained as illness as such crises are relegated outside the sphere of the ordinary and call for extraordinary methods, which only the diviner/herbalist for the traditionalists and/or prophets for many in the indigenous churches can fulfill. Here the Western trained doctor is at a loss.

Some prophets have become very popular in the urban areas because of their healing abilities, and most do not expect financial gain. Through their healing successes prophets often attract adherents to their churches and some achieve a special reputation for being effective in curing illnesses pertaining to the African cosmology. For example, couples who experience marriage problems may appear before the Bishop or come to the prophet to have the "bad spirit" removed--such a bad spirit may not necessarily be an evil spirit but an ancestral spirit who has turned against them and disturbs their lives. Special sessions are held to free people from drugs or alcohol addiction and here the church leader or prophet/prayer healer is active while the congregation sings to the accompaniment of drums and rhythmic movements; staves put against the person (this is not done when in the sea water because the water alone is strong enough), hands laid on the person, who is forcefully hit (often manhandled) on the body in order to get the evil forces out; loud, fast praying and shouting, which often ends up in glossolalia are all part of the whole procedure. Such sessions often have specific results not only in the lives of the victims/patients but also in the lives of those who witness these proceedings. When "the Spirit" and/or ancestor spirit mediate power to the victim/patient, the foreign evil spirits remove themselves. These are evil spirits which migrated into South Africa from neighboring countries, such as Mozambique, Zimbabwe and Malawi, mainly through the workers on the mines who come from these countries.

Possession by "the Spirit" implies being elevated to a higher level of spirituality, in which the limitations and weaknesses of the flesh are overcome. Healing and possession by "the Spirit" are especially typical of indigenized African pentecostalism. In most of the Zionist churches the ancestors also have a vital function as guardians, mediators, consultants, assistants in the diagnosis of the victim/patient's queries, and so on. The ancestor spirit in the context of the Zionist churches is usually not a possessor but, a mediator, except when an ancestor spirit takes hold of and instructs a person in these churches to become a diviner. (Cf. Lee in Beattie and Middleton: 1969, 200).

It is clear from the above that closer attention should be given to the ways in which the traditional healing methods find expression within the indigenous/independent churches. The significance of the prophet/prayer healer is so central to the physical and mental healing activities of a large number of the indigenous churches that it is a matter of urgency that attention be given to these activities. Less than two hundred psychiatrists are active in South Africa, which has a population of nearly thirty million. In a situation where two world-views-- the ontocratic and the secular meet, where so many socio-economic and political problems exist and where the most rapid social changes on the African continent are taking place, much psychiatric work--albeit indirection--is being undertaken in the indigenous churches. Whereas healing within most of the so-called historical churches is considered to be a kind of appendix to their church activities, healers in the indigenous churches receive great appreciation for their work. All the activities related to healing elevate religion to the dramatic in these churches, serving as a catharsis in the current chaotic situation in which their trusted traditions are attacked. Yet, it is precisely the combination of these old securities with what they find in Christianity, that helps them to meet this world of socio-economic and political insecurity.

The prophets/prayer healers take the world in which their people live seriously. The emphasis is never on "a pie in the sky when you die" but rather on the here and now. Theologically, certain issues may merit close scrutiny but, from a socio-psychological point of view, the prophet's position is firmly established in many indigenous churches.

HEALING PRACTICES IN THE AFRICAN INDEPENDENT CHURCHES
by
W.H. Wessels

Introduction

"Medicine born of necessity was at first magic, then a prayer, finally an art, and only recently a science." (Bromberg, 1937, p.27).

The words of Walter Bromberg reflect the need for healing practices among the Africans to incorporate magic, prayer, art and science. The African indigenous churches have realized the importance of including the magic and the art with the prayer when dealing with traditional African people.

A perusal of the literature reveals no previous psychiatric investigation of the knowledge and healing practices of the faith healers of the African Indigenous churches.

Method of Investigation

In order to investigate their practices, ten reputable faith healers from these churches in the Durban area were asked to complete a questionnaire with the help of a trained field investigator. Fifteen different, predominantly psychiatric conditions well recognized by traditional healers, were listed and five questions were asked about each. These were: a) How do you recognize it? b) What causes it and how is the cause best determined? c) Who should treat it? (A choice was given of iSangoma or inyanga or umthandazi/umpropheti or Western doctor). d) Why is this person best able to treat it? e) How should it be treated.

The fifteen conditions investigated were as follows: uhlanya, isidalwa, isithutwane, ufufunyane, idliso, izizwe iqondo, uvalo, umeqo, ukutwasa, indiki, ukudlula, abaphansi basifulatele, umnyama and umhayizo.

The sample was kept small because the questions were open, lending themselves to very diverse answers. The open questions had been necessary in order to determine the frame of reference of such an investigation. The results from this investigation will be utilized in future to plan a more comprehensive trial on a larger scale, with more specific questions and a choice of answers.

Discussion of Results

The faith healers (prophets) were asked to compare themselves with the traditional healers (diviners). They indicated that the main differences between prophets and diviners were that prophets go to church, pray and use holy water, whereas diviners use traditional herbs, bones and killing medicine.

TABLE I

Differences between faith healers (Prophets) and traditional healers (Diviners).

The prophet does not:

Use traditional herbs	67%
Use bones	60%
Use killing medicine	40%
Smoke snuff	7%
Make incision	7%
Divine	7%

The prophet does:

Go to church/pray	100%
Use "iziwasho"	47%

The traditional healer does not:

Believe in God/Christ   20%

The traditional healer does:

Wear beads   7%

The African concept of illness (Wessels 1985a) indicates the traditional African frame of reference concerning illness and misfortune. All people are obliged to prevent imbalance between themselves, their environment and the ancestral spirits by regularly performing certain rituals and using certain cleansing procedures. Should they fail in this moral obligation they become vulnerable to magical or natural influences.

Looking at the traditional classification of illness, according to Ngubane (1977), we find that the two main divisions are umkuhlane (natural illness) and ukufa kwabantu (African illness). African illness is that group of disorders believed to be peculiar to the African people and of traditional cultural aetiology. The natural group of illnesses are those that happen by chance. They closely resemble similar conditions in Europeans. (Wessels, 1976). Those that have relevance to psychiatry are the following: isithutwane (Epilepsy), ufuzo (familial and Genetic disorders), isidalwa (Mental retardation) and uhlanya (Schizophrenia). (Ngubane 1977, Edwards et al: 1982 and Wessels 1985a).

The natural illnesses (umkuhlane) are conditions that are present with psychiatric and physical type symptomatology. These conditions are best treated, therefore, by somatic treatments which may be stopped or changed as necessary.

Magic however, can also influence Africans, should they become vulnerable. This causes African illnesses (ukufa kwabantu), which give rise to psychological type symptoms that are best treated by ritual treatment, which should be persevered with, even if unsuccessful.

Certain psychosomatic conditions could also develop due to vulnerability, causing somatic symptoms, having both magical and natural causes, and therefore necessitating treatment of both kinds.

Table II shows a reasonably correct description of the symptoms of Schizophrenia. This corresponds well with the symptoms as recognized by the diviners. Looking at the causation of uhlanya, however, we find that the faith healers ascribe it to disobeying traditional customs, thinking too much with too many worries, witchcraft, or being possessed by evil spirits. This is at variance with the traditional concept that uhlanya is one of the conditions of natural causation and not one of the African illnesses.

TABLE II

Zulu name: "UHLANYA"

Traditional Concept: Madness

Psychiatric Diagnosis: Schizophrenia

HOW DO YOU RECOGNIZE IT?

Mad in the head	50%
Laughs or talks to self	50%
Talks nonsense	50%
Shabby appearance	40%
Avoids people	40%

WHAT CAUSES IT?

Disobeying traditional customs	40%
Too much thinking and too many worries	30%
Witchcraft or possession by evil spirits	30%

The faith healers have correctly identified isidalwa (Table III) as indicating a deformed person. Despite recognizing it as a deformity, they ascribe it to disobeying traditional customs in fifty percent of the cases. Only thirty percent recognize that the person was born that way. The traditional healer generally regards this as one of the natural illnesses.

TABLE III

Zulu Name: "ISIDALWA"

Traditional Concept: Retarded and/or Deformed

Psychiatric Diagnosis: Mental Retardation and/or Physical
                      Deformity

HOW DO YOU RECOGNIZE IT?

Deformed	100%

WHAT CAUSES IT?

Disobeying traditional customs	50%
God created them that way	30%

The prophets recognize the symptoms of Epilepsy (Table IV) very clearly but although half of them accept that one is born with it the other half ascribe it to stepping over muti. A further one-third blames it on an accident to the spine or brain. The latter corresponds with the Western medical concept of the causes of Epilepsy.

TABLE IV

Zulu name: "ISITHUTWANE"

Traditional concept: Seizures

Psychiatric diagnosis: Epilepsy

HOW DO YOU RECOGNIZE IT?

Falls down	90%
Body shakes	40%
Foams at mouth	30%

WHAT CAUSES IT?

Born with it	50%

Stepping over muti   50%

An accident to spine or brain   30%

The African illnesses (ukufa kwabantu) that were investigated can be divided as shown in Table V (Wessels 1985b):

TABLE V

Zulu name: "KWABANTU"

1.0 Spirit Possession

1.1 Ancestral spirit possession (ukuthwaza)

1.2 Alien spirit possession (ufufunyane, izizwe)

1.3 Wandering spirit possession (indiki)

2 Sorcery (umhayizo, uvalo, igondo)

3 Poisoning (idliso)

4 Pollution (umnyama)

5 Environmental hazards (umego)

6 Ancestral displeasure (abaphansi basifulatele)

7 Disregard of cultural norms (ukudlula)

Ukuthwasa (Table VI) is very well recognized by all of them as the ancestors having called the person to work for them. There is no agreement on how the condition can be recognized. This multiplicity of symptomatology is reflected in the diverse diagnoses attached to this condition by Western psychiatrists.

TABLE VI

Zulu name: "UKUTHWASA"

Traditional concept: Ancestral spirit possession

Psychiatric diagnosis: Atypical Psychosis or Severe Anxiety
                       Disorder

HOW DO YOU RECOGNIZE IT?

Called to work for ancestors   30%

WHAT CAUSES IT?

Ancestors want you to work for them   100%

Since ufufunyane (Table VII) and izizwe (Table VIII) are regarded as very similar conditions by diviners (Sundkler, 1961), it is gratifying to note that they are regarded similarly by the faith healers. However, there is a significant difference in the causation. Diviners generally regard the cause as alien spirit possession, in contrast to most faith healers who see the cause as "a man using muti to make a girl desire him." There is no difference in the symptomatology as described by the diviners and the faith healers.

TABLE VII

Zulu Name: "UFUFUNYANE"

Traditional concept: Possession by numerous alien spirits

Psychiatric diagnosis: Brief Reactive Psychosis
                         (Hysterical psychosis)

HOW DO YOU RECOGNIZE IT?

Crying or screaming	60%
Running around/away	50%
Easily startled	50%

WHAT CAUSES IT?

Man using muti to make a girl desire him	60%

TABLE VIII

Zulu name: "IZIZWE"

Traditional concept: Alien Spirit Possession

Psychiatric diagnosis: Brief Reactive Psychosis
                       (Hysterical psychosis)

HOW DO YOU RECOGNIZE IT?

Crying or screaming	70%
Running away	50%
Groan or belch after yawning	20%
React when shoulder touched	20%

WHAT CAUSES IT?

Man using muti to make a girl desire him	50%

Indiki (Table IX) is traditionally regarded as being due to possession by a wandering African spirit who has died away from home and for whom the proper rituals have not been done. People affected in such a way are regarded, after a cure has been affected, as the people best able to treat a person with indiki. This ability to work for the ancestors is recognized by the faith healers. Traditionally, the spirit possessions of ufufunyane, izizwe and indiki are seen as having very similar symptoms.

TABLE IX

Zulu name: "INDIKI"

Traditional concept: Possession by a wandering African spirit

Psychiatric diagnosis: Brief Reactive Psychosis

                      (Hysterical psychosis)

HOW DO YOU RECOGNIZE IT?

    Dreams of ancestors, snakes or izangoma   50%

WHAT CAUSES IT?

    Ancestors want you to work for them   100%

It is interesting to note that the next condition umhayizo, (Table X), is recognized by virtually all faith healers and is ascribed to a man using muti to cause a girl to desire him. This corresponds well with the traditional concept. The prophets, however, ascribe the same cause to the previously mentioned ufufunyane and izizwe. In Western psychiatric terms ufufunyane, izizwe and indiki are much more severe than umhayizo since the first three are regarded as of psychotic proportions corresponding to hysterical psychosis (Wessels, 1983).

TABLE X

Zulu name: "UMHAYIZO"

Traditional concept: Sorcery by love potion

Psychiatric diagnosis: Hysteria

HOW DO YOU RECOGNIZE IT?

    Scream/cry hysterically   90%

    Makes you run   20%

WHAT CAUSES IT?

    Man using <u>muti</u> to cause girl to desire him   90%

    <u>Uvalo</u> (Table XI) is described in the same terms, as far as symptomatology and causation are concerned, by both diviners and prophets. Both recognize it as a condition of fear or anxiety.

TABLE XI

Zulu name: "UVALO"

Traditional concept: Being frightened

Psychiatric diagnosis: Anxiety Disorder

HOW DO YOU RECOGNIZE IT?

Frightened/apprehensive	80%
Shocked	40%
Lose weight	20%

WHAT CAUSES IT?

Calling your name on <u>muti</u>	70%

    The causation of <u>iqondo</u> (Table XII) is recognized by only 40% of the faith healers as sorcery being practiced on a wife's lover by the husband. There is also wide variation in the symptomatology ascribed to the condition. This, however, corresponds with the traditional concepts. The condition is medically recognized as disease of the uro-genital system, often involving prostatic enlargement or venereal disease. Some cases of impotence have traditionally also been attributed to this cause.

TABLE XII

Zulu name: "IQONDO"

Traditional concept: Harm to a wife's lover by sorcery

Psychiatric diagnosis: Uro-genital Disease

HOW DO YOU RECOGNIZE IT?

Do funny things	40%
Pain/swelling genitals	30%
Talk/answer foolishly	30%

102

Venereal Disease	20%
Something inside stomach	20%

WHAT CAUSES IT?

Sex with someone's wife or girl	40%

In idliso (Table XIII) the symptoms and causation are agreed upon by both traditional and faith healers. This corresponds well with the Western concept of psychosomatic gastro-intestinal tract disorder.

TABLE XIII

Zulu name: "IDLISO"
Traditional concept: Ingestion of Sorcerer's poison
Psychiatric diagnosis: Psychosomatic G I tract disorder
HOW DO YOU RECOGNIZE IT?

Loss of weight	70%
Loss of appetite	40%
Tuberculosis	40%
Bloody Mucus/Vomit	40%
Coughing	30%
Chest problem	20%

WHAT CAUSES IT?

Inyanga's muti in food or drink	90%

The polluted state of darkness, umnyama (Table XIV), is usually contracted during periods of death and birth when the correct rituals have not been obeyed, according to the concept of diviners. The faith healers correctly identify it as the cause of bad luck and a condition which roughly corresponds with the Western concept of depression on a minor or major scale.

TABLE XIV

Zulu name: "UMNYAMA"
Traditional concept: Pollution causing bad luck
Psychiatric diagnosis: Depression (Minor or Major)

HOW DO YOU RECOGNIZE IT?

    Bad luck   30%

    Things never come right   30%

    People hate you   20%

WHAT CAUSES IT?

    Disobeying the ancestors   30%

    Bad ancestors creating bad luck for you   20%

The condition of umego (Table XV) is seen by both diviners and prophets as being due to stepping over a harmful concoction and causing swollen feet or paralyzed legs. It is interesting to note that thirty percent of the prophets state that one of the symptoms is "liquid inside you," corresponding to the Western concept of fluid retention (Oedema) causing swollen feet.

TABLE XV

Zulu name: "UMEQO"

Traditional concept: Stepping over harmful concoction

Psychiatric diagnosis: Oedema and paralysis of legs

HOW DO YOU RECOGNIZE IT?

    Swollen legs or feet   70%

    Liquid inside you   30%

    What cause it?

    You step over muti   100%

In the condition where "the ancestors turn their faces away from you," abaphansi basifulatele, reflected in Table XVI, the causation stated in forty percent of the responses of the faith healers was that your ancestors want you to perform a ritual. Traditionally, the cause is ascribed to neglecting to do so. Such a condition often leads to symptoms resembling minor or major depression.

TABLE XVI

Zulu name: "ABAPHANSI BASIFULATELE"

Traditional concept: Ancestral displeasure

Psychiatric diagnosis: Depression (Minor or Major)

HOW DO YOU RECOGNIZE IT?

Bad luck	90%
Cannot get a job	40%
Nothing you do comes right	20%

WHAT CAUSES IT?

Your ancestors want you to perform a ritual	40%

When ukudlula (Table XVII) is analyzed, there is complete agreement between diviners and prophets as to the causation. The symptoms they describe correspond with the Western psychiatric diagnosis of Obsessive Compulsive Disorder, sometimes reflected as Kleptomania.

TABLE XVII

Zulu name: "UKUDLULA"

Traditional concept: Disregard of ritual practices

Psychiatric diagnosis: Obsessive Compulsive Disorder

Kleptomania

HOW DO YOU RECOGNIZE IT?

Overdoing things when you don't want to	60%
Acts like a thief who can't stop stealing	30%
Does unusual things	20%

WHAT CAUSES IT?

Not mourning or keeping rules for someone in the family who has died	80%

Analysis of the treatment proposed for the disorders included in the questionnaire shows that, despite the fact that the diviners regard umkuhlane, or the natural illnesses as belonging in the domain of the Western doctor, the faith healers think that the diviner or prophet or ethno-doctor would be best qualified to treat these conditions.

TABLE XVIII

"UMKUHLANE" - Natural Illness

	Traditional Healers	Western Doctors
"UHLANYA"	100%	Nil
"ISIDALWA"	60%	40%
"ISITHUTWANE"	80%	20%

Informed diviners regard Schizophrenia, deformity, mental retardation and epilepsy as diseases treatable by Western doctors and not by traditional healers. On analysis of the group of African illnesses ukufa kwabantu, Table XIX), it is clear that the prophets regard themselves, rather than the iSangoma or inyanga, as being by far the best qualified to handle the culture-specific syndromes. Treatment of the culture-specific syndromes by Western doctors is generally regarded as less effective by both diviners and knowledgeable Western practitioners. The relative lack of knowledge about the ukufa kwabantu among faith healers is cause for concern.

TABLE XIX

"UKUFA KWABANTU" - African Illness

Who could treat it?

"ISANGOMA"	24%
"INYANGA"	29%
"UMTHANDAZI"	48%
WESTERN DOCTOR	9%

The most common answers as to why the different groups are best able to treat the different natural illnesses are presented in Tables XX to XXIII. The reasons given for these decisions clearly reflect the basic function and aptitude of each group. It is noteworthy that the conditions best treated by Western doctors, as reflected in Table XXIII, namely umhayizo, ufufunyane and izizwe, are all related in their symptomatology to the group of hysterical neuroses or psychoses.

TABLE XX

Why the "ISANGOMA" is best able to treat it:

Can use muti	42%
They know the rituals	15%
Can contact ancestors	9%
Can cause it so can cure it	6%

TABLE XXI

Why the "INYANGA" is best able to treat it:

Can cause it so can cure it	43%
Know the cure with muti	35%
Have anti-witchcraft muti	8%
Can plead with ancestors	5%

TABLE XXII

Why the "UMPROPHETI/PROPHET" is best able to treat it:

Is helped by God	45%
Can predict	20%
Can communicate with ancestors	15%
Can use muti/isiwasho	9%
Can make an altar	2%
Don't use Zulu medicine	1%

TABLE XXIII

Why the Western doctor is best able to treat it:

They have methods/machines	19%
They have medicines	19%
They are trained to treat brains	19%
Can "put in" blood	6%
Can use Western civilization	6%
No reason given but can cure"	

umhayizo, isithutwane, ufufunyane and izizwe

Table XXIV reflects the chief treatment methods advocated by the prophets. From this it is clear that they use vomiting most often, mentioning it first in eleven cases. This is followed by "holy water" in twenty-one percent of cases, prayer in fifteen percent of cases, inhalations and steaming in fourteen and twelve percent respectively and Western medicine in eleven percent. It is interesting to note that prayer is only third on the list of preferred treatments.

TABLE XXIV

Treatment methods:

	Mentioned	
	% Times	First
Vomiting	34	11
Holy water	21	0
Prayer	15	2
Inhalation	14	1
Steaming	12	0
Western medicine	11	1
Enema	6	0
Ropes	5	0
Purging	4	0

In analyzing the problems encountered by faith healers, as reflected in Table XXV, it is noted that religious problems such as "Holy Spirit" troubles appear only in forty-seven percent of cases compared to "trouble with the spouse" in ninety-three percent of cases. This is an unexpected finding in a consultation within a religious context. Seventy-three percent of cases appear to be suffering from depression, since "bad luck" corresponds reasonably closely with depression as defined in Western terms. This is very high in comparison to other figures quoted for the incidence of depression amongst Africans.

108

TABLE XXV

Reasons for consulting Faith Healers:

Trouble with spouse	93%
Work troubles	87%
Problems with pregnancy	80%
Trouble at home	73%
Bad luck	73%
Poisoning/evil agent	73%
Talking in sleep	73%
Barrenness	67%
Nightmares/visions	67%
Holy Spirit troubles	47%
Money problems	47%
Madness	47%

It is clear from Table XXV that the faith healers perform a very important task simply by being available to offer assistance to their people. It is heartening to know that such an important function is being performed by the prophets of the African Indigenous Churches.

Conclusion

In conclusion, it appears that prophets are slightly less knowledgeable than diviners about culture-specific syndromes; they use prayer less than expected and they do not accept that natural illnesses are best treated by Western doctors. It is, however, very clear that they fulfil an extremely useful function in assisting with the handling of day-to-day problems of living in the African community.

A SEARCH FOR ABUNDANT LIFE:
HEALTH, HEALING AND WHOLENESS IN THE ZIONIST CHURCHES
by
D. Dube

INTRODUCTION

African ideas about health are basic to the understanding of the healing work of Zion. The healing work of Zion is not an end in itself, but is a search for abundant life. Abundant life is synonymous with salvation.

The concept of life is bound up with health. A "healthy" individual is expected to go through all the stages of life. "Life" consists in harmonious adjustment to the visible and the invisible world. If this harmony is missing and health is impaired, attempts are made to find out who/what has impaired it, and also what can be done to restore the harmony (and, therefore, health). In this paper I discuss African ideas about health and the factors which account for impaired health. These ideas are basic to the understanding of the apparent "pre-occupation" with healing practices in African-guided church movements e.g., the Zionists. I shall also discuss healing as a life-restoring life-enhancing practice among the Zionists. I shall end this paper by assessing the importance of wholeness in African life. My observations outlined here are based on some research in the Durban Urban and peri-urban areas.

HEALTH

Sills (1968) citing the World Health Organization (1946) states that health is a state of complete physical, mental and social well-being and not just the absence of disease or infirmity. The implication is that when a person is healthy he will show this by active participation and involvement in his society.

Active participation defines his position and relationships in the society. On the one hand he finds fulfilment, and on the other he fulfils his society. Health, however, constitutes an ideal that can be approached but never attained in actuality. This is obvious when we consider the fact that illness affects not only the ill person, but also those with whom he is related.

Africans are very specific about health and its nature. Good health does not just mean a healthy body (Ngubane, 1977:29), Gumede, 1965:11). For Africans, health is defined in terms of the fulfilment of all the roles expected of a human person.

Notions pertaining to diseases will help us appreciate the African ideas about health. Africans view disease as not just a physical condition; it is a religious matter (Mbiti, 1975a 6:134). When a person falls ill it is believed that the balance between the human world and the spirit world has been affected. Health depends on being in harmony with or forming an integral part of the "life-force." Illness, therefore, is a lack of harmony brought about by different things e.g., one's wrong deeds, the malice of the enemies of society etc., (Dzobo, 1967: 12).

The idea here is that health, and, therefore, lack of disease, is believed to result from a wholeness which depends on man's relationship with the source of life (Otoo, 1967: 21). Any explanation of the causes of impaired health must of necessity be a religious explanation (Msomi, 1971: 10). The different health rituals that people perform are for the welfare of the individual and society. They are aimed at preserving and prolonging human life (Mbiti, 1975a: 135).

Africans believe in a balance between the visible and the invisible worlds. The net result of this balance is health and wholeness which find expression in participation in social activities. The invisible world influences the visible world.

Lack of harmony between these two worlds impairs health, brings diseases, and reduces chances of prosperity and good fortune (Gumede, 1965: 7,8). Good fortune and prosperity refer to material and spiritual blessings.

That diseases are believed to be caused by supernatural agents (Hoernlé, 1937: 227; Glick, 1967: 32,36) should not blind us to the fact that Africans distinguish between illness as a biological factor and illness as a mystical factor (Ngubane, 1977: 33; Glick, 1967: 35). Illness as a biological factor is treated and forgotten (Hoernlé, 1937: 227). This, however, is peripheral to our concern in this paper. Illness as a mystical factor requires cooperative responses from the sick individual's social group (Glick, 1967: 35).

Ngubane (1977) provides a useful analysis of categories of African notions of illness. Ordinary illnesses i.e., colds, coughs, etc., are ailments (umkhuhlane). These are diseases of African people (ukufa kwabantu). The causality philosophy is African and is based on the African world-view. There are illnesses which are associated with ecological dangers. Such diseases emanate from the fact that man and his universe are interrelated. Africans believe that plant and animal life affect the environment--whilst they take something from the atmosphere in which they exist, they give to the atmosphere something of themselves. The atmosphere is therefore full of substances which emanate from animals and plants. These are referred to as imimoya or imikhondo (i.e., winds/airs or tracks). Such substances can affect the health of persons. Illness, therefore, is a mystical force which threatens good health and upsets the rhythm of life.

Illness of the <u>ukufa</u> <u>kwabantu</u> variety requires special treatment methods. Whilst some African traditional healers can treat it, in urban areas there is fear of bogus doctors and the trade has become highly commercialized. The method they use to treat such illness is cause for concern. It is believed that they remove illness from the patient and when this is discarded it pollutes the environment. Since human life conforms to cosmic rhythms (Vicedom, 1976: 7), people will inhale this (<u>bakuhabule</u>) pollution as it intensifies in response to the changing seasons. The idea here is that the atmosphere harbors a lot of polluting substances some of which are discarded in the process of healing.

Health also depends on the disposition of the spirits to the living (Ngubane, 1977: 51). If the spirits are not playing their protective role, humans are believed to be prone to illness. The spirits are believed to be angered by failure to observe certain rituals and taboos. When humans fail to fulfil obligations which are meant to stabilize and formalize relationships, illness will result.

The notions of ritual impurity and sorcery underline much of the insecurity associated with life in the urban and peri-urban areas. People settled in townships for instance are not in a position to choose their neighbors.

It is very common to find that neighbors are hostile people or people who use dangerous medicines. Urban settlements are characterized by suspicion, mistrust and even lack of cooperation among neighbors. The result is that health is always in jeopardy; human relationships are in most cases enforced by means of mystical powers.

Ill-health attributed to ritual pollution and sorcery manifests itself in a number of ways, for example, sour relations; family tensions and quarrels; children becoming wayward and uncontrollable; prostitution and drunkenness, illegitimacy and poor parental control; barrenness and lack of good fortune. All these and many others are interpreted as states of ill-health which result from mystical causation.

There is a struggle for existence in the townships. People want to secure jobs and get promotion in their jobs. Good fortune, which is equivalent to good health, enables a person to be likeable and to be prosperous in his job. Some people will even use medicine to ensure success. Those who are unable to do so find themselves losing their jobs and not getting promotion. This is interpreted as ritual impurity. This is where the whole notion of blood comes in (Vilakazi, 1962: 93). Bad blood (iigazi elibi) makes a person to be unpopular. What he needs is healing i.e., cleansing his blood and restoration of proper health.

The very houses the people occupy in the township have changed many hands. The different occupants use different methods of making the houses habitable, for example, the ukubethela ritual to prevent attacks by mystical forces. Some of the informal settlements are on sites of old homesteads where people might be buried. Reports of mysterious noises and movements are a common feature of these settlements. This undefined mysterious force "into" (thing) is interpreted from a religious point of view. It becomes necessary either to exorcise this "into" or to close it off so that it does not disturb the living. The point I am making here is that settlements in both urban and peri-urban situations are attended by insecurity caused by fear of mysterious forces.

Our understanding of the whole concept of health pivots on our understanding of the whole idea of illness in African society. The Zionists understand health in this sense. Their apparent preoccupation with healing is an effort to restore man's balance with nature, the environment, his fellows and the invisible world. In the next section I examine healing, especially Zionist healing in an attempt to see how the Africans want to achieve wholeness.

HEALING

Our thesis is that Zionists see illness as a mystical factor which impairs health and prevents an individual from taking an active participation in his society and all that it stands for. This thesis underlines our definition of illness as a religious issue. Illness has a cause which is either human, superhuman or non-human (Glick 1967:3 6). In any event of illness it becomes necessary, therefore, to discover "who" caused the illness and then to treat it by removing or pacifying the cause of illness. Effective treatment will necessarily be a religious matter where the whole man will be treated, that is, his ailing physical body, his concerned "spirit" and his affected relationships. The idea therefore is that effective healing will take place in the community where both the visible and the invisible bases of such a community are involved.

The treatment of illness or disease will always reflect African ideas expressed in diagnostic statements about illness (Glick, 1967: 37). Treatment is designed to restore the balance of power between the affected individual and the antagonists of good health. The basic idea is to weaken the antagonist of good health and at the same time to strengthen the sick person (Glick, 1967: 37). The sick person's social group will be called upon to perform rituals or sacrifices in an attempt to save the victim.

Our contention is that African healing is an exercise in salvation. Indowa (1967: 63 citing Nadel (1954) suggests that:

... the whole economy of salvation is directed towards total well-being i.e., total good life. Treatment techniques and practices are aimed at deliverance from a particular adverse or unhappy situation. Since Africans view health "religiously," it stands to reason that treatment of diseases will necessarily be a religious undertaking. Treatment of diseases is in the final analysis concerned with personal relationships and man's understanding that he depends upon the supernatural for the satisfaction of his needs which transcend material needs.

I have deliberately quoted Idowu at length here to explain why in urban settlements African notions of diseases will persist and also to explain why Zionist healing, for instance, is found to be viable and preferred by many people, Zionist and non-Zionist. Also to explain the fact that the African world is primarily a religious world and every African is caught up in a "religious drama."

ZIONIST HEALING

Zionist healing must therefore be understood against this background. It is a search not only for African identity, but above all it is a search for salvation. The religious consciousness of the African is a very important factor. Becken (1971: 15) observes that Zionist services enable those who attend them to experience life by acknowledging with each other as human beings in their African identity. When they are in the service they experience healing which is something more than just being cured from a certain disease.

Becken (1971) has made a valuable contribution to our understanding of the African view of healing as reflected in the Zionist churches. Healing, as we have noted above, is in the first place religious, in that it means the restoration of good and healthy relationships with the source of being. When man's health is impaired, it suggests that there is a diminution of being. This means that the power supply from the source of being is tampered with. The Zionist service underlines the importance and the place of faith in the supernatural. There is an obvious belief in an ever-present God, a living God, who encourages participants to see Him as the focal point of all human endeavor, and the center of all life power. A sick person is not left on his own, neither is he held responsible for his condition; the whole groups intercedes on his behalf, supporting him when human and spiritual support is most needed. The authenticity of the Zionist groups lies in the fact that they:

> ... express their faith in the forms which are understandable by their members and by their environment: the symbolism of their clerical and congregational gowns in many colors with their specific meaning, the rich ritual connected with every service, the unreflected acceptance of the explanation and understanding of richness from their environment, all these are not syncretic remnants, but genuine results of the incarnation of the Christian message in Africa, which is more closely related to the understanding of healing in the New Testament (Becken, 1971: 16).

The emphasis on the religious nature of healing places man in an understandable position as regards his universe which is living and coherent and of which man is part (Dickson, 1984: 52). Africans believe in an ongoing communication between the supernatural and man. Whilst this is possible for everybody, it

is especially true of special persons who are thought to be in
touch with the unseen world so that they are in a position to
discern approaching events, read signals, use divination
techniques, or receive supernatural visitations in dreams or in
visions (Willoughby, 1928:1 13; Gumede, 1965: 13).

THE ZIONIST HEALER

The Zionist healer and prophet is a religious specialist who
stands in a special relationship with the source of being. The
calling of the Zionist healer (Hodgson, 1983: 23,24) shows
evidence of African understanding of the cosmos. It is
characterized, amongst other things, by illness, dreams, visions
and instructions. These features are an important aspect of the
religious life of most Zionists. Like a traditional diviner, the
Zionist healer is a point of contact between the profane and the
sacred world (Ngubane, 1977: 86).

The point we want to make here is that the Zionist healer
can be understood in terms of African religious consciousness.
His healing power is not isolated from his understanding of his
universe. Both the power and the understanding are of
supernatural origin and they are inspired by the spirit (umoya).
Zionist congregations accept the Messiahship of Jesus and
understand his relationship with God who is the source of life.

The authority and anchorage of the Zionist healer emanate
from his calling. His call is of a supernatural nature be this
in the form of dreams, illness or visions and instructions
(Sundkler, 1961: 114,115; Fernandez, 1973: 35). The call to heal
or to be a prophet emanates from the umoya (Spirit) which is sent
by the Supreme Being. It is for this reason that Zionists are
seen to be preoccupied with attempts at controlling and directing

umoya. The umoya is a life-giving and health-bearing force
(Kiernan, 1978: 28).

Virtually everybody has a messenger isithunywa. The
isithunywa is central to the healer's or prophet's call. It
provides an avenue through which supernatural communication takes
place. The Zionist definition of isithunywa includes what
Vilakazi (1962) calls inhliziyo which is the heart used
metaphorically.

UMOYA
The notion of umoya is central to the understanding of
Zionist healing. Umoya is built up and expended to offset the
effects of human and mystical agents which afflict the individual
(Kiernan, 1979: 13). Kiernan sees umoya as embracing "a whole
technology" of mystical powers and representing an array of
capacities, skills and instruments for fulfilling the work of
Zion (1978: 28). The emphasis here is on the understanding of
the universe and its effects on human persons. The umoya
transcends human existence. It is found everywhere. It becomes
effective as a personal power which is inherent in the different
objects the Zionists use. Becoming a Zionist therefore brings
with it the power of umoya. It "reawakens" and redirects one's
messenger so that relations with the supernatural are placed on a
sound footing.

"SPECIFICS"
Africans in urban and peri-urban settlements find themselves
in a hostile environment. The demands of the industrial world
leave the environment full of ritual impurity caused by mystical
agencies and failure to observe taboos. Active trafficking in
medicine and charms and fear or sorcery and witchcraft are a
source of insecurity (Kiernan, 1976b:3 54). This situation,

amongst other things, minimizes the chances of having good fortune and therefore affects the people's view of health. The use of what Kiernan calls the "specifics" is designed to cope with the hostile environment whilst at the same time enhancing good health. The "specifics," be they weapons (izikhali), or salt water and ashes (isiwasho), or forms of clothing (izembatho), are all meant to arrest or reverse all undesirable conditions (Kiernan, 1979: 13). The effectiveness of the specifics is believed to be the result of the work of the power of umoya.

One way of understanding the work of Zion is to look at the different types of "specifics" and how they are believed to be efficacious. Kiernan (1978) discusses the use of water and ashes in the curative work of Zion. His conclusion is that water has been elevated to a position of pre-eminence as a curative. My understanding is that water has always played an important role in African life. The myths of man's origin are associated with water. When relations are strained between persons, the ritual of ukuthelelana amanzi[1] (to pour water for each other) is performed. Although Africans do not trouble themselves with the chemistry of water, they do understand however that water which comes from "heaven" (izulu) has an important spiritual content because of its association with the air. When somebody with a recognized position pronounces a spell over the water, he activates the life-giving force which is a potential quality of water. The spell and the life-giving quality of water are inspired by the Supreme Being. It is the notion of relationships

---

[1]Sundkler (1961:232) discusses this point where he places emphasis on the role of water as a medical remedy. Ukuthelelana amanzi is meant to bring about reconciliation.

which manipulates the mystical powers of water. Water is closely associated with "heaven" and the source of being (Kiernan, 1978: 30).

The Zionists use water in a number of different ways in their healing and protective activities. As a "specific" water is used in the form of isiwasho where it constitutes a solvent for other ingredients. Kiernan (1978), Williams (1982), and Hodgson (1982) in their works indicate that isiwasho is not limited to one thing, neither does it always have a water base. It can therefore be ordinary water prayed over, water mixed with salt, ash, vinegar, lavender, sugar, wine, sea sand, white lime, etc., or it can be water mixed with Jeyes fluid, Dettol, methylated spirits, etc. The point I want to bring out here with regard to the making of the isiwasho is that there is need to bring about a working relationship between man and his environment. This is basic to Zionist healing. Health-enhancing activities start with attempts at striking a balance between man and his environment. Our contention is that the urban environment is a dynamic environment, always confronting man with new mystical forces. The nature of the Zionist isiwasho is such that these mystical forces can be arrested and reversed.

Williams makes reference to a variation of isiwasho which he calls ichibi[2] (1982: 153). His findings were that this is used by women who cannot conceive. Our understanding is that the Apostolic indigenous/independent churches prefer the term ichibi to isiwasho, and this is becoming popular even among non-Zionists. A secret prayer-group within the Congregational

---

[2] ichibi is a pool.

church in the Amanzimtoti area is referred to as ichibi basically because of the use of water that has been prayed over. The point I want to emphasize here is that water and any other items are believed to be effective in healing once they have been prayed over.

REFLECTIONS ON ZIONIST HEALING

It is helpful to consider Zionist healing as a defensive approach to treating illness (Williams, 1982: 152). Once powers have been conferred through a ritual act, e.g., prayer and the laying on of hands, such powers are believed to have a protective and a preventative function and are employed in the manner of weapons (Kiernan, 1979: 13,14). Weaponry which is used to ward off mystical attacks resides in clothing, staves, and flags. All these are prescribed in the context of public healing. This aspect has been brought to the fore by Kiernan.

Zionist uniforms play an important role as life-giving and life-enhancing objects (Kiernan, 1979 14; Williams, 1982: 213). Uniforms are meant to confer spiritual powers on the wearer. The prophet, inspired by umoya, plays a leading role in "discovering" the suitable color combinations to be used. It is sufficient here to point out that the prophet may recommend that a patient wear a permanent item of dress as a protection and deterrent against further illness. The color combinations have a specific purpose. The healer does not arbitrarily arrive at the colors required to be used by the patient. He arrives at this through communication with the supernatural which occurs during the healing part of the service. In addition to ordinary Zionist clothing, cords, sashes, and ribbons are prescribed and worn. It stands to reason, therefore, that even the outside appearance of a person can be subjected to the dictates of umoya. No two people will have an identical type of appearance. The uniform establishes the identity of each individual whilst at the same time linking him through umoya to the common source of all beings. An individual's item of dress contains his dirt (insila) which is of great mystical significance in African thinking. But above all it is life-giving and health enhancing.[3]

Another important aspect of Zionist weaponry is the staff (isikhali, lit. weapon). Most of the staves are fashioned out of wood. It is always wood which grows beside water. Whilst Kiernan's groups used reed in the making of their staves, it is a known fact that other groups use other types of wood, for example, umnyezane (Willow tree) (Kiernan, 1979: 15). The umnyezane tree, like the reed, is always found anchored in water. The umnyezane tree has twigs which bend easily. The emphasis here is on the significance of water in African religious thought.

Kiernan's groups adopted the practice of putting their staves together and leaving them at the minister's place at the end of each service (1979: 16). Each service would therefore begin with the ritual distribution of staves by the minister. In this sense, Kiernan observes, the service is a ritual enactment of stooling which is the quality of a reed (Kiernan, 1979: 17).

The minister assumes the position of the uhlanga from where members of his group break off. Africans regard anyone who is in

---

[3]Zionists are expected to put on all their uniforms when they attend services. During the ukuhlambuluka session a person who is not in uniform will declare angiphelele i.e., "I am incomplete." He owes the whole group an explanation of the reason of his incompleteness. This pertains also in the historical churches.

such a position as uNozala (begetter). Any begetter is saddled with power which is not of his own making, but which is supernatural. He exercises this power as delegated power and authority which is a sign of his contact with the supernatural.

The idea which emerges here regarding the staves and their distribution is that they are believed to be charged with power. The power they give to the Zionist does not come from the minister, but comes from the source of power, through the minister. When each individual finally receives his staff, he receives the power not only inherent in it, but which comes from the source of power. The Zionist sees the minister as just an agent and not the source of power. To suggest that the band is dependent on the minister who gives it new life, as Kiernan (1979: 17) does, is not an accurate assessment of Zionist commensuality.

STRENGTHENING RITUALS

Africans practice what might be termed the strengthening ritual (ukubethela) i.e., to fortify. This is meant to render a homestead and its inmates immune to mystical attacks. This practice of prophylactic treatment is not always a response to illness (Ngubane, 1977: 105). Zionist homesteads and houses are often distinguished by means of flags (Kiernan, 1979: 19,20). Flags are put on poles and planted at vantage points within the homesteads. In some cases they are put on the roof inside the house. The color and design vary, but the purpose remains the same, viz., that of repelling any danger aimed at the homestead and the inmates. Apart from the flags other methods are used to fortify homesteads and houses. Members of the Nazareth Baptist church inscribe on the doors of their houses the following words:

"Dumisani uJehova Amen."[4] These are words of response found in their liturgy.

THE COMMUNAL CONTEXT

Zionist healing takes place in the context of community which is expressed in the Zionist service. Our intention is not to discuss the order of service as such, but to mention those aspects which are relevant to this treatise. As part of the opening is the ukuhlambuluka (hlamba--to clean or to clear). This is an essential part of the Zionist service. It is here where each participant declares his physical and spiritual state of affairs. It is here where confessions are made and where ill-health is declared. In all-night services and other long services each participant concludes ukuhlambuluka by asking the congregation to join him in singing his favorite verse, i.e., hymn or chorus. A verse of this nature often expresses the inner needs of the participants. The effect of the ukuhlambuluka exercise is to create a sense of mutual trust and dependence and to anticipate in a positive manner the unfailing support of the congregation.

There is always a connection between the text and the healing activity (Kiernan, 1976b: 347). Preaching and healing are always seen as one ritual event which provides a framework within which umoya can act (Kiernan, 1976a: 357). It is this that gives direction and authority to the work of Zion. This more than any other thing emphasizes the fact that the Zionist church is an attempt at establishing an authentic awareness of the incarnation of the Word in Africa.

---

[4]Praise Jehovah Amen!

Mutual trust and community in Zion find further expression in the formation of the healing circle (Kiernan, 1979: 17,18; 1976b: 350). In the circle the Zionists achieve a degree of equality. Kiernan rightly observes that the circle is the very image of community; it has no beginning and no end. The sick and the weak kneel inside the circle. Those who have the power and the gift for praying for others step into the circle and pray for the sick. The whole exercise puts emphasis on the fact that participants in a healing service are in contact with one another and with the supernatural. The singing, handclapping and dance are expressions of mutual support and a desire to see "life" restored to those who are sick.

Praying for the sick involves touching the affected parts and sometimes remonstrating with the evil spirits or praying out loud. In some cases healers use their sashes and weapons in an imaginary attack on the evil spirits. The idea is that illness sits on certain parts of the body and in order to remove it, hands or items filled with umoya must be brought into contact with those parts. Since illness is "caused "by malicious agents, it can be exorcised by means of remonstration.

Kiernan discusses the closing of doors and windows tightly during prayer and especially during healing, and he concludes that the Zionists maintain religious exclusiveness (1974: 83,82). We want to point out here that healing is an act of divine intervention. During the healing session the divine presence must be acknowledged and secured. Visitation by the supernatural requires a guarantee of security. Zionists will often say that umoya is cowardly (umoya uyigwala); it can easily be disturbed by what goes on in the township. Our observation is that the closing of the entrance is meant to prevent outside disturbance. In fact this pertains even in other churches where a church elder is assigned to attend to the door whenever it becomes necessary to close and open it.

The Zionist congregation which Kiernan conveniently calls a band (ibandla) mobilizes communal fervor for the purpose of fighting against ill-health and everything which threatens life (Kiernan, 1976b: 354). Our observation is that health is a dynamic concept. Consequently, in the band, the participants achieve an inner transformation which, as an ongoing process, must always remain incomplete. The more involved a person is the nearer he approaches the source of life which inspires transformation. One aspect of this transformation is the sense of identity and community which finds expression in relationships between individuals. The work of Zion with its emphasis on prophecy and healing enforces the corporate nature of the Zionist community (Kiernan, 1976b: 354).

The umoya which is basic to Zionist activity and which provides an institutional framework for Zionist healing is not a personal gift. Healing is a collective working upon the individuals under the direction of umoya and the leadership of a prophet (Kiernan, 1976a: 360). The relationship between the leader and the congregation in Zion is based on collective "responsiveness." Kiernan (1976a: 363) correctly observes that the band manages spiritual forces for the attainment of group goals.

THE ROLE AND PLACE OF WOMEN

In the Zionist groups women figure prominently either as patients, prophets, or prayer women (Kiernan, 1974: 86). Women are in the forefront of contact with mystical forces which result from the indiscriminate use of umuthi in the urban settlements. They are the first to come into contact with evil spirits, and malihokha (unfortunate consequences). Their role as recruitment agents places them in a position where they are prey to ritual impurity and pollution. The situation becomes even worse if they belong to non-Zionist families (Kiernan, 1974: 87). Their exposure calls, therefore, for constant mystical treatment and strengthening.

THE HEALING SERVICE

African systems of kinship make allowance for the breaking up of the group once it becomes big. Smaller groups are effective in person to person caring and support. The domestic unit (indlu) retains its affiliation to the family, the lineage and the clan. The Zionist band is a branch of a church. It operates as an independent unit in many respects, e.g., in the distribution of social and spiritual rewards and the manipulation of moral and mystical bases of physical health (Kiernan, 1976a: 357). The use of the designation "minister" for every leader of the band is inaccurate. Even if he is a minister in the technical sense of the term, he cannot claim authority over the mystical powers of the band. The leader together with the participants acknowledge the Supreme Being as the source of power.

Our concern here is with healing within the Zionist community. The individual healers who work on a commercial basis are outside the scope of our exposition. It is important to keep this position in mind because the type of healing we are interested in is the one that takes place whenever the Zionists hold their services. It is healing which is not necessarily occasioned by illness. In most cases it is protective healing and preventative healing. When there is need for a more concentrated type of healing the whole exercise starts with the congregation and continues in a congregational setting. In an ordinary service, therefore, healing takes place towards the end of the service. By this time, the community will have been formed, the healers will have been gradually prepared spiritually, and the patients will have undergone a gradual process of incorporation in Zion (Williams, 1982: 131).

Zionist healing measures are effective in a community which finds itself disadvantaged. The definitions of illness and causes of illness extend beyond the practical and apparent physical and psychological symptoms to include socio-cultural and religious factors that impinge upon the life of individuals (Williams, 1982: 215). Their methods of healing make illness intelligible and capable of treatment. The healing instruments are expendable and are inexpensive (Kiernan, 1978: 31). This appeals to the poor masses in the urban areas. Even those with limited income resources are afforded an opportunity of fulfilling their health and life-increasing obligations when the healer prescribes manageable methods of staving off illness, for example, the use of chicken in an essential offering instead of a goat (Williams, 1982: 222). In African sacrifice it is believed that the disposition of the heart is more important than the material offering (Cf. Evans-Pritchard, 1956: 207). When a patient makes repeated appearances for treatment he establishes long-lasting relationships and is eventually incorporated in the Zionist community (Kiernan, 1978: 32). This relationship increases his awareness of his dependence on the source of being and the power which reaches him as a member of the Zionist community.

WHOLENESS
Life among Africans finds expression in the fullness of being. "Muntu" is a corporate personality (Goba, 1973). As a corporate personality Muntu interacts with his surroundings,

i.e., the social environment, the physical environment and the
spiritual environment. It is in this sense that man achieves his
wholeness. On one level he:

> ... is the supreme force, the most powerful among
> created beings. He dominates plants, animals and
> minerals. These lower beings exist, by Divine decree,
> only for the higher created being man (Tempels, 1959:
> 64).

At yet another level man defines himself in terms of his
involvement in the community (Goba, 1973: 67). He is born into
the community, and in his development he undergoes well-defined
stages within the community. He is not an isolated personality.
He understands himself and he is understood by others in terms of
his kinship ties. It is within the community where as an African
he learns to say "I am because I participate" (Taylor, 1963: 85).
He owes his existence to other people, i.e., his contemporaries
as well as the living dead. His life transcends death just as
the life of the community transcends death.

The nature of the urban and peri-urban environment is such
that it calls for solidarity and a social consciousness that
rejects and transcends individualism. The urban world which is
dominated by Whites and an impersonal type of existence is met by
Zionists in a dynamic attempt to establish a dynamic community, a
community whose foundation is caring concern. Suffering and all
the dehumanizing effects of urban existence call for a community
with a single purpose and a common commitment. This commitment
is in most cases a commitment to share in the suffering of fellow
Africans.

The above discussion places emphasis on the fact that in
African thinking, life is regarded as a whole and a person

becomes an embodiment of the community. Zionists are in search of wholeness of life. They regard everything which militates against their achievement as human beings as life-denying. Their very insecure settlement in townships and emijondolo (shanty towns) as well as in other people's backyards is life-denying. They start by examining themselves in an attempt to find a solution to their predicament. The work of Zion with its focus on healing is an attempt to search for corporate personality, because:

> (Jesus) challenged the whole man and all man's activities. He came to reclaim the entire person, the total history of the whole person, the sum total of his activities and aspirations--and in practical terms this means the whole community, the whole society, the whole humanity, the whole creation. So in effect He came to make men so totally and absolutely religious that no department of man should be left untouched by His Lordship, ... (Mbiti, 10973: 15).

This idea comes out clearly in the celebrational nature of Zionist worship where, despite the odds against which the participants operate, there is always a sense of joy, a sense of renewal, a sense of fulfilment and a positive anticipation. It is this positive anticipation which seeks to make of each individual a corporate personality.

Our contention is that the attraction of Zion results from the life-enhancing activities of Zion, viz., the management of umoya and healing. People are attracted to Zion not necessarily because they are ill, but because as Africans they are in search of good health with all that it means. Zionists, as Africans, imbued with a sense of religious consciousness organize their activities around African understanding of human existence. Some

Zionist homesteads especially in the outskirts of Durban are used as healing homes for patients. Williams (1982) calls these healing homes izigodlo (isigodlo--singular: izigodlo--plural). Homes of this nature provide the patients with boarding facilities and operate as communes. The patients are integrated into the household where they participate in the daily chores as human persons. In some cases their relatives make a monetary contribution to maintain the commune. The point is that whilst these people are being given treatment for their illness they are at the same time made "to feel at home."

The Zionists place great emphasis on relationships, especially kinship ties. It is in exceptional cases that a patient is removed from his social context. When a person is ill the cause for his illness is searched for within his social environment, of the family and the neighbors (Becken, 1971: 18). Some of the prescriptions suggested by the Zionist healers involve restoration of relationship ties.

CONCERN FOR THE PERSON

The concern for the "person" in Zionist healing activities cannot be over-emphasized (Becken, 1971: 17). During the time for prayer for the sick the patient's body is touched, there is confession of guilt, and "specifics" are prescribed. "Even the subconscious sphere of the whole person is touched upon when dreams are related by the members and explained by the healer" (Becken, 1971: 18). Healing, therefore, is successful not only in restoring physical well-being, but also in restoring a sense of and a feeling of oneness with the supernatural. A further dimension of healing is realized when the whole congregation visits the homestead of the patient. The healer plays a leading role in rendering the homestead safe for habitation either by removing the causes of illness or by making the other inmates of the homestead and the homestead itself strong against any further mystical attacks. Work of this nature is usually concluded by an ilathi worship (Williams, 1982: 146). This is a service of thanksgiving, when in real African style the whole congregation is entertained with a communal meal where the supernatural is believed to partake.

My contention is that Zionist healing activity is a reflection of collective responsibility (Cf. Williams, 1982: 178). An individual's illness has an effect on the whole group. It is common, therefore, at the start of the service to find a number of participants subdued and withdrawn. The reason is that a person's "messenger" is prone to being handicapped by other people's illnesses. The Zionists speak of the weight of such illness. This weight (isisindo) is mystically communicated. The metaphor of weight is not necessarily restricted to the concept of sin as Oosthuizen wants us to believe (1967: 119,120). It is this fact which makes the practice of ukuhlambuluka very important, and for that matter wholeness is not possible without it.

Wholeness is a dynamic concept, and healing ought to be understood in the sense that it is not a fixed point of perfect health (Becken, 1971: 20). The whole concept of wholeness reflects a new attitude to life. Life is seen on a sliding scale with death on the one end and increase in life on the other end. Good health, good fortune and therefore wholeness point to an individual's or a society's movement on the life scale. Illness, for instance, is a decrease in life and it means reduced participation and impaired wholeness.

The dynamic nature of the Zionist community is further reflected in the fact that the Zionist group is fluid and flexible (Williams, 1982: 213). The group is always adapting to a wide variety of challenges, e.g., social, medical, economic and religious needs of the participants. In Zion participants are promised physical health; they are provided with a community where each person enjoys recognition as a human being (Daneel, 1970: 23). The achievement of wholeness is obvious when instant status is offered to persons who live under the humiliation of being regarded as non-persons and "boys" and "girls" (Williams, 1982: 224,226).

CONCLUSIONS

Zionists adhere to recognized observations and taboos because they believe that ceremonial transgression is life-denying and impairs wholeness (Willoughby, 1928: 133). Ceremonial transgression is believed to destroy the prosperity of others, denying them offspring, physical and mental well-being (Tutu, 1970: 121). Africans are always in search of life enhancement i.e., increase in being (Tutu, 1970 122). They want to live as fully integrated members of the community and all that it means. Zionist healing is a question of reintegration and restoration of harmony and balance between man and both the visible and the invisible worlds.

To sum up, the chief desire of every African is life i.e., freedom from illness, good fortune, and above all communion with the supernatural. This is possible only if there is participation in all avenues of human endeavor and with the supernatural. The whole gamut of Zionist ritual is a search for wholeness and salvation. It is an exercise meant to reawaken in man his God-given responsibility of managing the umoya. The conferment of power through baptism must be seen as a method aimed at ensuring not only physical but psychic and ontological cleansing, strengthening and union. For Africans the concept of life is better illustrated by reference to the whole wealth of symbolism which plays a significant role in the rhythm of life.

BAPTISM IN THE CONTEXT OF THE
AFRICAN INDEPENDENT CHURCHES
by
G.C. Oosthuizen

Introduction

There are many reasons why African Independent Churches have grown from small beginnings to a vast movement in just over a century. Although there were already signs of independency in the 1870's, the churches started to proliferate only after Nehemia Tile established the Thembu Church in 1884 in the Transkei. The initial growth was, however, slow in comparison with later developments.

Whatever the reasons for the tremendous development which has led over 27% of contemporary Blacks to join independent churches maybe--there are many and it is not possible to discuss them here--one of the main reasons lies with the interpretation of baptism as a sacrament and a means of obtaining grace and numinous power. This symbol assists those who take part in it to receive the benefits for which it stands, namely, to be in the presence of the transcendent world which manifests itself through those various benefits bestowed generously on them, i.e., if they fulfill the necessary requirements such as fasting, attending the preceding nocturnal revival service, and confessing their sins.

Each symbol has a manifold of meanings; it unites heterogeneous realities in itself. It "constructs" a bridge between the micro and the macrocosms. In this manner it becomes the expression of the totality. As it gives expression to the manifestation of the transcendent, the symbol implies the continuing association of the people with the holy. It is related to the reality of a situation with which the human being is existentially involved.

This accounts for the variety of aspects related to the individual's life which is associated with baptism in the African Independent Churches, the sacrament which is called the missions' sacrament because of the decisive existential implications it had and still has in the life and work of the church in the African context.

The symbol is related to reality or the situation; it is not acknowledged with the mind in the first instance but in a psychical experience. It represents a complex reality which reaches out far beyond every expression in words. This is precisely the attitude to "baptism" in all its connotations at the sea. It is the symbol in the African Independent Churches which gives orientation and meaning; it changes chaos into cosmos. In their environment, work situation, living conditions and the foreignness of a secularized impersonal world, much of their inner equilibrium is disturbed and they receive through baptism the necessary orientation to continue. "Baptism" is thus a normalization act; an act through which balance is established; it has not only great psychiatric value but also great physical value because of the influence of the psyche on the body.

The symbolic religious geographical center such as a cosmic mountain, a holy city, a fountain, or the sea, establishes a central meeting place between heaven and earth, between transcendence and the here and now. In some religions the temple becomes the microcosmic image of the Universe, in others the cosmic mountain, and it seems that the sea has taken over this role in many Zionist churches. The sea has become for many the symbol of the presence of numinous powers.

Not only is the geographical association of the symbol of vital importance but also its association with the time in which the events first happened. Holy time is reversible and it repeats and represents the original time. With the new year there is the repetition of the cosmogony; with the Great Umkhosi among the Zulus the new time cycle was introduced. The original time, when the event occurred to which the symbol refers, is holy and strong and its reappearance leads to participation in its powers. What happened at the river Jordan and the Sea of Galilee during the time of Jesus is repeated today at the river and the sea, and Jesus spent more time at the sea of Galilee than at the river Jordan. John the Baptist baptized Jesus in the river Jordan; Jesus did much of His work at the Sea of Galilee. As a result of the symbolic repetition of the original, those taking part in the ritual at the Durban beach become part of early New Testament history.

Because baptism is to the Zionist a symbol of transcendence, not primarily of being initiated into the church, they are assured of the victorious outcome of the struggle of the divine powers against the demonic powers of darkness. They receive life through the removal of sins effected by baptism; they receive "the Spirit" because they have been cleansed and "the Spirit" is a source of strength.

Baptism in Zionist Context

The symbol of baptism among Zionists is strongly influenced by the Christian tradition, but they have given it an emphasis which it did not have in most of the established churches. In the mission context it is prominent because of its association with adult baptism and it is much closer to the early church's baptisms. Traditional African purification practices could also explain the emphasis put on this sacrament in the Afro-Christian context. It has, of course, also a Christian background as the sacrament of baptism was much more in the center in the life of the early church than is the case today.

This symbol which has such an amazing position within most of the African Independent Churches should be seen in Carl Jung's evaluation of the symbol over against the sign and allegory. For him there are two sides to the symbol--it could be a sign of progression which leads the human being to higher levels but it could also be a sign of retrogression to a lower level and become a dead form. There are two ways, according to Jung, of symbol formation depending on the increasing and decreasing of spiritual activity. The same outward form could be for the one a sign of spiritual expansion and for the other a shell from which the living content has long ago evaporated.

Much of the latter is true with regard to baptism in the Western world where for the late Karl Barth, the eminent Swiss theologian, a "baptized heathendom" exists. Over against this baptism has always been a dynamic sacrament within the churches in the mission context. The history of baptism within the church, before the modern scientific mind overruled everything, reveals the very central place it had in the church. It would be an interesting exercise to compare the approach of the primitive and early church to this sacrament when adult baptism predominated with what developed in the indigenous African churches where more adults received the sacrament than infants.

Symbols in African context

The question is: Are there certain symbols that speak very strongly to Africans and are these reflected within the churches? In spite of denials by some there is enough evidence of a specific traditional African approach. The independent African churches have a specific African character. This could be said when the African approach is put over against a western techno-scientific approach.

Certain symbols and images occur fairly regularly among African authors on this continent in spite of differences among them. Such symbols and thought patterns are unity, harmony, peace (many a child in Africa and especially South Africa bears the indigenous name for "peace"), the emphasis on life which comes through death and which is symbolically expressed in many of their rituals, the removal of the forces of darkness, the emphasis on humanity and personhood within the context of community, the role of water as a life-giving force.

These emphases, according to Jung's approach, are evidences of man's collective consciousness--they belong to the whole of humanity but could be and are so often suppressed by other symbols and thought patterns. But even post-modern man--man of the split atom, of quantum physics, of bimedical advance, the one-dimensional man--instinctively harks back to origins. There is an undercurrent within human existence like an undercurrent underneath the surface of the ocean which gives him a spontaneous sensitivity for a primal approach which finds expression in art, music, and dance; the emphasis falls on the emotional rather than the rational, on community rather than on individualism.

In spite of the strong emphasis in our time on the rational and the development of scientific and technological language, there are signs of reaction against this as is evident in the influence of not only Eastern but also Western mysticism on especially the youth. They look for identity, for new means of communication, for a sense of community, for a situation in which experience is central instead of belief and a person attains a new spiritual level through his experiences and himself becomes active to obtain what his religion professes. In communication the emphasis is on hymns, dreams, tongues; here liturgy is flexible, the service is "made", i.e., with no fixed liturgical order, with the emphasis on spontaneity. The self-propelled machines, computers, robots, the whole modern technology with its emphasis on a programmed existence, with a society overruled by production and consumption, gave rise to reaction from the youth many of whom found a haven in Eastern mysticism and Pentecostalism or "born again" movements. This development has been active for decades in the African Independent Churches but with their own type of reaction based on their own background.

Carl Jung's Explanation

What Jung, the real architect of modern depth psychology, terms the collective unconsciousness reacts against the ruthless repression of man's primitive self. It is through this primitive self that a man's personality could find its deepest expression, but it is not allowed to do so because of the straitjacket superficiality that overemphasizes the rational and what it can give (Cf. Jung, 1912, 1928, 1931). In Wandlungen und Symbole der Libido one finds for the first time Jung's hypothesis of the "collective unconscious" which contrasted directly with Freud's theory about the structure of the psyche. This was later translated, revised and published, and was entitled Symbols of Transformation: 1959. Jung stated in another work that "for Freud it (the unconscious) is essentially an appendage of consciousness, in which all the individual's incompatibilities are heaped up. For me the unconscious is a collective physic disposition, creative in character" (Cf. Jung: 1958 [1937]).

Jung investigated the collective unconscious, a limitless region of the psyche of which hardly anyone was aware before him. In his work he exposed the background to modern man's craving for meaning, which is one of great value in the analysis of such reaction of modern Western youth as is evident in Eastern and Western mystical movements and in the mysticism exemplified in the Afro-Christian religions. Concerning his concept of the collective unconscious Jung states: "Just as the human body shows a common anatomy over and above all racial differences, so, too, the human psyche possesses a common substratum transcending all differences in culture and consciousness. I have called this substratum the collective unconscious" (Jung: 1964). Freud found Jung's ideas totally unacceptable so that in 1912 they parted and Jung developed what has become Analytical Psychology. Jung's analysis has a definite bearing on the above-mentioned developments among modern youth and the African Independent Churches. Symbolism which is used by the African Independent Churches to penetrate deeper into their existential situation is not always understood by others outside their circles but they speak directly and strongly to many African people. For Western youth it is their communes; for the African Independent Churches it is their face-to-face congregations of which there are over one hundred and fifty thousand in South Africa, their baptisms and special ceremonies at the pools, rivers, mountains, elevated places, the sea.

The symbol must be understood in the context of the individual and the group. In the African Independent Churches uniform is not merely a piece of clothing that covers the body but a garb that elevates a person to the heavenly spheres; the staves are not merely sticks but vehicles of power, the "flag" is not merely a piece of cloth attached to a stick but an object which keeps the evil forces away; the "crosses" are not crosses in the traditional Christian sense but are resemblances of pieces of wood which symbolize the cancelling out of evil. One piece of cloth on the uniform represents disharmony, another put on this cancels this out and establishes harmony. The X symbol signified the cancelling out of evil. These pieces are in the form of the spokes of a wheel--after the equilibrium has been restored life

146

can advance again. Life symbolized by the circle can continue.
The sick usually appear at the place of baptism--the pool, river,
or sea--with crossless uniforms signifying that disharmony
prevails and penitence.

Usually the archbishop, bishop, or the baptizer, walks into
the sea with outstretched arms lifted upwards and a big cross
displayed on the back of his/her uniform. He (or she) challenges
the demons, monsters, and evil spirits of the sea. The fact that
the group moves rhythmically in a circle before the baptism, that
they plant candles in a circle, and that the person baptized in
the sea is turned round and round, shows how important the symbol
of the circle is, i.e., the symbol of harmony, of life and
perfection, of togetherness which is basic to the African sense
of community: it plays a greater role in the average Zionist
Church than even the symbol of the cross which is carved out or
fitted onto the "holy sticks." The circle is associated with
rhythm and rhythm is a means of making contact with the
transcendent power(s); healing is effected within a circle. The
circle is the most obvious place for the restoration of harmony.
In the circle they dance before getting into the water; they get
into the mood for the great event, namely the washing off of
their sins in the sea, the driving out of evil spirits, the
restoring of health, the receiving of the power of the Holy
Spirit; here transcendent power is relayed among themselves
thanks to the activities of the transcendent forces which are
either the Holy Spirit or the ancestor(s), or both; here in the
circle they act jointly before entering the water individually.

The idea of rebirth and the fullness of life

The idea of rebirth is uppermost in the traditional African
cultures. the rites de passage are associated with this cycle of
death and life. The rites de passage are closely related to the

ancestors; the ancestors mould the child in the mother's womb; they bring to life the dead person. The newborn baby is not accepted as being a person and as being associated with the life cycle until it is shown to the ancestors and until it receives a name; the young person has to die from the ways of the youth during initiation in order to get protection and real life within the community; death leads to after-life. This accounts for the central position that the rites associated with funerals take within the African context. The rituals of funerals are rebirth rituals. With most African peoples the corpse when buried is put into the grave in the form of a fetus. Death is a new birth.

Baptism symbolizes a transition from death to life which is effected through purification by fasting, washing, vomiting, and confessing of sins. Life is given through the water at the pool, river, or sea. The move one has of the fullness of life, the stronger one is, and the greater one's contact with transcendent powers. A situation of chaos is restored to cosmos; it could fade again but the restoration possibilities are always there-- fading and restoration itself is a cycle. Mass restoration gatherings during Easter is a familiar sight in South Africa and elsewhere. Such gatherings took place in the traditional societies with their First-fruit ceremonies such as the Umkhosi Omkhulu among the Zulu when they were "eating" with the ancestors, also the royal ancestors (amakhosi). Here much dancing, singing, and hand clapping took place.

Baptism as a symbol of death to life is so strong, that it has received a number of connotations within the African Independent Churches, such as connotations of rebirth, healing, power, and good luck, as well as connotations of being invited into the church, being purified from sin, being freed of evil spirits, and receiving "the Spirit" or Holy Ghost and becoming thereby enlightened (capable of visions) and able to prophesy. It has a strong rebirth emphasis among Zionists for whom new life, renewal of life over the forces of darkness and destruction (which overly refers to negative spiritual forces and covertly to the physical forces which govern their circumstances), is the main focus.

Baptisms by the sea are preceded by watch-night revival services at which the emphasis is put on the outpouring of the Holy Spirit or closer contact with the ancestors, when new life is conferred on the participants. Purification is central whether it takes place on the holy mountain or at the holy fountain or the sea. Whether they claim a river, a pool, the sea, or a mountain--it is not the place as such that receives precedence but its symbolic value. Fasting before and during the watch-night revival service which culminates at the sea, prepares for the gifts of baptism. Water mythology is not strange to the African--Zulu mythology maintains that man came out of a bed of reeds that were growing at a pool of water or a river. In African mythology running water and the sea played a definite role in man's origin. The reeds and the water of the river are closely associated in their cosmogony. Some of the staves are made of reeds and are used by spiritual leaders, which is reminiscent of John the Baptist at the river Jordan.

Baptism in historical perspective

It is necessary to look at baptism from the historical perspective and establish how baptism in the African Independent Churches fits into this context. From the point of view of the phenomenology of religion, baptism with its rich symbolism of removal of sins, resurrection, redemption, new creation, rebirth, eternal life, and immortality in which demons, chaos, and death, are overruled, belongs to the rites de passage.

John the Baptist proclaimed a baptism of repentance. In the Afro-Christian religions it is associated with removing all the forces which weaken a person and withhold him from enjoying the fullness of life and it gives him that fullness through ritual washing and cleansing and thus enabling "the Spirit" to do its work undisturbed.

In primitive Christianity baptism in the name of Christ was the main sacrament. A number of other words associated with it were used such as sign, stigma, name, redeem. The word for baptism (baptismos) is used in the New Testament also for ritual washing (Mark 7:4,; Hebrews 9:10) as well as for a sacrament which was related to the death of Christ (Mark 10:38f; Luke 12:50; Matthew 20:22f). The main contentious question initially in the church was whether "to baptize," meaning to immerse or to sprinkle. The African Independent Churches in general and the Zionist churches in particular adhere to adult baptism with regard to profession of faith and initiation into the church. Children are also "baptized" but then the emphasis is on being blessed, on being healed, on having power restored, and on being purified in sin. Baptism in running water is clearly mentioned in the Gospels (Mark 1:5,9; John 3:23).

Is there a link between John the Baptist's baptismal eschatology and the ritual of Qumran? John the Baptist most probably had contact with this sect--his baptism was a baptism of repentance (Mark 1:4). This is also found among the Essenes with whose immersion baptism John the Baptist also most probably had contact. Both baptisms effect God's forgiveness of sins, which takes place only on the condition of a "turnabout" (metanoia) in the lives of those who are immersed. Baptism is for John the Baptist preparation for the eschaton for which God baptizes the believers with the Holy Spirit and the unbelievers with "fire"

(Matthew 3:11). The Qumran people also spoke about a world fire on the one hand and a sprinkling with the truth symbolized by purification water. John the Baptist may have been a member of this sect, but he might have left them because he radically actualized the future events. This is why he did not live in esoteric isolation but called upon everyone to change his life and have himself baptized. While he emphasized that baptism is administered only once because of the imminent end of the world, the Essenes repeated continuously their baptismal immersions. Most probably John the Baptist was excluded from their group.

Jesus was associated with John the Baptist because of his baptism. Most probably he became indirectly acquainted with the Essene type of thinking. Like Jesus, they also saw the world and time in a dualistic conflict situation. His work is the removal of Satan's domination and the binding of Satan (Matthew 12:29). Their approaches, however, were completely different.

Of importance, however, is the fact that the Essene continuously baptized and did not take baptism as a sacrament which is administered only once. It has developed in the Qumran sect to a ritual without the emphasis on its eschatological significance. Baptism is an eschatological symbol--a sign which Jesus did not administer because He Himself will be the fulfilment of that sign--it is a seal of ownership.

Baptism as an initiation rite

The primitive church understood baptism soon after the first Easter as an initiation rite for the eschatological "Israel" (the remnant)--they were baptized in the name of Jesus. The combination of the baptismal act, forgiveness of sins, and giving of the Spirit, is pre-Pauline and has as motive the eschatological sealing of the baptized. From the baptismal confession in Romans 10:9 it is clear the Paul had in mind belief in and confession of the Easter events. In 1 Corinthians 6:11 the emphasis concerning the sacrament is placed on the washing away of sins, (this aspect is highlighted in the African Independent Churches "baptism" or ritual washings in the sea), on sanctification, and on justification. It seals an eschatological act, the christological eschatology which enables the baptized to take part in the death of Jesus and in His resurrection. Paul's understanding of baptism is rather the actualization of the once for all event of salvation (Romans 6:10 [phapax]) rather than an initiation act or washing away of sins. It is a symbol of dying with Christ, a certainty of the coming resurrection and the immediate beginning of a new life. Paul's baptismal theology stands over against Judaistic legalism, emphasizing the character of grace of this sacrament. Many of the African Independent Churches emphasize this latter aspect of baptism and the grace they highlight has both spiritual and physical consequences.

Although baptism signifies that the life of sin is broken, the Christian existence is an existence of paradox--the Christian has it and he has it not--he is sinner and not a sinner. This is expressed in the African Independent Churches through their repeated baptisms which have to wash away sins committed. Furthermore, Paul puts all baptized persons on the same charismatic level in spite of their variety of gifts (Romans 12:6ff; 1 Corinthians 12:4ff); each has a specific charisma (1 Corinthians 7:7)--there is no special class with charisma; no one takes special precedence in spiritual matters. In baptism all are equal; there is no special race. These aspects find expression in most of the African Independent Churches where various offices do exist such as archbishop, bishop, ministers, preachers, evangelists, prophets, women leaders; but none of these are elevated undemocratically above the rank and file

membership. Only in a small percentage of churches does one find
the leader as the sum and substance of the church with a position
of untouchable authority. Also among the African Independent
Churches, the sociological, biological, and other values are
superseded when members form a new community of those baptized in
Jesus Christ. Christology and anthropology are integrated into a
new order.

Magical conceptions

Already in the time of Paul magical conceptions prevailed
with regard to the sacramental character of baptism, such as
among the Corinthian gnostics. They maintained that baptism
guarantees that sin will not come over the sinner; i.e., it seals
a person against being sinful. This is, as indicated above, not
prevalent among the African Independent Churches for many of
whose members baptism has become a purification rite because they
take the consequences of sin and, more often, sin itself,
seriously.

The Corinthian congregation put forward four motives for
baptism, namely purification from sin, sealing with the name of
Jesus Christ, giving of the Spirit, and participation in the
death and resurrection of Jesus Christ. Not what the baptizer
does but what God does is of significance. In some African
Independent Churches much emphasis is being put on the
preparation of the baptizer, just as was the case in the
Montanist movement which Augustine had to confront. It is God's
grace and not the baptizer's background or act which makes the
sacrament effective. Belief goes with baptism and, for Paul,
God's presence in Jesus Christ is basic (2 Corinthians 1:21ff).
In his letter to the Colossians and Ephesians, Paul goes further
and states that being baptized is being buried and resurrected
(Colossians 2:12). It is not merely that sin is washed off but

that one's debt of guilt is nailed on the Cross, and the baptized takes part in the triumph of the Crucified over the powers of the world. The emphasis is not on "washing off" but on the Cross-- not on the pool, river or sea--an impression given by some of the African Independent Churches but on Calvary. The "washing off" emphasis on baptism at a place where numinous power is strong, prevails in some of the African Independent Churches. Many however put Calvary at the center.

There is no united doctrine in the New Testament concerning baptism--not among the apostolic fathers. The various views which emanated from eschatology, christology, and anthropology could not be harmonized. The new views that came forward with regard to baptism were related to the self-understanding of the faith which subjected the sacrament to intense theological thinking and discussion. The accent had already shifted in primitive Christianity with regard to the meaning of the sacrament. It was initially seen as participation in the gift of the eschatological salvation history and as an initiation rite which gives access to the gifts of salvation that could be offered within the church. The association of baptism with christology and anthropology was soon terminated and it became intertwined with ecclesiology, emphasizing ethics and repentance.

What Christ had done for man's salvation was in the background--in the forefront was the moral life of the person to be baptized, and his repentance. In this the church was the judge.

Baptism in post-apostolic times

During this period the various interpretations of baptism were finalized. The neglect of the eschatological self-understanding of the church resulted in its own sacramentalisation. Because of this, baptism and the Spirit were separated, highlighting two acts associated with this sacrament, namely forgiveness of sins through baptism with water and conveying the Spirit through laying on of hands (Acts 19:1-7). The African Independent Churches also highlight the latter act in their baptisms although one can lose the power of "the Spirit," and in order to receive it again, rebaptism, which is actually rededication, is necessary.

During the end of the first and the beginning of the third century, the baptismal ritual itself became established; namely, (a) laying on of hands and (b) baptism had to take place in running water as was already the case with John the Baptist (Acts 8:36; Hebrews 10:22). Many of the African Independent Churches administer the first baptism of the initiant only in rivers as they emphasize that this should be in running water; others maintain the water at the sea is always moving and that it is most appropriate to administer an initiant's first baptism at the sea. For some African Independent Churches the water should be undisturbed; i.e., nobody should as yet have entered it--this is why many baptize before or just after sunrise.

In the post-apostolic era the initiant entered the water and was sprinkled once while the baptizer pronounced the name of Jesus Christ over him (Acts 8:16). The baptism was in the name of Jesus--not in the name of Paul, for example (Cf. 1 Corinthians 1:13, 15). One specific section of African Independent Churches baptize their initiants in the name of their leader, but nearly all the African Independent Churches baptize in the name of the Triune God. The three acts in the baptismal ritual came as a result of the introduction of the trinitarian formula which was taken from Matthew 28:19. The African Independent Churches usually administer tri-immersion at the initial baptism but during the later "baptisms" which purify, drive out evil spirits, restore the power of the Holy Spirit, and heal, many immersions could be administered--in some cases over twenty immersions take place accompanied by the beating of the body, the drinking of sea water in order to vomit and get the evil out, and lying in the sea water so as to receive its healing effects and its power.

Infant (or paedo) baptism

Although child baptism i.e., baptism as an initiation act into the church, is not practiced in the Zionist churches in general, it is necessary to refer to this practice in the historical churches. What is called "baptism" with regard to infants, is actually the rite of blessing children practiced in adult baptism-orientated churches. Children of most African Independent Churches members are regularly "baptized" in the sea in order to obtain power, healing, and good luck, and to keep the evil spirits away.

The literature of the primitive church is silent on infant baptism; in fact, it is nowhere mentioned. Infant baptism is not historically anchored in the New Testament but has to be deduced theologically. Only in the last third of the second century is reference made to it, and in the third century it does come prominently to the fore.

Tertullian reacted against infant baptism on the basis of Matthew 19:14. Origen (250 AD) referred to the practice in 250 while Cyprian, born in the beginning of the third century, considered infant baptism imperative two or three days after birth, and to this his bishops agreed. In the 4th century it was a regular practice to baptize children of Christian parents. Late in the 4th century (about 381) Gregory of Nazianzus, bishop of Constantinople, expressed himself against infant baptism, whereas, according to Canon 3 of the Synod of Carthage (418), unbaptized infants were considered to be doomed on the basis of John 3:5.

As has been indicated, most of the African Independent Churches have the practice of blessing the child soon after birth through pouring water from a dish or bath over the child. This practice does not replace baptism which follows later, usually after puberty, and mostly after the age of fifteen.

The development of baptism in ecclesiastical-historical perspective

Brief reference to these developments will put various issues with regard to the Zionist practices in a clearer light.

The consensus is that adult baptism predominated up to the second half of the 2nd century. Justin maintained that infants were born without willing it but they should themselves be reborn willing it. To this most of the Zionist churches will agree. Children are "baptized" but here baptism is related to the receiving of the blessings which Christianity can give such as healing, protection from evil forces, inner strength, a good relationship with God--it is done in an ex opere operato manner. Only later can the child confess its faith and become a full member of the church after having received the baptism of faith.

Tertullian saw baptism as obsignatio fidei, i.e., sealing of personal accepted faith. For Zionists this takes place usually at the age of 12 but mostly after the age of 15. It was around 125 AD that children of these ages were baptized after instruction and if they had truly confessed Jesus Christ to be their Lord and Savior. After Augustine's doctrine of original sin and the consolidation of the State Church, the practice of infant baptism was fully accepted in the Western church. From the third century onwards baptism was increasingly understood as effective in removing original sin, i.e., in an opus operatum context. Infant baptism strengthened this approach with the result that it contributed to the corpus christianum fallacy. This fallacy could also become a predominant factor in African Christianity.

The early church fathers emphasized that with baptism a change of lordship takes place within the adult baptized. Not the demons, but God takes possession of him (Justin, Irenaeus, and others). Baptism is a seal (sphragis) which is assured through the holy names of the baptismal formula, anointment, crossing and/or the baptismal water. In this way the person is sealed as the possession of God or Christ; he is sealed off from demonic attacks, and angels and demons acknowledge him as God's child. For the gnostics baptism was the passport needed for the heavenly journey. African gnosticism will agree with this because of the purification from sin and evil which is effected and the evil spirits which are overruled. This is a transition from death to life, an emphasis put on baptism by the early church fathers. Baptism was a contract with God. For the African Independent Churches the contract stands if it has been entered into by those who are able to understand what it implies, and for them the contract includes many issues other than the death and resurrection in Christ. In most African Independent Churches there is hardly any catechetical instruction--what members get is through participation in the singing and the services.

Around 200 AD the emphasis was on catechetical instruction which eventually concluded with baptism. Nowhere was baptism considered to be a mere imitation of the New Testament. Origen understood the symbol (sumbolon) as complete and thorough cleansing through the Logos but as also giving power to the person baptized as a result of the pronouncement over him of the names of the Triune God. With this most of the Zionist churches will be in full agreement. For Origen the degree of cleansing depended on the attitude of the receiver. Many Zionist leaders go through even a week of fasting before they baptize people and expect such fasting from those to be baptized but not the same number of days: for the members these are usually fewer.

For Tertullian baptism effected forgiveness with absolute certainty even if an unrepentant person administered the sacrament. For him the baptismal water had wonderful power; it is a "holy stream," an eternal fountain, divine water; it is saving water of salvation, healing water (Cf. John 5:2ff; 9:7) or the fountain of life. Some of the Zionists attach such great significance to the purifying effects of water that it is used in the church after confession of sin and they drink it from small cups. Tertullian's emphasis on "holy baptismal water" could typify him as one of the earliest forerunners of the Zionist churches, indeed, the first "Zioni" in the Christian church. Also, according to the well-known church father, Irenaeus, baptismal water gives life, immortality. For Ignatius water in which the demons settled (also a Zioni belief) had to be cleansed and sanctified through Christ's baptism, through Christ's blood (Augustine), through the mediation of an angel (Tertullian) or the Holy Spirit (Ambrose) who moves over the water and who is responsible for the rebirth of the baptized. With this the Zionist churches are in full agreement. In the undisturbed water--some baptize from 4 a.m. on Sundays at the sea before it has been disturbed by bathers--which is blessed and sanctified by the baptizer, the flock are baptized and cleaned.

The gnostic Christians first consecrated baptismal water but from Tertullian onwards water was consecrated in the church. For the Zionists water at the pool, river, or sea, that has been prayed over is consecrated and the flag that they usually plant alongside them on the beach also keeps the evil forces away.

Baptism outside the established churches

Whether such a baptism is valid and thus acceptable was a real contentious issue in the church. With Cyprian "unbroken belief" of the baptizer and the receiver, which is only possible in the church, is necessary, and it was valid if done in the name of the Trinity or Jesus. Those against baptism outside the church were united in their belief that the receiving of the Spirit is possible only in the church.

The question arises at times in the various churches whether baptism in the African Independent Churches should be accepted. The ecclesiological norms apply and not necessarily the objective understanding of this sacrament in the context of the African Independent Churches. The question is whether the church is a church. Are the 3,270 African Independent Churches denominations (1980 census) with their 5.83 million members and adherents and their variety of practices, churches in the scriptural sense? For Calvin the church is the church where the Word is rightly preached, the sacraments rightly administered and discipline rightly executed. For Luther the first two conditions applied. Many established churches have problems with baptisms of some of the African Independent Churches. There is no justification for rejecting their baptism without analyzing carefully a specific church's approach to Scripture and its christology. From a phenomenological point of view their baptisms fulfil the requirements attached by any church to this act.

The opus operatum approach

During the Donatist struggle in the 4th century the opus operatum approach developed still further and was eventually highlighted in 12th century scholasticism. For the opponents of Donatism the impeccability of the baptizer is not an absolute precondition because God is the actual baptizer. (Optatus V, 4; deus lavat, non homo; therefore, sacramenta per se sancta non per homines). Baptism could after Augustine even be performed by a non-Christian as long as it was done in the name of the Triune God and accepted in faith.

The gnostics had various types of baptism such as water baptism of the mystery cults, fire baptism, and spirit baptism. Some African Independent Churches administered waterless baptism by laying on of hands, which is termed Spirit baptism, for example, the four million strong Kimbabwe Church in Zaire. In the third-century catechetical instruction before and after baptism was prescribed. Later the church's baptism was supplemented by other sacramental acts such as laying on of hands and crossing the forehead, which led to the disintegration of water baptism. Since the second century baptism had received the connotation of an initiation rite under the influence of the mystery cults and had received some mystery aspects: fire exorcism in preparation for baptism, prayers and fasting during the days before baptism (prayers and fasting before baptism with the African Independent Churches), watch-night service during the last night (very familiar with African Independent Churches-- umvusilelo, i.e., revival service), anointing the whole body as protection against the devil (also with some of the African Independent Churches), baptismal act with confession of faith, putting on white baptismal clothes, crossing processing of garlanded initiants in the church with candles under the leadership of the bishop (also with some of the African

Independent Churches at the sea, their baptismal "font"--they wear baptismal clothes and go in procession to the sea with the bishop of baptizer leading and "opening up" the water with prayer); there is also the kiss of peace with the congregation, and the newly baptized receive milk and honey.

During the third and fourth centuries Clemens and Origen understood baptism again as incorporation in Christ, the Logos. Cyril of Jerusalem and Basil saw it as death and resurrection with Christ, whereby the three acts of immersion signified the three days' burial of Jesus. The old ecclesiastical concepts of baptism in the West (the Roman Catholic Church of Cyprian and Ambrose) and the East (the Greek Orthodox Church of Origen and the Cappadocians) culminate in Augustine. He ventured to overcome their problems with the emphasis on the Word and the sacrament. Augustine maintained it is actually Christ who baptizes, who as visible word (visibile verbum) acts in the outward baptismal act (sacramentum) and as "invisible grace" (invisibilis gratia) completes the work of salvation (effectus sacramenti) in those baptized. The outward act (immersion in water and anointing) is only the symbol of the work of salvation. The work of salvation is seen in acts of cleansing and laying on of hands, and this implies (a) acceptance of the redemption work of Christ and reconciliation with God through giving up sinning and (b) building up one's spiritual life through receiving the Holy Spirit (infusio caritatis per spiritum sanctum, Romans 5:5) and becoming part of the church, the corpus or regnum Christi. This approach has influenced the more simplified liturgical approach to the sacrament of baptism. It had a decisive influence on the churches of the reformation.

The African Independent Churches in general differs from Augustine--the symbol is not merely a signum in the sense of a mere sign. Baptism has in itself dynamic value and it has specific effects which cannot be ascribed to a mere sign. They stand nearer to the gnostics and the scholastics who interpreted the act of baptism as freeing a person from guilt and punishment. The scholastics believed that through the eradication of sin and infusion of the "habitus" of a supernatural attitude (habitus virtutem) baptismal grace makes the baptized acceptable to God. Duns Scotus and the Nominalists emphasized that the water cannot effect the grace. For Zionists water that has been prayed over, and especially sea water, does convey spiritual benefits. They will agree with Thomas Aquinas that God is the Principal cause and the baptismal water the instrumental cause of the spiritual work of grace.

Even in the Middle Ages baptism was the main dividing line when so-called heretics and sects criticized the baptism practiced by the church--some rejected water baptism and practiced Spirit baptism through the laying on of hands. The Catharis advocated rebaptism because they rejected infant baptism. The African Independent Churches also rebaptize even if those who join them have been previously baptized. They will not accept baptism from a person whose morals and spiritual life are not on a par with their preaching.

The Reformers followed Augustine in holding that the sacraments are the visible word. The sign (water) and the word (the baptist formula) form an undivided unity. Luther defended infant baptism--God gives faith. He gives it to the children also. For Melanchthon baptism is necessary for salvation, also of the children. For Zwingli baptism is to turn around and live according to Christian rules. Calvin tried to reconcile Luther and Zwingli. The baptist act and the water are only signs-- baptism is not necessary for salvation which is bound to faith.

Only the ordained can baptize and baptism goes with rebirth, which takes place through repentance and personal faith; infant baptism remains incomplete until confirmation has been finalized with the candidate having to confess his faith personally.

Most of the African Independent Churches' ministers are not trained, neither ordained through the church but, as they maintain, through the Holy Spirit--which is unacceptable to most established churches. At every baptism the congregation has to devote itself anew to God's service and confess its faith. Only the blood of Christ and the Holy Spirit purify from sin--the water does not effect the cleansing and sanctification.

For Baptists adult baptism is the shibboleth. As for the baptizers of Zürich during the time of the Reformation, unbaptized children were not doomed. Jesus baptizes adults through the Spirit. Methodists baptize the children of converted adults. For the Pentecostals, Spirit baptism of adults is practiced. For the Salvation Army there is only Spirit baptism. With the Pietists the emphasis is on conversion and confirmation--they have a sacramental attitude to baptism. In the People's Church infant baptism is extensively practiced and mostly a mere convention. For the African Independent Churches, although it is widely practiced, baptism is not a mere convention--it has deep-seated significance.

Baptism and its dogmatic evaluation

Luther evaluated baptism as a means of grace as it conveys the salvation in Christ: the assurance of the forgiveness of sins. It is to be seen in conjunction with justification; it implies real renewal, rebirth (Titus 3:5f); it signifies inclusion in Christ and growth with Him (Romans 6:5); its emphasis is not on the formal joining of a church but it expresses inner oneness of the receiver with the church. In infant baptism the church represents the infants, and baptism has an objective validity and power, even if the faith of the baptized person understands it only later. A persons' faith does not constitute baptism but receives baptism. Infant baptism is associated for Luther with Christian instruction and education.

The once for all sacrifice of Christ on the Cross--our implanting in his life thereby assured and sealed--has taken place with such certainty and finality that there can be no question of repetition. Luther warns against superstition with regard to this sacrament--against believing, for example, that there is specific power in the water. He warns that it is not the outward water bath that cleanses from sin, but only the blood of Jesus Christ and the Holy Spirit; i.e., baptism should never be associated with any magical sources and effects. Baptism is not a second cause for a person's salvation alongside Christ. Baptism thus should not receive an independent efficacy but has meaning only in relation to the work of Christ on the Cross. The eschatological character with its emphasis on hope must be retained. Many African Independent Churches should take note of the possibility of being misled and seeing baptism as a means of obtaining some kind of transcendent power.

On the other hand, the established churches so often gave the impression that baptism has some special significance apart from its exclusive relationship to the Christ event and the gift of the Holy Spirit. While the Afro-Christian religions emphasize the importance of this sacrament and its deep inner relationship with the work of the Holy Spirit, there are factors which distort, in some African Independent Churches the meaningful work of the Holy Spirit as if it were associated with rituals that make use of magic. There is also the repetition of the sacrament in the African Independent Churches although some emphasize that the first is only an "initiatory" baptism in a river which is thereafter repeated at the sea. The repetition does have associations with magical power. Nevertheless, in spite of the many theological questions that do arise, the established churches should look at their own attitudes to this sacrament which has lost its centrality in the church. It is indeed a dynamic sacrament in the African Independent Churches--something which should not be overlooked.

Liturgical aspects

As in the primitive church so in many African Independent Churches a person to be baptized had to fast for a few days--the baptizer and members of the congregation had to share in such fasting. In the African Independent Churches some church leaders fast for five days before baptism, drinking black tea and water, while members fast for three days. Furthermore baptism has usually to be preceded by a revival service (umvusilelo) which could start on a Friday evening and continue to the Sunday morning before the participants leave for the place where baptism is administered. The service usually starts, however, on a Saturday night at about 21h00.

Baptism took place in the early church preferably where there was running water. Immersion three times was prescribed and the trinitarian formula was pronounced "over" the person baptized. In the African Independent Churches such baptism could also take place at the sea, as in the case of the The New Holy Church in Zion of South Africa, the leader of which stated that they do it at the sea because it is not easy to get an adequate spot at the river. On an occasion six new members baptized at the sea after the umvusilelo (revival service) were immersed three times, and the trinitarian formula was used, namely "In the

Name of the God, the Son, and the Spirit," If a running water
venue could not be obtained, the primitive church then had a
three-times sprinkling ceremony. Submersion took place in the
historical churches, but this was not the only valid manner of
putting a person into the sea. Immersion is, however, the only
manner accepted by the Zionist churches.

The order of baptism related in the Didache (i.e., teachings
of the twelve apostles) was as follows: instruction in baptism
was followed by fasting and praying for forgiveness of sins.
Thereafter came the baptismal bath where there was water.
Baptism was called illumination and through it rebirth took
place. After this the baptized were offered holy communion.
Thus, the baptismal act was not a mere signum but effectual in
changing the person baptized.

The baptismal order left by Hippolytus of Rome ($\pm$ 220 AD)
was of great significance to the old church. It also gives a
clear indication of how significant a place this sacrament
occupied within the church. Its reconstruction from original
Greek documents indicates that baptism then consisted of three
phases, namely:
I. Before baptism: Prayer was said over the water in the early
church (i.e., there was consecration of baptismal water; this
also occurs in the African Independent Churches--even when
baptism takes place at the sea the leader walks in and blesses
the water). In the early church undressing of those to be
baptized took place (first children, then men, then women, and
then all jewelry etc., was taken off; the Zionis also undress and
put their uniforms on for "baptism" which implies, for the
African Independent Churches healing, blessing, power, getting
the Spirit, initiation into the Church, etc). Consecration of
the oil by the bishop also took place in the early church (very

few Zioni churches consecrate with oil). There was renunciation of the devil (abrenuntiatio diaboli) by saying: "I oppose you, Satan, and all your pomp on all your angels;" this is found in worked out baptismal liturgies of exorcism--it is a personal rejection of Satan). Finally, there was first anointment of the baptized with the exorcism oil through the presbyter ("every evil spirit will depart from you;" in the African Independent Church the evil spirits (Zulu: imimoya emibi) are usually thrashed out of the person while he is in the water.

II. During baptism: The person whose clothes had been removed would be handed over to the baptizer (in the African Independent Churches a person leads the candidate to be baptized to the baptizer and after baptism leads the baptized person back to the group who normally sing choruses and clap hands while drumming and sometimes making rhythmic movements and dancing and running or walking in a circle). In the early church the baptizer would ask questions concerning the candidate's faith; then there would be three immersions after which would follow the reply of the person baptized, namely "I believe" (in the African Independent Churches this is usually done at the watch night service or at the beach or river just before baptism). Then the second anointment with the oil of thanksgiving through the presbyter would take place (this is not the case in the African Independent Churches). Then there would be drying and putting on of clothes of the person baptized (the African Independent Churches members usually change the wet clothes and wet uniform after baptism, with dry clothes brought to the place where the baptism has been administered).

III. After baptism: In the congregation laying on of hands by the bishop would take place as well as prayers for the descent of the Holy Spirit upon the candidate (such prayers in the African

Independent Churches are said before and during baptism and are also expressed in the choruses they sing). Then the sign of the cross would be made (not in the African Independent Churches). The kiss of peace (not in the African Independent Churches) and greeting would follow. The new member would be confirmed after baptism and would take part in the service that followed. During the neophyte mass that followed three cups were usually distributed: one with milk, one with honey, and one with water. (During the services of the St. John Apostolic Faith Mission a small cup of water is taken by each member during the service when members stand in queues to receive it in front of the pulpit).

Much of this baptist liturgy has gone astray in the churches of the reformation but has been retained in the Catholic and Eastern Orthodox baptismal rituals. It is significant to note that the African Independent Churches have revived on their own many aspects of this liturgy without having had real contact with most of these rituals. They compensate for what has been discarded of the rich traditional liturgical and ritual heritage they had, but within a Christian context. The above-mentioned Roman liturgy emphasizes that baptism is an act of forgiveness of sins, which was preceded by driving out of demons as an independent act. (The latter activity in baptism plays a great role among Zionists for whom Satan and demonic spirits are a reality). The "giving of the Spirit" in the early church was separated from the water bath while this is part of baptism in the African Independent Churches. Many church fathers had variations of the above-mentioned baptismal order. Baptism, as in the case of the African Independent Churches, was preceded in the early church by fasting.

During the fifth century and later baptismal and other orders and symbolic acts became more and more extensive. In the Eastern Orthodox Church exorcism also played a significant role. It seems that this would especially have been the case when adult baptism was still a significant form of baptism. When the catechumen was exorcised prayers were intensely said three times for the baptismal candidate; the priest then breathed in his mouth, on the forehead, and on his chest in order to drive out the evil and unclean spirit. Then followed the renouncement of the devil, the candidate facing the West, and then the acceptance of Christ, the candidate facing the East. On the question: "Do you believe in Him?" the catechumen confessed the Nicene Creed. All this was repeated three times. At the end the catechumen kneeled in prayer and the priest prayed over him that he might receive the blessings of baptism. Various ceremonies followed, such as washing after anointment, which took place eight days after baptism; then followed cutting of the hair of the catechumen. This was also part of the old church tradition. No distinction in the formula was made between infant and adult baptism--parents, godparents, or the congregation, stood in for the latter. In the Western church adult baptism slowly disappeared.

Opening of ears

In the Old Roman baptismal liturgy one finds, apart from the well-known aspects such as prayers and exorcism, also the apertio aurium (opening of the ears) in the third week of fasting when the baptized are officially made acquainted with the Gospel, the confession of faith, and the Pater Noster; further on, in the 7th week of the fasting, the Rite of Ephphata (i.e., "be opened," Mark 7:34) was observed by the priest; this refers to the opening of the ears in order to hear that which comes from God through words.

· The Zionists ritually open the ears of their prophets in the water when the baptizer shouts first in the one and then in the other ear in order to open them so that they can clearly hear what "the Spirit" says.

Salt and baptism

The Roman Catholic baptismal order in the Middle Ages not only included the consecration of the baptismal water (benedictio fontis) but had also a ritual blowing away of evil spirits (the African Independent Churches have a ritual "thrashing" of the body to get the evil spirits out--hitting on the shoulders and the legs while the person baptized stands or is lying in the water, even throwing sea sand on the legs of the person). There was blessing of the salt (with the African Independent Churches the water and the salt are blessed when the leader goes into the sea first; fresh water is often salted); there would be salt in the mouth of the baptized (the African Independent Churches drink water mixed with salt or sea water which is a precious commodity for those far away from the sea;[1] helps them to vomit, (palaza) out the evil and to clean their stomachs (isiwasho); ordinary

---

[1]On 7 July 1985 a group of Vendas were at the Durban Beach. They had left Louis Trichardt on Friday the 5th of July at 18h45 for Johannesburg where they transferred to the Durban train which departed on the following day at 10h15, arriving at Durban station on the 7th of July at 06h50. They walked to the beach, arrived at the North Beach at 08h10, spent the rest of the day in and at the sea for baptism, i.e., to receive power and good luck and to get "the Spirit." The spokesman emphasized that they do this for the sake of the children also, so that they also may "get the Spirit." According to the spokesman they came specially to the sea because it has power; it has salt in it--the sea purifies! They took water and sea sand with them and were looking also for shells. The church to which they belong is The Revelation Apostolic Church in Zion.

water is often mixed with ash for medicinal purposes). In the above-mentioned Roman Catholic baptismal order the salt was considered to be the salt of wisdom, however not as numinous power but as illumination; liturgically salt was considered to be indispensable (as in many African Independent Churches who mix water with salt when sea water is not available)--salt makes food palatable, removes what is unsavory, has a purifying effect, protects from decomposition; is a symbol of consistency; it had to be added to the Jewish and non-Christian Roman sacrifices and the Old Testament salt covenant symbolized the stable and consistent bond which God entered into with his people (Numbers 18:19; 2 Chronicles 13:5 cf; Mark 9:50). With the African Independent Churches salt refers mainly to special power but also to its purifying and protective aspects such as providing protection against the activities of evil spirits. Since the 5th century the baptismal water was taken from consecrated water, i.e., water which the priest had exorcised by adding salt and blessing to it.

As in the case of non-Christian Rome where the newly born received consecrated salt on the 8th days (dies lustricus), so also the catechumens received consecrated salt before baptism and after this exorcism was ceremoniously executed--special power was ascribed to salt. The blessed doctrine (Titus 1:9) which the catechumens received keeps the souls healthy and gives the necessary wisdom for salvation; this was symbolized by salt which is called sal sapientiae, medicina perfecta and propitiatio in vitam aeternam. The purifying power of salt was acknowledged in the Old Testament (Cf. 2 Kings 2:19ff). Because of this it is used to consecrate water which was used not only for baptism but also for the consecration of the place on which the church would be built and of the church itself.

The liturgical use of salt, which Luther recommended in the first edition of Taufbüchlein (1523), is omitted from the second edition (1526) and later editions of the baptismal orders. The use of salt has disappeared among the reformed churches. The question is: How and why did it become prevalent among the African Independent Churches?

What has influenced these churches is the special power and purification aspects of salt, it seems, and what is stated about salt in the Bible, as in the following examples:

And every obligation shalt thou season with salt ... with all thine offerings thou shalt offer salt (Leviticus 2:13) ... it is a covenant of salt for ever before the Lord for you and your offspring with you (Numbers 18:19). "Bring me a new bowl, and put salt in it" .... Then he went to the spring of water and threw salt in it, and said, "Thus says the Lord, 'I have made this water wholesome; henceforth neither death nor miscarriage shall come from it.'" So the water has been wholesome to this day ... (2 Kings 2:20, 21, 22). Ought you not to know that the Lord God of Israel gave the kingship over Israel for ever to David and his sons by a covenant of salt? (2 Chronicles 13:5). But its swamps and marshes will not become fresh; they are to be left for salt (Ezekiel 47:11).

In the New Testament the Christian witness is symbolized by salt (Matthew 5:13); they are admonished to have salt in themselves (Mark 9:50); their speech should be "seasoned with salt" (Col. 4:6). Salt, however, can lose its power. For the African Independent Churches it does not lose any of its effectiveness in the sea.

Consecrated water and baptism

The major precondition of African Independent Churches' baptisms is that the water has to be consecrated--even the powerful water of the sea. The baptizer enters the sea first and--some do so with outstretched arms--blesses the water before baptism. This water to which ash is often added is also used for healing purposes. They dance regularly around water to be used for healing purposes; the dancing is accompanied by singing and drumming.

The consecrated water (aqua benedicta) of the Roman Catholic Church has its forerunner in Jewish and non-Christian washing. With Tertullian and the Apostolic Constitutions, washing before prayers and the Eucharist was most probably still done with unconsecrated water but since the 5th century the baptismal water used was from consecrated water. From the 8th or the 9th century consecrated water was included in sacramental acts and was considered to have an enlightening and a remedial and sanctifying influence. This is precisely what the African Independent Churches emphasize--the consecrated water gives them "the Spirit" of which the burning candles, planted in a circle or otherwise, are a symbol; it is used for healing and it symbolizes spiritual devotion. Exorcism played an important part in the baptismal ritual of the early church as it does within the African Independent Churches context.

The Reformation counteracted the emphasis on baptismal water apart from moving away from the elaborate liturgy regarding baptism. The Zionists reinstituted not only an elaborate liturgy but gave a dynamic significance to baptismal water. Luther's Taüfbuchlein and the Common Prayer Book of 1549 which is related to Luther's Taufbüchlein of 1526 were still the nearest to the old liturgy. Bucer, Zwingli, and Calvin moved the furthest away as they took only the Bible as their norm. Calvin's rather extensive baptismal order of 1543 excludes any reference to traditional rites and rituals but ventures to give a clear biblical exposition of the sacrament of baptism. During the Pietist era in Europe a conflict arose concerning exorcism as part of the baptismal order. A variety of Lutheran baptismal orders developed, and in 1961 a unified baptismal order was decided upon by the United Evangelical Church in Germany.

House baptisms and baptisms of the sick in African Independent Churches had a definite influence on the "democratization" of baptism, i.e., it became less controlled by ecclesiastical authority. The African Independent Churches developed this further. Most of their church leaders had no theological training; others had hardly any schooling or very little (the average being about standard 4). They emphasize the work of the Holy Spirit as being the main factor in their ministry.

The "secularization" of baptism was partly due to the church; there is a rite, for instance, associated with the baptism of church bells. Zionists baptize their holy staves and crosses (with which they inter alia touch a sick person or to whom they relay power); their flags (which, even if they are sometimes not opened and planted alongside the circle where they gather at the beach, are also baptized) and they themselves are baptized in their uniforms.

The blessing of the mother after baptism became increasingly a custom in evangelical congregations and therefore a new element in baptismal liturgy. In some of the African Independent Churches this happens after a child-birth when the mother is received into the group; also, after the death and burial of a close relative, those who have been closely associated with him or her are not immediately allowed into the church after the funeral. In the African Independent Churches such persons are often baptized the second or third week after the funeral and are then accepted into the group. Death magic has to be removed first.

Baptism and the circle

Often the group gathering for baptism at the water first turn in a circle; they start slowly and gradually they gain momentum and run faster. The circle is the symbol of perfection, and in it they make contact with the transcendent. Here the Spirit comes to them and so often they repeat just these two words many times in a chorus: "Come Spirit" (Woza umoya, woza umoya). When an individual turns round at speed on his feet, it is a sign of the entrance of the Spirit.

Flag

The flag does also play a role in the baptist ceremonies of some African Independent Churches. Some bring the flag to be baptized in the sea--it is folded and tightened with strings. Others plant it alongside them on the beach or the place where they baptize.

It is not certain were the flag originated from--most probably from John Alexander Dowie who started the Zionist movement in 1896 in Chicago and whose church is the initiator of the movement in South Africa. He introduced the flag in his church. The use has, however, undergone a transformation.

The flags have various functions: (a) they open the way for the believer to the place of public worship; (b) evil spirits are removed from a place of worship or baptism through the flag;

(c) they are planted near the place of worship or baptism as a sign that the place is safe and that the various liturgical and ritual activities cannot be obstructed by evil forces; (d) those who wish to receive catechetical instruction gather at the flag; (e) it also serves as a protection against witchcraft; (f) it could also be a sign of the power of the prophet or leader to cure disease, or to confer "the Spirit," and it may be in various colors, mainly blue, green, yellow, and white--seldom in black or red; (g) the colors serve different purposes in driving away evil spirits, and often depend on the dreams or revelations of an exorcist. Black and red medicines among Zulu people are so-called "hot" medicines which have to be cooked and which stop the disease while white medicines are "cool" medicines which cure the person. The flags have the softer colors which are associated with trust, love, and purity, as in the case of the uniforms.

Flags are put on top, or in front of houses where they serve to ward off evil. In some cases the flags are detached from the flag pole or staff to ward off the intense dangers, for example, at the moment of internment at a burial service. Flags are prominent on many huts and houses where lightning is experienced as a real danger.

Thus, because exorcism plays such a significant role among the African Independent Churches, the flag will have a place at the baptismal ceremonies of many of the African Independent Churches. It is often the only "watch dog" over their possessions on the beach while they are singing and handclapping and drumming in or near the water with the baptismal ceremony in progress.

Baptism in the mission situation

Baptism acquired in many ways its own specific character in the mission situation to such an extent that it has been referred to as the mission sacrament. It signifies inclusion in the body of Christ, being included in the corpus christi mysticum, and at the same time becoming a member in the ecclesia particularis. A new community is formed which often meant in the alienation from traditional structures, customs and groups. It is in a specific sense a rites de passage. It has often led to tension as non-Christian initiation rites have been discarded, different theological accents have been highlighted, and quick and mass baptisms have been organized. Furthermore, the large number of ex-non-Christians who had their longest and often deepest religious experiences in the traditional religion also created problems.

Adult baptism predominated during the first centuries of Christianity; the same situation prevailed in the South African situation during the initial and later impact of Christianity among black people. This accounts for the inclusion of some traditional emphases also in the sacrament of baptism with many of the African Independent Churches. In the West, infant baptism, which predominated for ages, was streamlined especially in many Protestant churches which initiated mission work among Black people, and with many in Western churches it became either an act of respectability or, to a certain extent, merely a custom. The symbol has retrogressed in the sense that it has lost its content for many. It has already been indicated that this sacrament is of great dynamic significance within the African Independent Churches context. The new baptismal name the baptized in the mission received further distinguished them from the rest, and this also was an indication of the change in them.

This change has been with some not such that it has completely penetrated the magical traditional heritage, for example, the interpretation of the baptismal water as being effective in itself, i.e., if it has been prayed over. Such an approach could have a negative bearing on the relationship between baptism, the Word, and belief. It has to be emphasized that baptism is only necessitas praecepti not medii. The emphasis on Spirit baptism, that baptism should bring "the Spirit," is often referred to in the choruses sung at the place of baptism.

Baptism in the mission demands decision which means breaking with the old spiritual forces and separation from the old traditional community. Baptism draws the line between the old traditional ways and the new life, and often activistic baptismal names are coined by the baptizer or the baptized person, which is just as characteristic as the significance of abrenunciation in the baptismal act.

Through baptism into communion with the new Lord a new community is constituted which gathers round "mission stations." This community has its separate forms and structures. It is precisely such a community that many of the African Independent Churches have become. Christianity could easily be nationalized, as has been the case where the traditional heritage has become more prominent than the basic tenets of Christianity. The relationship between baptism and belief thus becomes a problem. Syncretism also plays its role, and traditional religious aspects often play a role in the Christian expression of their faith-- these aspects occupy in some of the African Independent Churches such a predominant role that questions are asked such as: When is the church no longer the church? Do these aspects obscure or assist the understanding of Christianity--are they obstacles or not? If they are to a certain extent obstacles, would it be wise to eradicate them considering the fact that many find personal, psychological, and social benefits through them, through, for example, belief in ancestors, belief that the sea has special powers such as healing powers (also psychic healing), and that through dancing and praying and laying on of hands and baptizing one gets "more of the Spirit."

A further problem that does arise is the practical problem of the separation of the sacraments. Without an acceptable baptism no other sacrament could be validly received. In many of the African Independent Churches Holy Communion plays a much lesser role than baptism. In the Protestant churches Holy Communion usually takes place four times a year while baptism is administered at least once a month. Baptism has the connotation of a rites de passage while this is not the case with Holy Communion.

Where infant baptism predominates the church could develop into a people's church. Family solidarity plays in this connection a significant role. In such a situation family ties are so strong that the exclusion of children of non-Christian parents from baptism is found to be unacceptable. Where the "power" of the sacrament is underestimated (of which some of the African Independent Churches accuse the established church) reaction and secession could follow as the feeling is not to limit the gift of God's grace. The "cognitive" approach to baptism in Western context is mainly due to the fact that the Western churches did not have the corrective influence of adult baptism. This has also become evident in the established churches which were founded by mission societies among the Black people. Missions were often strict in a legalistic manner concerning the devaluation of baptism--the missionary and his flock often differed on the norms applied. People wanted baptism because of the dynamic value they attached to it and which was lacking according to them in the "mission" churches. They went to those churches--and are still going--where they experience the positive and dynamic effects of baptism, and understood in those churches. For many the African Independent Churches understand the essence of baptism far better than the missionaries and the missionary-originated churches, in spite of the theological problems raised by some of the African Independent Churches in connection with this sacrament.

Baptism at the North Beach Durban and its various connotations

Baptism is here used in the wider connotation because this is how the African Independent Churches evaluate this sacrament-- it is dynamic, it could be repeated, and it is associated with holy water. The best is to let them speak for themselves. Fasting precedes baptism as well as revival services.

There are various reasons for baptizing:
1. When a person is initiated into the church he/she is baptized--either at the sea or at a dam, a pool, or a river. For some, such baptisms preferably take place where there is running water, implying that the "initiatory" baptism should take place at a river and later "baptisms" at the sea. Others consider baptism at the sea as also taking place in running water.
They usually baptize in the name of the Father, the Son, and Holy Spirit.
2. "If somebody backslides the person is brought here to be baptized in order to wash away the sins ... are very hard to ... take out of a person"--according to the "prophet" of the Apostolic Full Gospel Church of Zion. This "prophet" is a plasterer. The office of "prophet" is a very important

one--he/she diagnoses the disease, reveals secret sins, experiences visions, explains the meaning of dreams, etc.

3. They are baptized to get new life according to archbishop Phewa: "When they put you down you are dead; when you come up you are new ... impilo entsha. We pray for a person that he gets new life!"

4. You must give them power. I have already baptized them once--after that I give them power." According to a minister of the Bantu Christian Church in Zion.

   Great emphasis is put in the African Independent Churches on the acquisition of power (amandla) through baptism at the sea. Power is obtained not only through immersion, "thrashing out" the evil spirits, and laying on of hands but also through swimming in the water with their uniforms on or just lying in the sea sand so that the waves go over them-- this is a familiar sight at baptismal ceremonies. Just being at the sea in a uniform even without entering the water, gives power. Two elderly Zionist women, for example, visited the sea; both put their uniforms on but only one entered the water--the other maintained that merely being present there in her uniform gave her power and a good feeling.

5. Getting "the Spirit" or Holy Spirit (umoya oyingcwele) is an important theme in all baptisms. The choruses also reflect this. The Holy Spirit reveals to them secrets at the sea. One said to me, "I see you are a church man; the Holy Spirit told me that." When they are baptized, candidates usually spin around, which is a sign of the Holy Spirit entering them; other shake, which is also evidence that "the Spirit" has entered them.

6. The Secretary of the St. Matthews Apostolic Church of Christ in South Africa at Sebokeng, the Black township that erupted in violence this year (1985) stated: "We came specially to

baptize in sea water. We believe in "spiritual water." Our members drink the sea water in order to palaza (vomit); this works the stomach, it cleanses everything ... it strengthens one's manhood.... We can have another baby again ... baptism gives one inner wellbeing."

7. Infant baptism is combined with baptism of children who have just passed the puberty stage. They were baptized in the church when they were small and are now baptised in the sea. They are called aside at the sea and instructed before the sea baptism by a khokheli (a Mama, a female leader).
    While this baptism takes place a group sing with candles in their hands:
    Thina(we) ... Ewe(Yes) ... Ewe(Yes) ... Thina(we) Nkosi yami (My Lord).
    The candles in their hands are symbols of the light that the Holy Spirit gives. Often the candles are put in a circle on the sand. The candles also assist the minister or prophet to see invisible things as well as to look into the future. Often candles with various colors are used; white candles always symbolize the presence of the Holy Spirit when lit. Those with other colors represent the ancestors of the person to be baptized or healed (for example yellow or green) and another color represents the ancestors of the baptizer or healer. It is important that these ancestors work in harmony, otherwise the work of the baptizer or healer will be ineffective.

8. Exorcism is deeply associated with baptism--hitting a person on the shoulders, on the arms, on the legs, accompanies the baptismal act. Away from the sea or water "holy" staves are regularly pressed against a patient in order to remove the evil spirits. Often the "baptized" (especially after this procedure) will say "I feel free." The staves are usually not pressed on a person in the water; they are only held

sometimes in an upright position by those who take part in
the ceremony. Away from the sea the staves are pressed on
the patient when they dance round him, but this has not been
observed after numerous contacts with Zionists at the sea.
The staves have either a cross on top or a copper or bronze
circle with spokes and on top of this a rooster made of the
same metal; or the top, if made from a twig, is bent in the
form of a circle.

One respondent had a uniform made of sugar bag material.
His explanation was "it will help me when we want something;
or when bad spirits come, nothing will happen." In
traditional society such evil spirits were an omnipresent
reality and various rituals were performed to ward them off.
When entering the sea one sometimes hears the chorus:

Zonke izinto zaluhlaba   All the things of the world
zidukisa umoya wona   take your strength/spirit away.

9.   Sick persons are brought to the pool, river or sea to be
"baptized" i.e., to receive the power from the water. Sin
and sickness are correlated--sin weakens a person physically
and psychically--and baptism removes sin so that the sick
person is strengthened.

Even sick babies are brought to the sea to be dipped in its
water; for example, upon my asking a parent why he and his
wife brought such a sick baby of about nine months to the
sea, the reply was: "The prophet said that she has to be
brought to the sea and be put into the water, to get power."
The diagnosis and instruction of the prophet is accepted as
if from a specialist. The father said that the medical
doctor using white (Western) medicine "cannot get nothing"
i.e., he could not diagnose the sickness of the child. Such
baptisms give life--impilo entsha.

10.   (a) There are also ecumenical gatherings of the African
Independent Churches at the sea where they are baptized

together in order to get "the Spirit." They come in contact with "the Spirit" who strengthens the bond between them.

(b) Interdenominational gatherings of established churches among Black people take place at the sea; for example, a group of about eighty from the Orange Free State, Lesotho, Johannesburg, Pretoria, and Bophuthatswana gathered in February 1985 and again in February 1986 at the North Beach. Not only were they from different churches such as Catholics, Methodists, Reformed Church of Africa (NGKA), Anglicans, etc. but they were Zulus, Sothos, Tswanas, and Xhosas. The spokesman, a Reformed Church of Africa (NGKA) member from Bloemfontein stated: "Once a year, the last Sunday in February, we come to the beach to get sins removed and to restore and strengthen our relationships. We are all friends and relatives." They did not perform the baptismal act stating that they were baptized but went into the water so that it covered their bodies, singing hymns while clapping hands and praying. The sea thus strengthens the bonds between families and friends as it does with those in the African Independent Churches who come to the sea mostly as house congregations.

11. (a) There are those who come to the sea unaccompanied by a minister or leader. Two young men, Jetro Mtsdhali and David Nene, for instance, came from a men's hostel situated in a black township. After putting their gowns on over their usual clothes, they went from the ablution block down to the sea where each lit a candle. Both came to receive power and good luck and to pray for their families whom they left up country and to have the evil spirits removed in the sea. They conducted their own special ceremony.

(b) A group of Xhosa domestics came from a white residential area in Durban one Sunday morning to the beach to receive power. Here they prayed and here they were strengthened merely by being at this spot.

(c) Established church members come to commemorate their ancestors who have passed away, for example, one group who sat in a circle with three candles in the center and with a cross planted in the sand. They were mainly Anglicans and Catholics. It was a special occasion at which a woman prophet took the lead. Chicken meat was in abundance--it took the place of a sacrifice to the ancestors.

(d) There are those who only touch the water, for example, a KwaMashu Prayer Group's spokesman said: "The sea water is holy water but we do not baptize, we only touch it."

(e) Another group from established churches came to the sea to pray for those unmarried young girls who fall pregnant-- some thirteen years of age--and who sometimes destroy their babies or who subject themselves to dangerous abortion practices.

These mentioned examples show what place the sea (in these cases) is in the lives of even members of the established black churches: it is a place of communion with the ancestors, a place where they get strength and also the spirit.

12. Baptism also implies getting rid of traditional medicines and traditional medical practitioners whose office is more extensive than just healing; they "prophesy," i.e., see things and are general consultants. One leader stated: "We throw the isangoma (diviner) things into the sea and then the umoya of Jesus comes to us."

13. The ancestors are also present at the sea; they protect those baptized from drowning. Their protection--even if they were not Christians when they passed away--are accepted by their Christianized progeny even at sea.

14. Dancing and rhythmic movements accompany most baptisms. Dance is the most universal of all acts and in dancing the dancers are protected from dangers, evil spirits, and it strengthens and brings down numinous power on objects or persons round which they dance such as the container with water and the sick person. In the church which was established within the sphere of Hellenistic culture, dance was a significant aspect of the service and even bishops such as the famous John Chrysostom, took part. In the Hellenistic mystery cults it was a sacral phenomenon. From the Synod of Aquiles (318) to the Council of 680, a struggle reigned in the church for three hundred years about dancing in the church. At the latter Council the standpoint of Augustine prevailed namely chorea est circulus, cuius centrum est diabolus and so dance was forbidden absolutely. The Zionist will say in the center of the circle is power and the Spirit--not evil. During the whole of the Middle Ages dance was considered to be suspect while Calvinists maintained it is sinful. Dance is movement and the dancer-- although he may dance in a circle the center of which becomes the focal point--himself becomes a significant factor in the act. It gives the dancer a certain feeling of freedom.
Dance is rhythm in which all sense of space and time could be lost and contact made with the transcendent world. This makes dance inevitable in the African Independent Churches. Before going into the water those to be baptized sit, walk fast, or run rhythmically (a form of dance) in a circle.

15. The flag, staves, uniforms and robes are "baptized"--this is not a secularization of baptism as in the case of the bells being baptized in the church, but it has a deep meaningful background for those who take part in it. It is an act of transferring power to these objects so that they can fulfil

their specific tasks effectively. Even the money which will be put in the offering plate at the service at home is taken into the sea. A Zionist bishop's wife, wearing a diviner's band round the neck and left arm, threw muti (medicine) into the sea into which she then dipped two roosters which were to be taken back home to be sacrificed to the ancestors.

16. Fasting for days--leaders up to seven days before baptisms are performed--is one of the major prerequisites for effective baptisms. Those to be baptized and those who take part in the baptismal service also fast, although for a shorter period of about three days.

17. The most important prerequisite for an effective baptism ceremony is the umvusilelo--revival service--at which the participants prepare themselves to receive "the Spirit" as well as to be in a position to receive the other mentioned blessings which baptism brings.

The context in which baptism is evaluated is so intense and so extensive that this sacrament cannot be described with full justice in the language and terms of most of the historical churches. It has much more meaning than they ascribe to this sacrament, as is evident from the above exposition. The main question regarding the African Independent Churches is not whether the historical churches accept their evaluation and use of baptism but whether, for them, baptism has a positive meaning and role in their situation. It certainly does provide direction in the lives of many African Independent Churches members in South Africa. It relieves their tensions, frees them psychically from the forces of evil, heals them, strengthens relationships, gives them an insight into their destiny and strength for the road ahead. It offers them the guidance of the Spirit and an acceptable framework to work in over against the one experienced in daily life which often means confrontation to them, and alienation and subjection and frustration. Here they learn the power of positive thinking without ever having read Norman Vincent Peale or such people who offer their spiritual remedies for coping with the pressures of the modern world--they have found their own remedy in what the church terms a sacrament and what for them has a medical, psychical, spiritual, and a social and even an economic connotation. Here the secular is not dissected from the spiritual.

PART THREE: ZIONIST HEALING AND OTHER
       INDEPENDENT CHURCH PROCEDURES

INTRODUCTION

Miss M.B. Motala begins this section, which has papers on specific Independent Churches, with another empirical study. Her subjects were female members of the largest South African Independent Church, the Zion Christian Church, and what she sought to discover was whether membership of the church played a positive role in their lives. The results are fascinating and once again raise many questions for further investigation.

Dr. Felicity S. Edwards then presents a detailed study of amafufunyana spirit possession based on her own observations of the phenomenon in the Western Cape. The paper is rich in detail and discusses the treatment of the "illness" by Zionist prophets as well as reflecting on its meaning in terms of Western understandings of society. In particular, Dr. Edwards draws attention to the socio-cultural confusion experienced by many Africans and the personal stress which this creates.

Dr. Hans-Jürgen Becken's paper concentrates on the ama-Nazarites but in doing so illustrates the dyanmic nature of theology within African Independent Churches and their holistic approach which refrains from separating theology from everyday affairs. In this context healing is a natural aspect of theology, indeed, theology seems meaningless unless it addresses the need for health and wholeness. Healing is therefore seen as a visible manifestation of both forgiveness and salvation, a perspective which Professor Becken believes could invigorate Western churches where the importance of healing as part of the Christian message has been largely lost.

The last paper in this section deals with the role of music and dance in Zionist healing. Here Mr. B.N. Mthethwa presents an inter-disciplinary study of religious ritual as found in the church of the ama-Nazarites. The paper draws attention to a neglected aspect of African Independent Churches and demonstrates the musical genius of Isiaha Shembe, the founder of the ama-Nazarites. Reading this paper, one is reminded of the role music has played in many religious movements from Luther's reformation to the Wesleyan revival and the birth of the Salvation Army. Here, surely, is an important cross-cultural topic which deserves considerable attention in the future.

THE RELATIVE INFLUENCE OF PARTICIPATION IN ZIONIST CHURCH
SERVICES ON THE EMOTIONAL STATE OF PARTICIPANTS

by

Miriam B. Motala

Almost thirty-seven years ago, Sundkler suggested that a study of the indigenous churches and urbanization would be worthwhile if it were treated in all its implications and its sociological setting (Sundkler, 1961). He stated that the churches were "adaptive structures" in city life in South Africa, but offered no further evidence.

Since then, very little has appeared on the subject of the role of indigenous churches in the urban situation. Kieve, (1959), discussed this matter briefly, and stated that in urban and industrial areas in Africa, "sects patterned along tribal lines have developed to meet the psychological needs of detribalised Africans." More recently, Thomas (1970), pointed to the functions of religious institutions in assisting women to adjust to the pressures of urban life. His seems to be one of the few studies which attempts to deal systematically with this subject and to produce evidence. The remaining literature on urbanization in Africa is disappointing for its failure to deal with the subject except peripherally. Unfortunately, when the subject is raised, the indigenous church movement is frequently only discussed in relation to the rural situation left behind and is not viewed as an important part of the urban environment.

The Indigenous Church Movement

The indigenous, or independent, church movement has been described as a Black response to the alien world of urban values. According to Norman (1981), independent churches have appealed to the poorer, less-educated sections of the "emergent Black proletariat," uniting their members, even over tribal and linguistic barriers, in a sense of personal significance, overcoming for many of these people, the anomie of existence in the cities. In the African styles of worship and healing, the

Black workers found some consolation for their loss of their traditional values.

Leaders have typically been drawn from exactly the same class and type as ordinary members: men/women who have experienced the common deprivations and disorientations of their followers, yet men/women marked out by the traditional Nguni gifts of prophecy and healing powers.

The extraordinary vitality and the extent of the independent church movement has frequently been attributed to the race issue in South African society--to see these churches as a withdrawal into a world of their own values by those excluded from political life by Whites. This certainly was the view of Sundkler (1961). Noticing that independent churches were a feature of several African countries, he probably felt that the larger number of these churches existing in South Africa required special mention. He decided that the "root cause," was "the color line between White and Black."

As the independent church movement is not organized on a tribal basis, it weakens the movement's capacity to become involved or concerned with political issues which are in any case defined by a White society.

Hanekom (1975), noted in his study of an independent church (the Zion Christian Church), that "as gevolg van hulle stam en tradisionele agtergrond is die lede van die Z.C.C. oor die algemeen nie geinteresseerd in politiek nie."[1] The independent church movement seems to be a Black response to an alien world of urban values, that could lead to an integration of personality.

The Zionist Christian Church--Usually known as the "ZCC"

The ZCC is concerned with life in an urban society. Its origin lay in dissatisfaction with the pietism and individualism of the mission churches. Eiselen (1967) wrote "To these tribes with their communalistic outlook came the missionaries to win individual souls for Christ. They came to teach a people, where individual personality counted for little and private interests were made subordinate to those of the group, that a man must leave his father and mother and family in pursuit of his own salvation."

Ndebele (1972) encouraged Black Africans to turn their backs on all the Western churches as he believed that these churches had been shorn of all emotional content. He emphasized that a genuine religion would spring out of Blacks' own circumstances. He added, "it should be a religion that will find God through man, and not man through God."

The Zionist churches offer the possibility of finding God through man. In the Zionist churches, communal loyalties could be re-established. These are used to lighten the burdens which are part of everyday living, not in the promises of eternity.

---

[1]Translation: "As a result of their roots and traditional background, the members of the ZCC are, in general, not interested in politics."

At this stage, it is necessary to establish who the Zionists are. Zionists or ama-Ziyoni as they call themselves can be recognized by their long white, green and blue, garments with green or blue sashes. Kiernan (1974) stated "As with the traffic light in more prosperous cities, their very visibility is a symbolic expression of certain aspects of the experience of urban living." According to Kiernan (1980) they are more or less exclusive groups in which women outnumbered men. They made converts among the adult population of the city, attracting them mainly through a healing service and thereafter offering them mystical protection against the hazards of city life, and, through the practice of a puritan ethic, providing collective support against the ravages of poverty.

A review of relevant literature and the researcher's own observations indicates that the Zionist church integrates healing with worship. In the Zionist church, healing is directly associated with worship and with the practice of religious belief--a blend of traditional Zulu custom and the Christian doctrine of the Holy Spirit (UMoya).

Healing during these services can be direct or indirect. In indirect healing, it is not necessary for the healer(s) to be aware of the specific complaints of individual persons. They are healed through the power of the Holy Spirit, UMoya, acting through the agency of healers and of the church congregation as a whole. Direct healing takes place when the healer is specifically aware of the person's complaints and prescribes specific cures for them.

In healing, the congregation of the Zionist church plays a supportive role. Edgerton (1971) has suggested that some of the important factors in "primitive medicine" are the roles of suggestion, faith, confession, catharsis and group support. Much of this is reinforced by the Zionist congregation: the common belief suggests the efficacy of faith-healing, and members are encouraged to have faith. At the same time the church services have a catharsis function as confession, singing and dancing are encouraged.

The relative effect of participation in Zionist church services

Briefly the study was an investigation of the relative effect of once-weekly participation in the Sunday services of an African independent church--the Zion Christian Church, and how this participation influences the emotional state termed "affect." Affect is defined as an emotional state in its discernible psychological rather than physiological and/or situational aspect.

Subjects of the Study

The subjects were ten Black, female domestic servants, working and residing separately from their families (parents, spouses, siblings and children), in an urban area, Durban's central business district, for a minimum period of three years. They earned between R50 and R60 per month.

In Group A--were five women who belonged to the Zion Christian Church.

In Group B--were five women who belonged to Western mission churches.

80% of the women in Group A were financially supporting two or more family members with their monthly salaries.

In Group B, only one woman was supporting two family members on her monthly salary. The remaining women were self-supporting.

In both groups, 70% of the women have had no formal education, while 30% have had two to four years of formal school education.

Research methods

A tape recorder was used to record the ZCC services. Two notebooks were used to record pertinent details. For four weeks the researcher observed and recorded sessions of Group A's church services. Thereafter, in the initial interviews with individuals from both groups, group members were told that they would be:

a)   asked to describe their emotions,

b)   asked to mention any external situations (for example, arguments with employers, friends, financial difficulties, and other problems) physiological aspects (physical illness) and any internal aspects (bad or good dreams; feelings of happiness, sadness, or neutral affect).

These aspects are necessary in determining whether internal or external circumstances are responsible for the person's emotions.

Questioning of group members on the aspects concerned with their emotions, was carried out on a once-daily basis, six days a week and twice on a Sunday (morning and evening).

Members of Group A, attended ZCC services for approximately three hours on a Sunday afternoon.

After a fifteen-day climatization period, the investigation began for a seventeen-day period. Results were based on data collected during this second period. Group members were not aware of when the actual investigation took place. A nonrandomized pretest-posttest control group design was used. The difference between Group A and Group B was that the former were participants in Sunday church services of a "band" of the ZCC, while the latter was not.

The Results of the Study

The results revealed that members of Group A reported more positive emotional responses than Group B.

When Group A members reported changes in emotional responses of a positive nature (due to affect), Group B members reported changes in emotional responses, (generally due to external circumstances). In addition, over a period of fourteen days (excluding the three Sundays on which services were held), members of Group A reported more positive emotional responses (due to affect and external circumstances) than members of Group B.

External circumstances appears to have had a greater influence on the emotional responses of Group B members than on members of Group A, over the fourteen day period.

Discussion

The findings suggest that participation in the once-weekly services of the Zionist Church has a positive effect on affect.

Attendance at Sunday church services at the ZCC seems to have led to spiritual and/or emotional upliftment of Group A members, while this was not the case for members of Group B who participated in the Sunday services of Western mission churches, although both groups shared similar day-to-day experiences (for example, financial difficulties, disagreements with employers, bad news from home, physical illness and so forth).

Observations of Zionist church services, indicates that this independent church allows for the release of tension and frustration through dancing, singing and confession (the participants talk about their problems during the service and through the use of prayer, God is invoked on, to render assistance or a solution). The members of Group A, as participants in Zionist church services do not have to search for emotional outlets to alleviate their frustration. Sundkler (1961) believed that the Zionists have succeeded in "building a world apart, an emotional Utopia."

One can therefore agree with Kiernan(1978) when he stated that the Zionist services must be analyzed as a powerful emotional experience rather than as a purely intellectual exercise. This powerful emotional experience could possibly change effect, in the case of members of Group A.

In the case of members of Group B, attending services at Western mission churches does not offer group members a significant amount of emotional release from their day-to-day problems.

External circumstances appear to have had a lesser effect on the emotions of Group A members but a greater effect on the emotional responses of members of Group B.

Members of the ZCC are resourceful and take social responsibility for one another's needs. This is done in the following ways: Firstly, the Zionist congregation is encouraged to act as a family, and to support and sympathize with fellow members. Secondly ZCC group members are encouraged to make friends within their church. In a small group, members are able to feel at home. The group is able to give both moral and material assistance in times of need, and assists individuals in their adjustment to city life. Thirdly, Little (1965) pointed out that the Zionist church offers supernatural protection to members through church membership and attendance at services. Lastly, the ZCC congregation also assists members in practical ways to deal with the urban situation. For example, members may be assisted by getting information about the urban situation.

These factors indicate that membership in the ZCC and participation in the services help individuals who are placed in the urban situation to adjust and not allow external circumstances to influence their emotions to too great an extent.

Therefore, external circumstances have less influence on the emotional responses of Group A members.

In the case of the members of Group B, the transient nature of their social relationships, the absence of a family-like bond, protection and practical help often impairs their ability to divorce negative external circumstances from their emotions.

Like many research studies, this one has numerous limitations. In this study, a non-randomized pretest-posttest design was used. As subjects were not randomly assigned to groups, it was probable that the groups were not equated. As a result, generalizations to other groups would not be possible. Ideally, a group of subjects who belonged to a Zionist church should be compared to a group of subjects who belong to a single Western mission church.

A variable such as race could have influenced the results. Subjects in both groups may have responded differently to a researcher who belonged to their race group.

The researcher could have indirectly interpreted the data in such a manner that the results indicate significant differences between both groups.

Subjects in Group A were observed as well as interviewed, while subjects in Group B were only interviewed. This additional exposure may have influenced the results.

The additional questioning on Sundays may have made subjects aware of the hypothesis as well as influencing the manner in which subjects responded on Sundays.

The researcher did not assess the personality of individual subjects. Personality testing may have been relevant in determining whether a subject's emotional responses were characteristic of her personality or not.

Conclusion

The study that was conducted and on which this paper is based was of an exploratory nature. It did not deal specifically with independent healing systems and therefore references made to independent healing were incidental.

The researcher's own shortcomings made the study simplistic, biased and limited at best.

The only value in presenting a paper of this nature is that it is an attempt to make people aware of the existence of the independent churches in South Africa. Too frequently, people who have seen the Zionists conducting their services in the open have merely regarded the proceedings as somewhat bizarre or have been extremely amused because these church services are unconventional. It is therefore important to educate people so that they can understand that the estimated six million Black South African men and women who belong to the independent churches find meaning in their lives through being part of the movement.

AMAFUFUNYANA SPIRIT POSSESSIONS: TREATMENT AND INTERPRETATION
by
Felicity S. Edwards

Amafufunyana spirit possession is a relatively new phenomenon and very little has been published on it. I first encountered it when investigating the theology, rites and particularly the healing practices of Zionist congregations in Grahamstown in the mid seventies. At a conference in Grahamstown in 1975 Dr. Harriet Ngubane (Sibisi as she was then), the Zulu anthropologist, gave a paper on Zulu Cosmology in which she spoke of amafufunyana possession, and in the same year she published a paper in the volume Religion and Change in Southern Africa (edited by Whisson and West) on Spirit Possession and Zulu Cosmology. In this paper Ngubane discusses amafufunyana as first occurring in Zululand in the late 1920s or 30s, suggesting that it was "introduced into South Africa by people who live to the north." She interprets the phenomenon in relation to recent changing social conditions in Zululand (Sibisi, 1975).[1]

My work has been in the Eastern Cape, with one case in Transkei. In the Eastern Cape it is said to be "a new thing" by both Zionist Independent Church leaders and amaggira (diviners). It is reported to have spread from Zululand,[2] occur frequently in the North and North Eastern Transvaal, and it appears to be on the increase. I have encountered amafufunyana in individuals and

---

[1]This is a shortened version of a paper delivered at the Fifth Annual Congress of the Association for the Study of Religion (SA) at the University of Durban-Westville in July 1983 and published in Religion in Africa, 5, No.2, 1984. It is based on research supported by a grant from Rhodes University, and I would like to thank both that Institution and my Xhosa informants.

[2]I have been informed by Professor G.C. Oosthuizen of the Department of Science of Religion, University of Durban-Westville, that this particular kind of spirit possession originated in Mozambique.

on a mass scale, where it is claimed that four hundred people were affected. Also there is a situation intermediate between individual possession and mass outbreak where quite a large proportion of a particular population group, finding themselves in a common undesirable situation, have fallen prey to this kind of spirit possession.

Amafufunyana spirit possession, as I am using the term in the main part of this paper, must be clearly distinguished from any kind of ceremonial spirit possession, from possession by ancestor spirits, from any kind of shamanistic possession, and from possession by the Holy Spirit. In contrast to all of these we are concerned here with an illness, a syndrome with a fairly standard pattern of symptoms. The most characteristic diagnostic feature is that, at the climax of the disorder, voices are heard speaking from within the patient. The other features stand out: (1) the voices heard are not those of the patient himself; (2) typically the voices become agitated and aggressive in the presence of "church people" or when prayer is made, and (3) at a particular stage of the illness the patient may evince inordinate strength. These characteristics put a amafufunyana spirit possession in line with the New Testament narrative of the man possessed by demons and out of whom Jesus cast the unclean spirits (pneumata ta aktharta), as they were called, restoring him to his right mind (Mark 5:1-20 and parallels in Luke 8:26,29 and Matthew 8:28-34). In the Matthean version there are two demon-possessed people "so fierce that no one could pass that way." The face-value similarities with the New Testament accounts may be an added incentive to prophet-healers of Zionist-type independent churches to make a speciality of healing. or attempting to heal, cases of amafufunyana spirit possession by exorcism in the name of Jesus, along with other supportive forms of treatment. Zionist church leaders see it as an important part of their calling to do battle with the evil agencies of the spirit world and to restore harmony within their community.

There is a basic unanimity among informants as to how the evil spirits are introduced into the body of the victim. You go to the grave of a person who has recently died and collect from the surface of the grave some of the imbovane (ants) crawling there. If there are no ants you can take a piece of animal fat, put it on the grave and wait a while. In due course ants will come up to get the fat and these you collect. The presupposition is that the ants have been eating the flesh of the corpse so that in some way (perhaps pars pro toto), the ants are conveyers of the spirit of the dead person. These ants are ground up along with some of the earth from the grave and mixed with particular herbs procured from an ixwhele (herbalist). I have not identified the herbs but it is said that they are plants which typically grow in Zululand. A recent local Grahamstown variation, as an alternative to getting ants from a grave, is to go to the scene of a fatal road accident or a stabbing and to scrape up some of the blood from the road. The blood is said to work similarly by being a conveyer of the spirit of the person killed. The ground-up mixture, idliso, then has to be surreptitiously introduced into the food or drink of the intended victim. After it has been ingested, the stomach of the victim begins to swell as if filled with wind, and he experiences severe abdominal pain. At this stage the spirits are said to be growing inside the body of the victim and he becomes weak and emaciated. It may be that he will develop an enormous appetite and eat voraciously while at the same time becoming thinner, weaker and more emaciated. The spirits are thought to be using up the nourishment in the food as they grow stronger and more powerful. The victim now presents as physically ill and psychologically

212

disturbed. He exhibits antisocial behavior, is confused, moody and frequently depressed.

The next stage is where the victim goes into a state of extreme agitation. He may become violent and lose control of himself altogether as the spirits within him, so it is said, take control of him. He may charge about the house, breaking things up as he goes and resisting with prodigious strength all efforts to restrain him. I was told, for instance, that in one case it took five men to hold down a thirteen-year-old girl possessed by amafufunyana spirits. The victim may rush out into the street and run up and down; for this reason the amafufunyana phenomenon is sometimes known as "running-about disease." At this point there is frequently a tendency to attempt to commit suicide. One girl drank down a bottle of paraffin and another in this stage of violent agitation kept trying to throw herself in front of oncoming cars, saying that the spirits inside her were telling her to do this. The spirits are said to be all the time under control of the person who sent them, so this behavior on the part of the victim is predictably exactly what the sender wants.

The third stage is the climax of this episode. The victim falls down not only from exhaustion but in some kind of unconscious state and at this point the voices begin speaking from inside the victim's body; the voices are apparently audible to anyone who is present. It is said that the spirits seem to be using the vocal chords of the victim, but the sound that comes out is definitely not the victim's own voice. A young girl may speak with a man's voice, or several different men's voices. Ngubane reports that in Zululand the person may be "possessed by a hoard of spirits from different racial groups. Usually there may be thousands of Indians or Whites, some hundreds of Sotho or Zulu spirits" (Sibisi, 1975). My own encounters with amafufunyana have been in Xhosa-speaking country where the possessing spirits are less sensational, but it is reported invariably that the spirits speak not only in Xhosa but mainly and particularly in Zulu, and they identify themselves by Zulu names. Because in the Eastern Cape it is understood that amafufunyana has spread from Zululand, the acceptance of the tradition that it is a Zulu disease may influence expectations that the spirits will speak in Zulu. While the spirits are in this speaking phase they will answer questions put to them by those present; for instance, they will say how many they are, they will sometimes identify the person who has sent them and they may announce that they have been sent to kill the patient. When this acute stage passes and the victim regains consciousness, he has no recollection of what has happened to him and knows nothing of the voices.

In any particular case, once the voices have developed, the time has come for treatment. Consultation with a Western medical practitioner is pointless because such people are operating within a totally different reference system which takes no account of the spirit world, while Black priests and ministers of the mainline churches are considered to be too Westernized to be of any use. Interestingly, priests of the Order to Ethiopia, which is an independent church and all Black, fall into the same category of being out of touch with the Xhosa frame of reference. The choice then is between an iggira (i.e., a Xhosa diviner) or a Zionist healer. In the Grahamstown area the amaggira for some reason are wary of amafufunyana cases (Cf. Schweitzer, 1977), whereas Zionist church healers make a speciality of treating them. As I suggested earlier, this particular type of spirit possession is so like the New Testament counterpart as to present a particularly attractive challenge to the Zionists; the phenomenon straddles their traditional religious world-view and their Christian experience. An interesting possibility is that there is a connection between the Zionist predilection for treating this particular kind of spirit possession and the spread of the disease westward from Zululand. Since both Zionism and amafufunyana spirit possession spread from Zululand at about the same time, it could be that the Zionists "brought it with them."[3]

A prophet healer in Grahamstown, who was an ordinary Zionist minister when we first became friends but who has recently become the archbishop of his church (the Apostolic Holy Church in Zion), has had considerable experience of amafufunyana, and I happened to be on the spot when he was involved with a case. Both symptoms and treatment turned out to be fairly typical. The healer, Mr. N, was called early one morning to the home of a patient, Mr. M, and found him lying unconscious on the bed. His relatives said he had been behaving in a violent and agitated manner all night and when morning came he had lost consciousness. Mr. N. told me the next day, "He had a very faint heartbeat. The whole of his body was flexible (i.e., limp), and when I listened to his body there was a sound as though he was going to die. Mrs. T (the patient's sister-in-law) and her friends were crying. I told them not to cry. Instead, let us pray. Then I tied him with a cord and prayed for him. I pressed him on his stomach. When I did this I heard a noisy sound come out of the stomach. When I listened to his stomach I heard voices in the Zulu language. One said his name was Khumalo (a Zulu name). I asked them in prayer, 'What do you want?' In reply the voices said they were sent to come and kill this man. Then I commanded them

---

[3]A suggestion made to me by Dr. J.P. Kierman of the Department of Religious Studies, University of Natal.

to come out of the man in the name of the Lord. They shouted 'we will never go out.' When they said that I felt my voice rising higher and higher. I took water, prayed over it and gave it to the man to drink. I made him stand on his feet and I shook him violently. I put my hand on his breast and wind (umoya = wind or spirit) came out through his mouth, very strong. Then he spat out something. After that he was calm and I left him."

Two days later, on the Wednesday night, this patient was treated at the weekly healing service which I was able to attend. The main healer was the visiting president (mongameli) of the church, assisted by Mr. N and another healer. The patient was prayed for as he knelt between two lighted candles and the mongameli listened for voices in his stomach. Then the mongameli picked the patient up bodily and heaved him onto his left shoulder, holding him there for some time. The position was like that of a mother winding her baby, perhaps precisely to get the wind/spirits out.[4] While the patient was being held aloft by the mongameli, Mr.N. vigorously massaged his thighs, and he explained afterwards that the amafufunyana spirits go out of the patient through his legs, leaving them weak and in need of strengthening by the healer.

After being put down the patient was bound with a prayed-for cord and was made to whirl around on the spot faster and faster, while the drum was beaten and the congregation sang with increasing intensity. In the heat of this, Mr. N. brought the patient gently to a standstill and covered the patient's head and

---

[4]This explanation was suggested to me by Professor M.G. Whisson of the Department of Anthropology, Rhodes University.

shoulders with his own robe while he prayed intensely. The symbolism of covering the patient with the healer's robe is firstly to prevent, by the power of the Holy Spirit, the amafufunyana spirits from spreading to members of the congregation; when the spirits come out from the patient they, like their New Testament counterparts, are looking for somewhere to go. Secondly, by covering the patient with his robe, Mr. N. understands that he is imparting to the patient his own wholeness and integrity.

Finally in this treatment, after a lot of typically Zionist laying on of hands, which is a kind of therapeutic massaging, thumping and pummelling of the patient, and after the typical "dancing in a circle" (ukugida) which symbolizes wholeness, the patient collapsed to the floor. As he lay inert the mongameli knelt and bent over him, his ear close to the patient's stomach, listening intently. After Mr. N. had also listened to assure himself that there were no more voices, the patient was hoisted to his feet by the cord around his waist and his treatment was concluded with a quiet blessing. In this case the patient made a good recovery and was soon able to resume his job as a hospital orderly.

I have analyzed this example of typical Zionist treatment of amafufunyana spirit possession (Edwards, 1983). There is just one feature to point out here: the spitting-out or vomiting of an object of some sort is important both diagnostically and therapeutically. It indicates both that the patient had been dliswata, given idliso poison, and that the resulting evil spirits have now left him. The nature of the object vomited varies enormously. Exactly what is vomited does not matter. What is important is that the vomited object is the concretisation of the evil which has been within the patient's reality and which has now been dramatically ejected and got rid of. Examples are needles, a beetle (Qongqothwane) and little round shiny stones. Why does amafufunyana spirit possession occur? I can only offer some suggestions on the basis of which a pattern or typology seems to emerge.

The first type of amafufunyana spirit possession is where there is a history of disturbed interpersonal relationships, and it may be that the animosity generated reaches an intolerable level. A "poisoned relationship" with another person may be "concretised by the poisoning of his body," resulting in the possession state (Cf. Schweitzer, 1977). A commonly cited reason for breakdown of relationships is jealousy over an attractive girl friend or husband, a good job, children doing well at school, good sons who send money back from the mines, and so on. In this type, the good fortune of A is resented by B who is then believed to have set in motion the process of destruction by amafufunyana spirits with the intention of killing A.

Taking further the logic of this type of amafufunyana spirit possession, it could be that a person, T, being more fortunate than her neighbors, becomes a "target of suspicion" of having attained her advantageous position by sorcery (Cf. Chilivumbo, 1976, 78). To this stress-producing situation of being advantaged but afraid of losing what she has, T's response is the amafufunyana possession syndrome. Since this is a socially acceptable illness it is more likely to arouse compassion than censure in the community. It will at least account for the psychological crisis she has got herself into, and, because of the communally accepted aetiology, not she but a jealous member of the community will be held responsible. In order to distinguish different types, I am calling this amafufunyana spirit possession Type 1. There could be a complex ethno-pathology here similar, perhaps, outwardly, mutatis mutandis, to the Western "Room at the Top" tightrope-walking between precarious success and incipient downfall, not to mention those by whom that downfall is contrived.

A second type is where the alleged "victim" is in a situation with which he or she is psychologically and personally unable to cope (amafufunyana spirit possession Type 2). The jealousy motive (amafufunyana spirit possession Type 1) could overlap with the intolerability situation (amafufunyana spirit possession Type 2) if, for instance, animosity between husband and wife results in wife allegedly sending amafufunyana spirits to husband. Typically, however, amafufunyana spirit possession Type 2, moving into victim/patient status occurs when there is no longer a sense of order and manageability in the person's life. Examples here would be the schoolgirl who finds herself pregnant by one of her teachers (loss of order) or the young colored girl who is being brought up as the adopted daughter of a Black family and finds herself increasingly unable to cope with her experience of being different (loss of manageability). In this case the adoptive mother is the sister-in-law of the man whose treatment for amafufunyana spirit possession was described above (does amafufunyana spirit possession run in families?) In this kind of case where the amafufunyana patient is in an intolerably difficult situation three very significant things can happen. Firstly, diagnosis can be made that the the patient is suffering from a recognized Xhosa illness. Such diagnosis restores a kind of order to her life and takes the focus of attention off, in the first case the disorderly pregnancy, and in the second case, the mockery incurred through being a different kind of person, or coloured child in a Black setting. Secondly, with Type 1, responsibility for being unable to cope is taken off the sufferer (because she has allegedly been dliswata, poisoned). Thirdly. there is the treatment whereby the spirits are removed from the patient's body and are seen to have come out (in the material objects vomited out), allows the person to make a fresh start and get a hold on life again. In terms of Western psychiatric terminology, amafufunyana spirit possession is classed as brief reactive psychosis--brief because if treated appropriately the prognosis is good.

Ngubane (1975) suggested that amafufunyana spirit possession "seems to be an aftermath of colonialism, related to intrusions by alien peoples into a culture or society." So as a result of a higher degree of mobility, industrial development and so on, the competition from foreign intruders--Europeans, Indians, as well as from, in Ngubane's context, fellow Zulus--for jobs, housing, land, etc., increased the experience of insecurity to an intolerable level. Failure to cope with the socio-cultural disruption, and with the resultant insecurity, spiralled into increasing psychological disruption. The form in which this insecurity concretised in the illness indicates the nature of the disorder; i.e., alien spirits in the body parallel alien intruders in the social structure. To her suggestion could be added the sense of loss of control over one's life and destiny. The possessing spirits are, temporarily at least, in the driving seat, and the syndrome is thus a way of saying to society, "Look, I am not in control of my own reality."

This kind of interpretation accords fairly well with the state of affairs in a sector of the Keiskammahoek community, around St. Matthew's Mission, where the is amafufunyana possession on a wide scale among young unmarried girls. The social structure there has been disrupted, not by alien intruders but by the exodus of many of the men. As in so many other communities the exigencies of the migratory labor system have precipitated the previously well-defined social system into a state of confusion. The responsible and able men folk of the community have gone to work at the mines, and these are precisely the men who, as fathers or elder brothers, would have protected the young girls, or as younger men would have married them. As it is, those men who are left tend to be the irresponsible ones and many of the girls find themselves with illegitimate children. The insecurity-tolerance level of these young unmarried mothers is low, shame and/or guilt is high and they present with amafufunyana spirit possession. I am planning to do field work in this Keiskammahoek area in the near future. At present I foresee that this would be amafufunyana spirit possession Type 3, which is similar to Type 2 but on a group scale, with all the possible reinforcement, imitation or inspiration that may be going on there.

Finally there is mass amafufunyana spirit possession (type 4) as in the case of the two-year long epidemic at Lamplau Junior Secondary School in the Macubeni District of Lady Frere. Lady Frere is in Transkei and the people are Xhosa-speaking. Here I was told that four hundred children, the entire school, had been possessed by amafufunyana spirits--not all at once but in groups where a few would set others off. When possessed by the spirits the children not only spoke in Zulu but wrote their November examinations in Zulu--or rather wrote Zulu nonsense on their examination scripts. The outbreak started in 1981 and was still going on in 1983 at which point overseas leave curtailed my investigation of it. This case has some particularly interesting features. Unlike the other cases which are considered to be a matter of sorcery--that is to say, the manipulation of materials or entities with the intention of causing harm, this case was openly alleged to be the result of witchcraft, and three local women were named as responsible. The details of this case are documented in a previously published paper (Edwards, 1984).

To complete the suggested typology there are two further categories where the term amafufunyana is used in a weak sense, in my opinion by extension from the strong or original sense as outlined in the cases above. Neither of these milder disorders appears to involve evil spirit possession as such, and the "victims" are hysteric rather than psychotic.

In type 5 the term amafufunyana is used for the effect of what might be called a love potion. For instance, if I am a young man and I want a certain girl to fall in love with me, what I do is this (so a Xhosa informant told me--and this is just standard run-of-the-mill sorcery): I cut my hand and take a little of the blood, put it in a teaspoon, mix it with some dirt from my armpits and a little of my saliva. I have to add a bit of Xhosa herb, isivamna, which I get from an ixwhele and to make quite sure, I top all that with some dirt from my nails. I put all this in some sweets and give them to the girl. When she has eaten the sweets the girl will behave as though she is out of her senses and she will fall crazily in love with me. She will be suffering from a kind of mild hysteria, isiphoso, and all these highly personal ingredients will make her think only about me.

Another possibility is that a love potion of this sort can be blown in powder form from the man's hand while at the same time speaking the girl's name and the medicine will then be "carried" to her. Such tactics can also be used to ensure that a wife or girlfriend remains faithful when the man goes away to find work (Kruger, 1974).

Also mentioned by Kruger is what would be Type 6 which is a
more serious disorder, also brought on by idliso, a poison
obtained from a herbalist. This is not a spirit possession
state. There is no question of voices, and in Western
psychiatric terms the condition would be diagnosed as hysteric
with dissociative episodes.

Types 5 and 6 have been included for completeness because
use of the same term amafufunyana for such a wide variety of
conditions can result in talking about very different kinds of
phenomena under the same name and thinking one is talking about
the same thing. A typology of this kind I have suggested is
merely one of the means by which one type of amafufunyana spirit
possession can be distinguished from another, but there is a
great deal of overlap between categories and much more work needs
to be done.

My interim conclusion is that amafufunyana spirit possession
Types 1-4 is a constellation of stress-related phenomena
associated with socio-cultural transition. Colonialism and
post-colonalism have meant relatively rapid transculturation. In
traditional society, personal identity, security and meaning are
found much more in community structure with its well-defined role
boundaries and integrative social framework than is the case with
the individualism of the modern West. Hence the result of social
disorder accompanying cultural transition is all the more
devastating to personal wholeness. It seems to me that the logic
of amafufunyana spirit possession requires links to be identified
between socio-cultural conditions, including political elements,
and traditional understanding of harmony, misfortune and the
spirit world. At this state I would say with confidence that in
many instances amafufunyana spirit possession is evidence, in the
Southern African context, of one of the ways in which humankind

deals with conditions where the threshold of psychological tolerance has been overstepped. There are probably parallels in other cultures. In this phenomenon, the illness is structurally and perhaps even causally related to the belief system. The question remains as to why in some individuals or groups such ethno-pathological syndromes spring up, whereas in other individuals or groups psychological viability is retained in the midst of socio-cultural confusion and personal stress.

TYPOLOGY OF AMAFUFUNYANA SPIRIT POSSESSION

Type 1 "Victim" envied by someone in the community	Blame put on an evil intentioned person who has sent the amafufunyana spirits	Focus on fear of attack or retaliation
Type 2 "Victim" personally unable to cope with situation	Development of ASP syndrome (a) gives socially-acceptable reason for illness (b) releases patient from responsibility (c) offers therapeutic way out.	Focus on survival and restoration or order and sense of control
Type 3 Group of "victims" unable to cope (as above) e.g., Keiskammohoek situation	As Type 2 but group phenomenon	As Type 2
Type 4 Mass amafufunyana possession e.g., the Lamplau Junior Secondary School situation		
Type 5 Term amafufunyana used in the weak sense for the effect of a "love potion"	Differentiated from Types 1-4 by no suggestion of evil spirit possession being involved	Focus on evoking or retaining of love

Type 6 Term amafufunyana used for condition also caused by idliso but without spirit possession	Could be similar to either Type 1 or Type 2 but differentiated (a) as hysteric rather than psychotic and (b) no alleged spirit possession involved	Focus could be as Type 1 or Type 2

AFRICAN INDEPENDENT CHURCHES AS HEALING COMMUNITIES
by
Hans-Jürgen Becken

The two decades which I spent in Zululand are already "church history" in the perspective of contemporary researchers engaging in the study of African Independent Churches in our time. However, I cannot escape the fact that my close contact with this movement in the past has been not only an experience which I would not wish to have missed, but also a fundamental influence on my thought patterns and my theology. The African Independent Churches taught me to understand a facet of Christian faith which appears to be underdeveloped in my Western tradition, namely the aspect of the church as a healing community. Working on this tenet after returning to Europe, I became convinced that this message is not only important for the solution of South Africa's burning problems but also for the relevant proclamation of the Christian faith in the church world-wide.

Thus, this contribution by a guest from overseas to a symposium of South African specialists in field research on the African Independent Churches could mean a dialogue between this isolated group and relevant research in other parts of the world. It might also add an historical perspective to your deliberations. To avoid the danger of presenting old stuff only, I have attempted to update my studies by regular visits to the present scene, and to get acquainted with recent developments in the field through contacts with the African Independent Churches.

When visiting South Africa again in February 1986, I watched video tapes on the activities of the African Independent Churches and very early one Sunday morning, I was taken to the Durban beach to meet different African Independent Churches communities who attended to their water rituals at the shore of the Indian Ocean. The white city of Durban was still fast asleep when Africans in their colorful uniforms faced the rising sun and were fascinated by the eternal rhythm of the tidal waves washing their feet. Their holy sticks and flags were stuck in the sand somewhere higher up, watching over their small parcels of property, while the Black Christians stood in ranks along the sea, singing and dancing, preaching and praying, and dipping individuals into the rolling waves. A magnificent spectacle indeed! A new form of holistic healing ministry.

Amidst all these worshipping groups whom we interviewed, we found two Zulu girls who romped happily in the waters. On our enquiry they answered: "No, we are not ill; we merely recreate our ama-ndla (energy)." To me, these two girls were eye-openers in understanding what was happening on the beach that morning. I had to ask myself: Why do we make such a fuss about the African Independent Churches' activities at the shore when we ourselves regard the Golden Mile of Durban as the ideal spot to go for our own recreation?

Certainly, when going there, we do not wear cassocks and sticks, but comfortable bathing costumes. However, what is so wrong about these African Independent Churches singing their hymns to praise the Lord who gave us the sun and the sea for relaxation and to strengthen our health? Is it so serious a mistake to express our common Christian faith in their way, even if we in the mainline churches customarily restrict the confession of our faith to worship in church buildings and, perhaps, to devotions at home?

I claim that this holistic aspect of the message which is communicated by the African Independent Churches in their ritual way is an essential in the good news of Christ. In spite of their exotic disguise, our independent brethren and sisters could help us to appreciate that, in essence, the church is a healing community. This insight may enable us to see in this movement not just a strange phenomenon; rather, it might help us to perform our task as the Christian church in our country and in our times, according to the call and the commission of our Lord.

The discussion of this issue is gaining momentum in the theological studies of the church universal, not only in Europe and America but especially also in the "Third World."

In January 1985, an international conference on mission studies took place at Harare, Zimbabwe, where I had the honor to chair a workshop on "the church as a healing community." The findings of this study group start with the provoking theological statement:

Recognizing the brokenness and afflictions of the world in which the church finds itself and of which the church is part, and remembering the healing ministry of Christ which he committed to his church, we conclude that healing is an essential function of the church. In describing the essence of the church, the element of healing is of equal importance to Word and Sacrament (Mission Studies, vol 2, No.1, 1985, p.82).

This is not the place for me to discuss the far-reaching consequences of this statement emphasizing the role of the people of God as his missionary team in communicating reconciliation, health and peace to humankind. Rather, I wish to underline the importance of health and healing as observed in the African Independent Churches for the proclamation of the Word of God and the practice of the church universal.

During my last visit to Durban, Professor Oosthuizen took me by car to Ebuhleni, a new settlement near Inanda which the Nazareth Baptist Church established under the leadership of the

Reverend Amos Shembe. At the entrance we saw the more-than-life-size statue of the founder, Isaya Mloyiswa Mdliwamafa Shembe, in shining white stone. Next to it, the village of closely packed tent-huts reminded us of the shacks at Crossroads. Even the water is sold at four cents per eight gallons. It is the same blend of the spiritual life with the hard facts of daily life that marks this African Independent Church.

The leader of the church was not in. However, we met Petros Dlomo (74 years old), the archivist. He complained bitterly that in the course of the succession struggle after the death of Johannes Galilee Shembe, the documentation of the church was destroyed. He reminded me that in 1967 I did a series of interviews with members who testified to the deeds of their leaders, and he requested me to help him with copies of the old transcripts.

Back home in Stuttgart, I traced the requested papers in my old files. The old carbon copies were yellowed and brittle, besides which they were on the old-fashioned full scrap size and thus did not conform to the standardized modern files and photostat equipment. However, I succeeded in reproducing them in a readable way. My Zulu was still good enough to understand the testimonies given by the old men and women praising the mighty deeds of God through their revered leaders, Isaiah and Johannes Galilee Shembe.

To them, there is a logical difference between sin and disease, between forgiveness and healing; however, their holistic world-view does not allow them to separate the two, for they belong together. These people live in full accord with the closing of the last hymn (No.242) in the IziHlabelelo

zamaNazaretha, or Zulu hymnal of the ama-Nazentes, which ends
with the words:

> And sins may cease and also all diseases.
> Purity and good health may dwell with us.

Another observation struck me: they do not regard their
salvation (uku-sindiswa) as static; rather, they see in it a
dynamic process. To them, it is not illogical to report "I was
healed and I am healthy to this day," and in the same breath to
tell of another disease from which they were saved. Salvation
does not immunize Christians; rather we are always in need of
forgiveness and healing. Adapting an old doctrine to the
holistic African context, we understand that "Christians are
healed and at the same time in need of healing."

A number of those witnesses in 1967 stated that their
conversion was prompted by a dream experience. Listen to the
experience of Mrs. Bertina Luthuli of Illovo Beach (Mbumbulu
District):

> I know this father (J.G. Shembe) well, I witness to his
> great deeds. I was ill in Zululand. He came and
> entered the house in which I lay ill and he interceded
> for me. When he left, he enquired from me: "Does your
> strength not yet return?" I replied: "No, not even a
> bit." Then he said: "I see that it does not yet come
> and that you progress very slowly."
> When he had left, he came to me in a vision while I was
> sleeping and, dreaming, I saw him entering the room
> while I was on my bed. I saw him like coming from a
> baptism; he handed to me the stick which he usually
> carries if he intends to baptize. I grasped it. He
> said (in my dream) that I should not let loose. I kept

it, trembling. Then a door opened there near my head,
because there he went out taking my disease away.
On the next morning, I walked around the whole
courtyard. Thus from this day onwards, I was always of
good health.

However, dreams are not so typical in the conversion reports
as it is generally accepted. It is also difficult to find a
model according to which the reports are given. Every one is a
fine cabinet piece of personal experience by itself. Abraham
Ngrobo of Hlabisa District records the experience of a young
crippled man of the Mkhwanazi clan who was healed by the Father
after gathering and burning the thorns of the Izingayi trees at
Thembalihle.

Not every witness spells out clearly the relation between
healing and salvation. People have blamed the African
Independent Churches for this lack of theological
explanation--which they share, however, with the Gospel records
of the healing ministry of Jesus. Now the evangelists of old,
like the African Independent Churches of our times, are confident
that the connection of forgiveness and healing is always
understood, even if they witness it only occasionally. One
example is the record of the preacher (un-shumayeli) Daniel
Mpofana of Harding, Natal. Of his own experience, he stated that
he was healed from his "black blood" when I. Shembe baptized him
in the river, and that this experience made his wife and his
children also join the Nazaretha Church and abstain from
medicine. And when reporting about another man suffering from
spine trouble, he remembered the following dialogue:

Shembe enquired from him what was wrong. Thereupon the
man said: "I have sinned, I had intercourse with a
married woman." To this, Shembe replied: "The Bible

says: "The man who confesses his sins and parts with them will be forgiven." Indeed, you will be healed. After these words, I observed the man rearing, I heard a noise: du--du--du. I was tempted to run away. However, this noise marked the returning of his vertebrae to their normal position. The man stood and praised the God of Shembe saying: "Now I am healed." His name was Mlandu. Before, he was not a Christian.

As with events in the earthly ministry of Jesus, people are always amazed that the mighty word conveys healing, even in the absence of the healer. The same preacher of Harding has a similar story to tell:

One day in the year 1932, we were in the Anglican congregation Madonela, Mzimkhulu District. There came a man by the name of Nyambose, alias Mtethwa, who reported to Shembe: "My daughter is ill; already for four years she is chained." Shembe was in a hurry to reach the train for Durban, and therefore he commissioned us, two men, to tell the father that he should take off the chains from his daughter for she had now been healed. We went to the place and told him the message of Shembe. By this word alone, the girl was healed and she is even today of good health and has five children.... She was saved at the very hour when Shembe said this word.

Evidently, these reports are shaped by the terminology and the concepts of the Gospels. Superficial Western observers got the impression that here Jesus Christ had been supplanted by a "Black Messiah." The opposite is the case: the African Independent Churches take seriously the statement of Paul that, today, Christ speaks and acts through his body, namely the church universal. Consequently, the church, according to their understanding, is the community of healed healers who exist for the salvation of other people.

When I asked J.G. Shembe to explain to me his understanding of healing, he replied--and this text is in the quoted collection which we shall now return to the Nazaretha archives:

We cannot explain it. We believe that anyone can lay hands on a sick person who is a Christian and that person would get healed, provided that the person laying hands has enough faith in God, faith in Jesus Christ. The whole idea of healing comes from the teachings of Jesus Christ: Go ye in all the world and preach the Gospel, lay hands on the sick; if they will believe, they will be healed. When people start explaining these faith healings and so on scientifically, I do not believe it; it is impossible. We do it blindly. It is a matter of faith. I believe that anyone with enough faith in Jesus Christ is in fact a healer on other people, may be a child or may be an old person, it makes no difference. But once we start saying that I know what I am doing, there is no faith in it, and there is no Christ in it.

It was actually at this point, that Shembe suggested that I tape statements of his flock who "could explain better what they had experienced" in their holistic conversion.

In this connection, it will be of interest to quote another section from the report on the missiological conference at Harare. Dealing with the question of Faith Healing, the findings of the workshop had this to say:

We understand the term Faith Healing as using the dynamics of prayer and community support to directly

calling upon the power of Christ as an agent of healing. Faith healing is to be considered as an important aspect in the concept of Christian healing and is applicable in every kind of brokenness. Some important aspects of Faith Healing are:
- it acknowledges the supernatural factor in healing,
- it ought not to be performed by amateurs, and
- it also has political implications for the medicine of poverty.

Faith healing is understood as supportive to the healing process but not an absolute substitute for medicine (Mission Studies, vol. 2, No.1, 1985, p.83).

This statement includes not only prayer but also community support in Faith Healing. And, indeed looking through our recently retrieved records, now twenty years old, we find a remarkable emphasis on the element of fellowship experience in the event of healing and salvation. Welbourn and Ogot rightly speak about the African Independent Churches as "a place to feel at home."

In welcoming the suffering person, the congregation makes him/her feel comfortable and plants in the patient a sense of confidence and hope. In the record of the Indian lady, Samaria Joseph, she remembers the day when she visited Shembe for the first time. She was suffering from not having children, even after thirteen years of matrimony. There she was offered a reed mat with the words: "On this mat are sitting beautiful children." And when Shembe entered, somebody whispered to her: "There comes the messenger of God who brings good news for you."

In worship, Christians as members of the Body of Christ have direct access to the Father in heaven. In our records, the

African Independent Churches members often remember very vividly their experiences in the healing services. Alvina Mdletshe of Matuba remembers:

> I know the great father Shembe already since I was a child aged fourteen. From birth I suffered chest and ear pains. At night, I had ear ache, and water running from my ears. We were living at the farm Cannes; from there we went to the assembly at Linda. The great father came and called the sick. I also went and he prayed over me and over all the people: "Let all diseases go out from these people." When the assembly was over, we returned home. On the way, I still felt chest pains. However, when I arrived home, the ear aches and the chest pains stopped, and I was healthy up-to-date.

And in a similar vein, others report on their healing experiences in the course of the great festivals of this church. It is essential to note in all these cases that the community character of the African Independent Churches has not only a religious but also a social aspect, which in itself already has a healing quality.

All these records are now twenty years old. However, the African Independent Churches are still moving on. I suppose that we will not do justice to them by eliminating the healing phenomena, impressive as they might be to Westerners who have lost this experience in their spiritual life. It seems to be more adequate to appreciate how these churches are realizing their Christian faith in the day-to-day normal life; how they acknowledge and celebrate the presence of Jesus Christ also in events which we would call secular. It is only in this holistic context that heir healing ministry gains momentum.

I do not advocate that we should imitate the African Independent Churches' practices. However, being convinced that the commission of the Lord--"Go and heal" is not outdated, I trust that the church and her members will in time recognize their function to communicate health and salvation to diseased human beings, to broken societies, to the world and even to the divided church with its contradictory theological currents. In this way, the African Independent Churches may be able to help the church of Word and Sacrament to rediscover her essence as a healing community.

MUSIC AND DANCE AS THERAPY IN AFRICAN TRADITIONAL SOCIETIES
with special reference to
the iBlandla lamaNazaretha ('the Church of the Nazarites')
by
B.N. Mthethwa

Introduction: Some Zulu Music Concepts

In dealing with the issue of music and the church in Southern Africa, one is immediately confronted by the problem of musical syncretism between Western and African music. These two musical traditions, analytically, belong to the same musical "species." They both carry the same music elements of rhythm, harmony and melody. However, the ratios between the music elements differ. African music can overemphasize rhythm and harmony, whilst most Western traditions lay stress on harmony and melody. Other music parameters like dynamics, tempo and timbre, play a role in both genres.

In this short paper, I shall first mention a few concepts found in Zulu music (which overlap with other African musical practices) and discuss the value of music and dance in traditional societies. From this I shall lead into Shembe's interpretation of dance in Christian worship and its value as a therapy in healing.

In Southern Africa, the baroque Christian hymn is perpetuated by the notion that it represents "proper" Christian singing. Besides other historical factors that contribute towards preserving the baroque type of hymn, the baroque musical style per se was designed to appeal to human emotions. Tonality or sense of key is important and the top voice, that is the soprano voice, carries the melody or tune of the song. The soprano melody is harmonized by the lower voices, these being alto, tenor, and bass. This hymnal arrangement of singing leaves many people with an illusion that this is the only style in which choral music can be expressed. Melody in these conventional (baroque) hymns is governed by the harmonic progression.

Harmony in Western baroque music is a counterpart of human emotions. This type of harmony is known as cadential harmony which creates a body response of tension and relaxation. Taking into account the congregational context where repentance and contrition are supposed to prevail, the effect of harmony (tension-relaxation) on the congregation becomes transformed into a religious experience. Hence the common saying that we would not go to church if there was no music.

In Zulu, harmony of any musical tradition is called isigubudu and this word means a beast with converging horns so that the horns overlap or touch the skin of the animal. Zulu harmonization considers tonal relationship of notes as well as timbral correlation. The two factors--being call-and-response, and singing at a range where one's voice is comfortable--oppose the convention of singing in four parts. Consequently, Zulu harmonization exceeds four voices. Harmony might be called isigubudu because people prefer to form a semicircle when singing in harmony. Harmonious music is referred to as ukudla kwendlebe, which means "food for the ear," and philosophically, harmony probes the inner feelings. "Nice" music must be "painful" and the desirable pain is indeed harmonic intensity. The baroque Christian hymn with its tension-resolution cadential harmony is musically not foreign to African masses. Sadness expressed in music must train the ear with blending harmonies. In Western music, sadness is basically vested in the minor mode. The minor keys in Zulu carry unmusical notes which must be avoided at all costs! Perhaps the only weakness or clash between Western and African music, insofar as African participants are concerned, is lack of rhythm in Western music.

Western music throughout the ages suffered the suppression of rhythm, which was regarded by the early church fathers of the middle ages as an evil element. Western hymns in, say three-four tempo (three pulse measure), for Zulu musical taste have no rhythm. A song of worship, in Zulu traditional terms, must carry a good harmonic structure and a strongly felt underlying rhythmic pattern. Harmony strengthens the interpersonal communication in a musical rendition. The rhythm of a song of worship must unfold, as it were, its dance counterpart. The dance is beyond group solidarity; as a product of music, it attains a new level of communication between the group and their God.

The Value of Dance in Traditional Society

Zulu life, basically, cannot be divided into secular and sacred. Zulu dances are clearly divided by the insiders into spectacular and ritual dances. In a spectacular dance like indlamu, the dancers entertain their audience. The unseen ancestors may be present if they so wish, but they may not influence the creativity of the dance leader. The commander of the dance creates his own variations and teaches his group. No outsider can dance with a particular ndlamu group, without having practiced with them. A lot of rehearsal and drillwork goes into this type of dance, and improvisation is minimal.

The ritual dance lacks spectacle. It is the dance performed by the living and the dead. It therefore becomes imperative for the living to perform the dance as it was performed in the "beginning" of time, so that all the long-dead who are present will be able to participate comfortably. Zulu ritual dances are not performed for the ancestors. The dead are a reinforcement in a dance which is dedicated to God.

Zulu prayers are realized at two levels. The first level is a prayer to ancestors to intervene for the living; at second level, the living and the dead pray together to their God. An anthropological view would see the intervention by ancestors, which is localized to the family, as belonging to the private sphere. A prayer to God would be categorized as a public matter. Serious issues such as drought are a national concern where both the living and the dead must sing ihubo to their God (Callaway, 1970: 409 translates ihubo as a magical song).

Music and dance in Zulu conceptualization cannot be separated. Dance is a product of music. Each given song must be able to unfold its own dance form. People will say "sisina igama," meaning, we are dancing a particular song. Both act as catharsis and are also closely related to physical and mental healing.

Zulu ceremonies are diverse, the most common being the wedding. There are numerous ceremonies, lasting months, leading to the actual wedding. All these ceremonies lead to ukusina (dance) by the newly weds. The most common Zulu expression used in determining the stage of the marriage ceremonial procedures, is to ask: "Umakoti usesinile?" Has the bride danced?

After the ceremony incorporating the ritual dance, other functions take place. The question, "Has the bride danced?" underlines the very fact of social reality that no man, witchdoctor, diviner, chief or priest can solemnize a wedding. It is the dance, ukusina that sacrileges the marriage.

The Meaning of Religious Dance in the Nazareth Church

Isaiah Shembe started preaching Christianity in about 1900. About a decade later he founded the Nazareth Church. Shembe's mission was to reorientate the European missionaries and persuade them to teach the "gospel of the heart"--that Christianity demands change of heart and not change of culture, as had been the case with the early missionaries. The odds of achieving his goal were too great for the prophet Shembe.

Firstly, he had not been converted into Christianity by any person, but by visions. This lack of Christian referee seems to me to have illegitimized him among fellow-Christians.

Secondly, he was a semiliterate trying to argue with the educated; and thirdly he was an African debating with White people in a land ruled by White supremacy. The founding of a church was therefore accidental.

Having honored the Western style of worship, where people sit down, sing and listen to a priest, I think that there must have been a conflict in him as a Zulu person and a Biblical scholar. According to Zulu custom, the highest offer to God is a ritual dance and, according to Christianity, in many passages in the Bible, God must be worshipped with music and dance![1]

Consequently, in the Nazareth Church, as in all African Christian churches, God is worshipped in ukukhonza, that is, congregational type of worship. The Nazareth Church differs in that, besides the congregational type of worship, it also incorporates the sacred dance, ukusina. Some may see these two types of worship as a mixing of the new and old, that is religious syncretism. I hold the view that the so-called religious syncretism is a reconciliation of the Western and traditional Zulu type of worship.

---

[1]Psalm 149:3; 150:4; Ecclesiates 3:4; Jeremiah 31:13; Lamentations 5:15; 2 Samuel 6:14,21; Exodus 15:20; 1 Samuel 18:6; 1 Chronicles 15:29.

In Zulu traditional life, ukukhonza means to sit with one's countrymen in front of a chief or king. In such a situation the important issue is to be there. A small pot of beer may go round as a form of social drinking. Philosophical arguments prevail. An old man for example, may demand from the others a definition of say, "hardship." An hour might be spent on that discussion. People do understand that the chief or his regent is not God; but their gathering with him generates spiritual powers. The Christian practice of congregation and priest is therefore acceptable, except for the fact that the preacher delivers a one-way speech which may not be interrupted by any questions.

Shembe introduced the ukusina type of worship after more than twenty years of preaching. It was then the late twenties and the Nazareth Church was over ten years old. The ukusina dance had been preceded by the European type of procession.

For an African, the most frustrating thing about European processions, military or religious, is that these splendid processions "march past," building up an expectation for the climax of it all: the dance. But no dancing ever takes place, and the feeling of "emptiness" persists afterwards! It is an anticlimax!

Shembe was a great creator of music and dance. In introducing ukusina for Christian worship, he in fact modified the old Zulu ritual dance, isigekle. This dance is the product of a song type called ihubo. The composer therefore created new ihubo with biblical lyrics.

The fact that the melody in these dance hymns resembled old Zulu war songs and that the dance patterns were suspiciously similar to the old Zulu izigekle, did not arouse any misgivings either in the prophet or his followers because the so-called ancient pagan dances were indeed ritual dances to UmvelingqangiU, God Eternal. To the Zulu the melody or tune is the "path," indlela, and the lyrics are the song. The words may be fitted onto an existing "path" (melody), if their mood matches it.

Shembe started the sacred dance with isigekle, a continuation of an old tradition. The different types of worship of congregational and sacred dance resulted in the prophet's hymns being divided into izihlabelelo nezingoma (hymns and dance hymns) (J.G. Shembe, 1940: V). Later on the other hymns, not originally meant for dance, were made to realize a dance counterpart by some inventive dance leaders. The dances today are therefore in two styles: isigekle (the original dance) and what people call ukusina okwejwayelekile, (the ordinary or common dance).

The basic difference between the two dances is that isigekle is generated by a purely indigenous musical genre. The "ordinary" is a product of the Euro-African hymn. In watching these two dances, one soon realizes the cyclical nature of isigekle and the controlling chord progression of "ordinary" dance. Consequently, isigekle as a dance, lends itself to improvisation. The other type is improvised to a comparatively lesser extent.

In the so-called orthodox Christianity, there are many rituals such as procession, sacrament and baptism. All these are also found in the Nazareth Church. According to the African traditionalist view, these are not the best that Christians can offer to the service of God.

The prophet Shembe tried to practice what the Bible says, rather than "interpreting" the scriptures. As part of this endeavor, he changed the day of worship in 1913, from Sunday to Saturday. He further changed the procession in the late twenties; he changed the process to an actual religious dance which inter alia strengthens the dancer against the weakness brought about by the forces of evil.

I have mentioned the two types of worship, ukukhonza (congregational type) and ukusina (religious dancing). Every member of the church must attend Sabbath worship. Non-members are also free to attend. Members are expected to lead a Christian life and to prepare themselves spiritually for the Sabbath. However, some members may find themselves at work on the day of worship, leaving them with little time for Sabbatical meditation. However, since the main Sabbath service commences between 1:00 and 2:00 p.m., depending on the particular temple, most people would return from work in time to catch the main service. The fact that they attend directly from work does not bar them from worship.

Those who participate in what I regard as the higher order of worship, that is the sacred dance, must first undergo some ascetic seclusions. Thus not every member may take part--the preliminary catharsis is essential. The dance itself is not easy to master. In my own observations, years of practice are necessary before one can fully master it. The question of musicality of an individual plays little role, because in this part of Africa the common belief is that if you talk, you can sing; and if you can walk, you can also dance.

The standard books for members of the Nazareth Church are the Holy Bible and Isaiah Shembe's hymnal. Apart from the biblical reference to sacred dancing, Shembe's hymns frequently refer to the dance as an offer to God. Hymn No.124:4 for example reads thus:

Ngomsinela obongekayo ngingasenanhloni

Phakamani masango, phakamani singene

Translation:

I will dance for Him who is praiseworthy

Lift up ye gates, lift up so that we may enter.

The gates are those of Heaven.

In the Sabbath hymn, stanza 9 also refers to the dance:

Mbongeni ngezigubhu nokusina

Ngokuba umusa wakhe uhlezi phakade

Translation:

Praise Him with drums and sacred dance

For His mercy is eternal.

Christian rituals sanctify the living, but they are limited to this world. Ukusina is practiced here and into the hereafter. It links people with their dead, with their angels and with their God here on earth. It is therefore beyond death. It has a tremendous cathastic effect because through it contact is made with the Creator and those forces which are well disposed to one's physical and spiritual well-being.

In actual practice the dance does not interfere with the Sabbath worship. The dance may take place only after instructions from the titular head of the church. Any day of the week, except Saturday, may be chosen; but Sunday is most popular. In the Nazareth precepts, the six days of the week must be spent doing constructive work. If a particular day has been spared for religious dancing, then the dance becomes the work of the Lord.

Once made, the arrangement for the ukusina is irreversible. Thunderstorm or any violent element of nature cannot stop the dance. Spectators can disperse when rain comes, but the participants of the dance will continue because the dance is not for spectators. In fact, the discomfort suffered by the dancers strengthens their spirituality and reminds them of the object of the ritual dance.

Before the dance, each group gathers at a specified time for a short prayer. The prayer is held at the temple where Sabbath worship takes place. This particular prayer requests God to accept the sacred dance and specifically to make the participants dance for Him, and not for spectators and cameras.

The dance costumes are divided into African traditional regalia and Western type of dress. Men wear kilts, which suggests Scottish influence, and also Zulu traditional costume. People who are not Zulus--like Xhosa, Swazi, Shangane--are free to wear their own traditional dress. This practice of choosing one's costume at a given occasion, underlines Shembe's doctrine that God wants the heart and not a particular culture. Indian members that I know of use Zulu traditional costume. One finds transformation of meanings in traditional items such as Zulu beadwork. Today, Zulu beadwork has been replaced by greeting cards. This art, besides the ornate appearance, was meant for transmitting messages. For example, a woman would send a message to her fianacé reading thus:
     "I love you, I yearn to be with you."
The same bead patterns in a religious context would say:
     "I love you my God, I yearn to be with you in Heaven."

Coming back to ukusina; at midday each group leader is free to stop his/her group for a lunch break. In the evening, when the dance must come to an end, it is not the dance leader who orders a stop, but the titular head of the church. Only he may do so because he is the one who authorized the dance in the first place. After having spent the day on the work of the Lord, the dancers expect "payment" as it were, in the form of a blessing. The titular head or his duly appointed representative blesses each group before they can stop, by the phrase, INkosi inibusise! which means, "May God bless you all!" The response is a cry of "Amen" because the end of the sacred dance is indeed the end of a long prayer that has lasted a full day. The blessing thus bestowed rewards people's lives here and now. But most importantly, ukusina declares their membership in the heavenly hosts. It is as if the dancers have been registered in the heavenly holy book.

In fact, a very ill individual with a premonition of death will expect to hear the drums of the sacred dance. These will be drums of heavenly hosts coming to meet the departing spirit. When the dying Nazareth says "I have heard the drums!," he/she declares the faith which mocks death as in "Death where is thy sting, grave where is thy victory?" The person knows that he/she is going to Heaven, for these cannot be the drums of the devil. The devil can imitate God's notes in music, but he dare not imitate God's rhythms and holy dances. These are indeed divine and cannot be tainted with evil.

Religious Dance and Healing

On the question of religious dance and healing, ukusina cleanses people of their physical and spiritual ailments.

Looking at it from an outsider's view, the sheer physical strength exerted in the dance can only come from a healthy body or the exercise will leave an ailing body in sound health.

Spiritually, ukusina is preceded by harsh asceticism, including confession of sins and forgiveness of those who have trespassed against one. Whilst the primary object is to belong to Heaven, the path leading to the dance is for those who are pure in spirit.

God, according to members, is for abundance and happiness. Visitations by the demons manifest themselves in poverty, disease and quarrels within the family.

People rehearse ukusina in their homes with their children, for self expression, and they also practice on Saturdays after the Sabbath meetings, in order to while away time; but most important is the fact that they remark after each rehearsal that they have "dusted off the demons."

A family with endless problems of disease, extreme poverty and endless quarrels, may invite members of the church to come and conduct a prayer in their house. This privilege is not restricted to members only.

When people arrive at the house, they rehearse the dance rather casually before the actual formal church service takes place. After the service they may continue again with ukusina. Religious dancing on such occasions is regarded as rehearsal because the genuine dance can only be authorized by the titular head of the church.

In spite of all that, it is still believed that the dance has power to drive away demons. The devils are frightened of a formal church service, but after the prayer they might come back. On hearing the drum sound, they are supposed to run away for good because ukusina cannot be tainted with evil.

People envy those who have been able to participate in an official dance. It is common practice among families to encourage at least one member of the family to prepare for ukusina because there is bound to be peace and happiness in the family.

Ukusina is regarded as the highest religious experience, but it is also understood rather indirectly, that it imparts "good health" to the community.

Summary and Conclusion

Shembe endeavored to follow biblical commands to the letter. From his Zulu and Sotho culture, he removed those elements that were against scriptural teachings. The Zulu religious system regards music and dance as the highest form of worship through which a wealth of blessings can be obtained. The Bible supports the worship of God with music and dance. Shembe modified the Zulu sacred dance isigekle and left out the non-sacred dances.

Religion and culture are inseparable. The so-called orthodox Christianity is permeated with cultures of mother countries. In African terms, offering music without dance to the Lord is not enough. Western hymns and Western musical styles are not the best that Africa can offer to the service of God.

The notion that Zulu and other African religious dances are evil results, I believe, from some early presumptions that African cultural practices are basically evil. Sub-Saharan African history did not begin with the arrival of Europeans four hundred years ago. I cannot imagine how religious ecstasy can be expressed without a thanksgiving holy dance in Africa. I have witnessed the most orthodox Christians beating their "bibles to pulp" at night revivals and improvising a dance to the Lord!

256

Shembe's dances are a public matter, and religious ecstasy is expressed in other churches in some kinds of dance movements.

I therefore foresee an escalation of religious dancing in all African Christian churches, which will, indeed, be following Shembe's style of worship. To me, this will not be perversion of Christianity, but an enhancement of Christianity in Southern Africa. In years to come, when Africans become less ashamed of their culture, Christian drums will thunder across the sub-continent with all Christians "drumming" the earth with their feet (as it is said), in holy dancing. African Christianity cannot survive without religious dancing.

PART FOUR: AFRICAN HEALING AND WESTERN THERAPY

INTRODUCTION

In the final section of this book the papers raise many important questions about the relationship between traditional African healing, the healing practices of African Independent Churches and Western psycho-therapy. The result is a stimulating debate which raises many, many questions for future consideration and research.

The first paper, by Ms. I. Mkhwanazi, discusses the role of the traditional iSangoma as a therapist. Although there are many cultural differences between the Western therapist and the traditional healer, it becomes clear that both deal with essentially human problems and that the success of both is to a large extent based upon the empathy of the healer/therapist for their patient.

In Ms. H.B. Mkhize's paper the ways in which traditional healing finds expression through the incorporation of Christian beliefs producing the "prayer-healer" is examined. Here again, through the careful examination of one highly suggestive case history, the reader is forced to reflect on the role of empathetic understanding and human interaction in the healing process. And again, behind the cultural facade of ancestors and traditional beliefs one sees a common humanity.

The next two papers by Drs. Cheetham and Griffiths are powerful examples of what happens when Western psychiatrists apply their understanding of psycho-therapy to African traditional practices. The results are a creative interaction which enlightens the reader by forcing him, or her, to reflect on the healing process itself. To aid in this reflection, the authors have provided a schematic presentation of their arguments and comparisons which greatly assists the reader to think critically about the issues they raise.

Dr. M.V. Gumede then presents a creative article in which he continues the reflection on the differences and similarities between traditional and modern healers. He places the practice of traditional healing firmly within the social context of modern South Africa and challenges us to think the cost of medicine and the role of the medical profession in society.

Finally, Dr. Edwards once more presents a challenging reflection upon her fieldwork and the relationship between traditional healing and Western therapy. Here we see the importance of studying religion in a comparative perspective and the need to develop cross-cultural studies for the benefit of all

THE ISANGOMA AS A PSYCHOTHERAPIST
by
Ms. I. Mkhwanazi

There are a variety of traditional healers in the Black Community of Southern Africa. West (1975) mentions three types: the faith healer, the prophet, and the iSangoma or diviner.

The faith healer belongs to a mission or an independent church, and the power to heal is believed to come from God. A period of training as a faith healer may or may not be necessary.

A prophet is a healer, found mainly in Zionist Churches who has the ability to predict, heal and divine. A prophet belonging to a church, draws his healing powers from God, but the power may come from God through the more direct agency of some guiding ancestor or ancestors. Prophets undergo training by another prophet and claim their healing work is led by the Holy Spirit.

The iSangoma, or diviner, may or may not belong to a particular church. Her healing power is not said to be Christian, but rather to come directly from the ancestors.

The life and history of a diviner are in many respects parallel to that of a prophet and include a call, a period of illness which can be successfully treated only by another diviner.

The iSangoma relies to a large extent on divination to discover the cause of discomfort. The iSangoma serves many functions in the Black community. As the link between the ancestors and the living, he/she is able to interpret the messages of the ancestors. This is done by means of a special concentration of power within the iSangoma which enables them to understand and do things which are beyond the conception of ordinary mortals. The diviner is able to see into the past and the future and is therefore consulted in all matters in which people require advice or have to make a choice. The iSangoma is also consulted when people feel they are being bewitched and when things go wrong in their homesteads.

The success of the iSangoma in therapy is based on the fact that he empathically understands the sufferer's problem in terms of their world-view. And because diviners are able to understand the activities of the ancestors and to interpret their wishes or orders to their clients, the latter look upon them with awe and respect, believing implicitly in, and acting upon what diviners prescribe.

The iSangoma is not expected by the community in which he or she practices to be otherwise employed. They always have to earn their living by being actively working as a diviner. Diviners are thus regarded as professionals within African culture. An operational definition of the iSangoma can be made in relation to the functioning of the Western trained psychotherapist. Unlike the highly private nature of the Western therapist, however, the Zulu iSangoma always functions in full view of the client's extended family or kin system. Thus the iSangoma's clients are never treated in isolation but as integral components of a family and of a community at large. The iSangoma can therefore be seen as a family and a community psychotherapist because his or her treatments are carried out at home, in close contact with the client's family. This strategy has a therapeutic value, because the therapy takes place in a natural home atmosphere, with the intention of creating a warm and non-threatening environment.

Mkhize (1981) is of the opinion that, in a particular cultural group, any healing system that attempts to understand a person in terms of his own world-view will be experienced as enriching and meaningful. An understanding of the world-view of the client as the client sees it is said to be a primary requisite in effecting meaningful therapeutic change. The Zulu iSangoma seems to be in a better position to understand the behavior of his or her own people than the Western psychotherapist because he or she shares their culture.

During divination, the diviner usually labels the condition from which the client is suffering and suggests the first steps for their management. The naming process is one of the most important components of all forms of psychotherapy and may, in and of itself, be effective in alleviating many of the client's problems. The very act of naming is, therefore, therapeutic.

Being able to assign a label and point out a cause or an offending agent indicates to the client that someone understands and also implies that something can be done to alleviate the suffering. In most cases of divination, the diviner names the illness in terms understood by the client. The diviner tells the client what caused his or her problems and prescribes their treatment. In fact, Carstairs (1955) is of the opinion that as long as the client's problem or illness is nameless, the client will feel desperately afraid, but once its origin is defined and the appropriate measures are taken the client can face the outcome calmly.

Healing rituals therefore move through three separate stages:
> (i) The illness is labelled with an appropriate and
>   sanctioned cultural category;

(ii) The label is ritually manipulated or, to put it another way, culturally transferred;

(iii) A new label, such as cured or well, is applied and sanctioned as a meaningful symbolic form that may be independent of behavioral or social change.

It is therefore important that the therapist knows the right name for the illness and, in order to know the right name, shares some of the client's world-view concerning the illness itself.

The psycho-therapeutic implications of traditional practice are that the cause of the problem is always explained, and that ways of dealing with it are always given. This in itself is therapeutic. Just knowing that a reason and a coping procedure exist brings about some satisfaction. Relief occurs if the diagnosis is meaningful to the client; that is, if the world-views of the healer and the client in some measure coincide.

Power is an important factor in traditional therapy. The basic relationship between the diviner and the client is authoritarian. As a result the direct contact or communication between the diviner and the client is highly directive. The implications of an authoritarian relationship in traditional settings is considerably more positive than would be the case in Western settings. The client expects direction and relies on the healer for instruction during the treatment session. Thus the iSangoma assumes the culturally-supported personification of a wise, detached but empathic and warm person who provides all the necessary gratification for his client.

The diviner is an expert to whom the client attributes superior knowledge and or ability and he or she is seen as a provider of information previously unavailable to the client. Within this therapeutic relationship, the client depends upon the diviner for help in reaching his or her goals and for information about how to achieve them.

Since the iSangoma is seen as a bearer of authority and power, it is difficult and perhaps impossible to eliminate all authority and power from the diviner-client relationship. Thus, power and authority may be viewed as the theme in traditional therapy.

The therapeutic effect comes basically from the client's belief that the healer is a powerful person. The diviner claims supernatural power and supernatural sanctions for his or her therapeutic activities. It is this source of power that attracts people to the diviner when they are faced with frustrations.

The diviner also uses the technique of suggestion in his or her practice as a psychotherapist. Direct suggestion may be intentionally or unintentionally employed by therapists, Western or non-Western, in the course of their contact with their clients. In the case of the diviner, such suggestion may take the form of a direct command, such as an assurance that "you will get well." The prestige and status of the iSangoma enhances his or her power of suggestion and the client's hope of getting well. Also in wide use by diviners is the giving of charms, amulets and rings, together with the suggestion that the illness or the problem will not recur.

According to Torrey (1972), certain paraphernalia are used by therapists in different cultures to increase a client's expectations. As indicated previously, the iSangoma uses colorful regalia, an impressive headgear and an array of equipment. All these suggest a man of great knowledge, which gives the diviner an immense advantage over the ordinary Western therapist (Gelfand, 1964).

The colorful regalia gives the diviner an imposing appearance and self-confidence which conveys an air of absolute certainty that he or she knows what is wrong and how to make it right again. Diviners therefore stand out as different in their communities. They are accorded respect and sometimes fear (Frank, 1961). The image of omnipotence accorded the iSangoma is an essential ingredient of his or her therapeutic success.

Symbolism is yet another technique used in the diviner's therapy. Symbolism exists in the form of rituals which are believed to bring about certain desired states, such as symptom removal or contact with ancestors. Rituals are only effective, however, insofar as they do not conflict with the client's other expectations and beliefs.

Cheetham and Griffiths (1982) state that any therapeutic intervention contains some healing ritual. Therapy through rituals is based on a group of symbols and beliefs, some of which are general in scope and others specific to a particular society or ethnic group. The specific aim of the rituals is to purify or exorcise. This should be distinguished from the therapeutic effect which involves understanding of the social and psychological principles at work in the society.

It is only through the performance of rituals that people experience that feeling of belonging together and of being in direct contact with the ancestors. During ritual ceremonies, people often experience this feeling as togetherness in an enriching and fulfilling manner (Mkhize, 1981, p.81).

Within the Zulu cosmology there is a belief that performance of a ritual strengthens the relationship of a person with his or her ancestors. Ceremonial offering can thus be considered as therapy and most rituals are done with a therapeutic intent. These ritual sacrifices are for the Zulu people a communication model for their relationship with the ancestors. Pleasing the ancestors has a therapeutic effect, especially when one believes that one's misfortunes are due to a disturbed relationship with the ancestors. A sacrifice which forms the bond between humans and a deity is absent in modern Western practice, though it is a crucial psychological point in most African societies (Cheetham and Griffiths, 1982).

The diviner may move his client into his or her own home and spend periods with him or her each day as he or she carries out therapy. Treating the client at home also makes it possible for the diviner to enjoy frequent informal contact with the family, using suggestion and assurance, while encouraging and supporting the client's belief in the protective and therapeutic power of the healer. Treating the client in a family environment fosters a warm non-threatening, atmosphere and also gives the diviner an opportunity to observe as an outsider the social situation of the client, and to gauge the extent of tension and anxiety that may be contributing factors in the client's illness (Ngubane, 1977).

Though the diviner-client relationship is authoritarian in form, the diviner is also able to provide a non-threatening safe atmosphere by accepting, and understanding the client's problem. This is because the traditional healer is well versed in the client's cultural beliefs, thus making communication based on empathic understanding more meaningful.

Research into the effectiveness of psychotherapy has established that the greater the cultural and personal similarity between the healer and the client, the more effective the therapeutic techniques. Of interest, in relation to this view, is the fact that the traditional healer always carries out his functions within the whole cultural setting, giving primary importance to the whole cosmology of the person and refusing to treat the client outside a cosmological system.

In traditional healing, therefore, the interplay between client, healer, group, and the world of the supernatural, serves to raise the client's expectancy of cure, helps harmonize inner conflicts and reintegrates the person with their group and the spirit world, while supplying a conceptual framework to help this along and stir them emotionally. In the process, the method used combats anxiety and strengthens the person's sense of self-worth (Hammond-Tooke, 1975).

The function of the iSangoma in Zulu society is consequently of paramount significance because it is the iSangoma, possessing the capacity for divination and for meditation with the ancestors, who acts as the final arbiter in matters of sickness and health.

In particular cultural groups, any healing system that attempts to understand a person in terms of his or her own world-view will be experienced as enriching and meaningful. An understanding of the world-view of the client as the client sees it is thought to be a primary requisite in effecting a meaningful therapeutic change. The iSangoma seems to be in a better position to understand the behavior of his or her own people because he or she shares the culture of his or her clients.

A research study to investigate the therapeutic methods of Zulu diviners was undertaken in Durban. The study was prompted by the need for greater clarity regarding the role of the iSangoma, or the function of the iSangoma as a psychotherapist in his own community. It also addressed itself to the problem of whether the iSangoma embodies the three facilitative conditions of empathy, warmth and genuineness in his practice as psychotherapist. The research was thus concerned with examining the concepts of empathy, warmth and genuineness, and evaluating their specific contribution as active ingredients in psychotherapy.

Therapy sessions between diviners and clients were video taped and brief segments of therapy were rated, using Truax and Carkhuff's (1967) scales of empathy, warmth and genuineness to establish whether the isangomas approach embodied these three therapist conditions.

The concepts of empathy, warmth and genuineness were selected for investigation because they are generally considered to be of great importance, and it was thus a matter of interest to establish whether they are present in the practice of the iSangoma.

Four raters listened to 3 x 5 minute segments from each therapy tape. The first segment came from the beginning of the tape, the second segment from the middle of the tape and the third segment from the end of the therapy interview. The first five minutes of each segment were rated for each of the three therapeutic conditions of empathy, warmth and genuineness, yielding twelve ratings per therapy session.

Statistical Analysis

An analysis of variance approach was used to determine the extent to which different raters (or judges) agree in their ratings.

Inter-Rater Reliability: Coefficients of the Final Rating Procedure.

Dependent Variable: Empathy

Segments	Reliability Coefficients
I	0,566
II	0,779
III	0,862

Dependent Variable: Warmth

Segments	Reliability Coeffecients
I	0,881
II	0,791
III	0,863

Dependent Variable: Genuineness

Segments	Reliability Coefficients
I	0,828
II	0,337
III	0,612

The reliability coefficients all indicated an acceptable interrater reliability.

For comparison of the different segments with one another, t-tests for dependent measures were computed and the results were:

Variable	Mean	Standard deviation	t-value	2-tail probability
Warmth I	3.15	0.962	-3.64	0.022
Warmth II	4.25	1.016		
Warmth II	4.25	1.016	-3.50	0.025
Warmth III	4.95	1.230		
Empathy I	2.3	0.647	-4.62	0.010
Empathy II	4.05	0.570		
Empathy II	4.05	0.570	-2.5	0.065
Empathy III	4.7	1.022		
Genuineness I	2.35	1.069	-4.23	0.013
Genuineness II	3.6	0.576		
Genuineness I	3.6	0.576	-2.87	0.045
Genuineness II	4.65	0.675		

The results with respect to the mean levels of empathy, warmth and genuineness ratings for each segment in the final procedure are graphically summarized in figure 5.1

Figure 5.1

Results of the mean levels of the therapeutic conditions of empathy, warmth and genuineness for each segment: final procedure

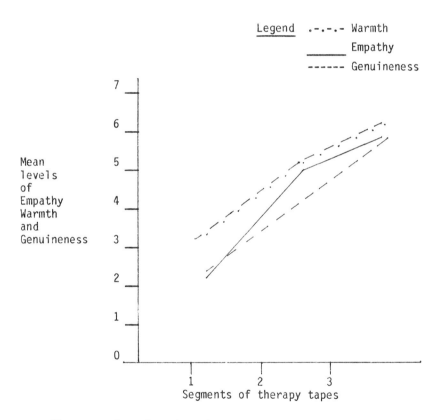

These results showed an improvement in the presence of the facilitative conditions of empathy, warmth and genuineness from

segments 1-3. All were significant at the 0,05 level of significance.

This study demonstrated that therapeutic facilitativeness is not as consistent as one would predict. There is a trend for maximal therapeutic conditions to occur in the middle and later segments of the therapy interviews. According to Garfield and Bergin (1971), clinical experience would suggest that this pattern of therapeutic functioning is based on the therapist's need to have a "warm-up" period early in the therapy interview in order to assume the client's emotional set. Also in the early therapy interview the therapist often does not have enough data from his clients to be able to "tune in" to their phenomenology. The perception of the raters is therefore that of an increase in the facilitative conditions of empathy, warmth and genuineness as therapy progresses. The anticipated results of the increase in the facilitative conditions would appear to mean an increase in confidence and satisfaction in the diviner's therapeutic power.

According to this study, it would seem that the three conditions of empathy, warmth and genuineness are present in varying degrees in the therapeutic practice of the iSangoma. The study also seems to reveal that the effectiveness of the diviner depends not only on his or her training and on other sociocultural determinants of the client's image of the diviner, but also on certain personal qualities and attitudes. The diviner, besides being persuasive, charismatic, self-confident, directive and authoritative, may also be said to be emphathetic, genuine and able to display controlled warmth to his or her clients.

No claim can be made however that the study approaches an exhaustive examination of the factors that influence successful therapy outcome. The iSangoma's role as a psychotherapist can also be discussed in terms of Torrey's (1972) components of the psycho-therapeutic process. Torrey (1972) has suggested that the components of psychotherapy are universal and comprise:

> (i) a shared world-view: that is a common language, common culture, beliefs and values;

> (ii) personal qualities of the therapist which make the professional relationship acceptable to the client and family;

> (iii) the aura of the therapeutic setting, linked to the status and qualities of the therapist; and

> (iv) particular techniques of therapy.

A common world-view is shared by the patient and the traditional healer/psychotherapist. According to Torrey (1972a) Bührmann (1977; 1982), Cheetham and Griffiths (1980) and Frank (1961), for the therapist to be effective he or she must be attuned to the beliefs, values and expectations of the people he or she serves. The therapist and the client should furthermore, be able to understand and appreciate each other's cultural values. The therapist should not have too great a socio-cultural distance from the client.

The iSangoma shares the same culture, common systems and traditional beliefs of his or her client and therapy is given in clearly explicable terms. Also, since healing should take place within a meaningful cosmology, it is posited that the traditional healer is often the best person to act as an integrating agency in the client's society. The qualities of the diviner/therapist are also important in therapy, as are factors such as regalia, proven powers of divination and social status in the community.

The attire that the iSangoma uses in therapy demonstrates dignity and majesty. The diviner's paraphernalia, which gains its power from its culturally determined symbolic meaning, also helps to arouse the client's expectancy of help. The expectations with which the client enters into the therapy situation are important. According to Frank (1961) the higher the expectations the better the outcome. The client's expectations of help may also be raised by the healing rituals/techniques prescribed by the diviner, and many rituals make a strong aesthetic appeal. The performance of rituals lies in the client's expectancy of help, based on the client's perception of the diviner as possessing healing powers derived from his ability to communicate with the ancestral world.

According to Frank (1961), the following are common to all psychotherapies: an emotionally charged, confiding relationship; a therapeutic rationale accepted by client and therapist; provision for new information; strengthening of the client's expectations of help; provision of success experience and facilitation of the emotional arousal. In terms of Frank's criteria, parallels may be drawn between the traditional healer and the Western-trained psychotherapist. The therapeutic relationship is in both cases open, frank, confident and respectful, while interpretations made within a particular world-view represent the main source of new information. The traditional healer's explanation of the cause of the client's problem, the ancestral influences, ritual observance and supernatural causes all provide the appropriate rationale in the African context. However, psychotherapies based on Western causation may be ineffective for patients in cultures that attribute mental illness/misfortunes to, for example, spirit possessions.

The results of the survey and the discussion thus suggest that the universal features of psychotherapy may be seen to be applicable to the function of the traditional healer, and much of his or her activities are clearly psycho-therapeutic, as in all cases of therapy. The diviner's emphasis is on providing warmth, support and reassurance, while restoring confidence in a familiar and comforting way.

EFFECTS OF PSYCHOTHERAPY
(after Wittkower & Warnes)

ISANGOMA		THERAPIST
a.	Rationalization of fears	Rationalization "Id-Ego conflict"
b.	Suggestion through prestige	Suggestion by prestige
c.	Projection onto deities	Displacement ("Id impulsive")
d.	Displacement onto "scapegoat"	Displacement ("parental deprivation")
d.	Displacement of attack	Displacement of attack ("mature defenses")
f.	Penance by sacrifice	Penance by sacrifice (time/fees)
g.	Symbolization	Symbolization (Id ego superego)
h.	"Undoing"	"Undoing" (regression/free association/ talking through)

THE UMTHANDAZI - PRAYER-HEALER

by

Ms. H. B. Mkhize

INTRODUCTION

Concern with whether Black Africans still use indigenous healers or not has been superseded (Edwards et. al., 1983, Mkhize 1981; Ngubane 1977; Watts 1980). Generally the trend is towards the recognition of traditional healers and a vague form of integration in the mental health team. Presently a great concern prevails amongst clinical psychologists and psychiatrists about the related issue, the relevance of Western methods of healing to Black South Africans especially those who are illiterate. (Bührmann, 1984; Kruger, 1984).

There is, however, a strong need for researchers to refine and clarify their thinking by articulating the factors that make indigenous healers popular amongst Africans. This is particularly important because arguments like "Black Africans still prefer to use their own people" inevitably serve an ideological purpose and distort the reality of life and health care provided by separate Departments of Health. For example, they may create an error of thinking that in cases where both practitioners are equally available, Black people would still prefer indigenous healers.

It is interesting to note that historically both the state and the Mental Health profession did not recognize the value of indigenous healers. In fact they were persecuted. Indigenous healers were said to be aggressive, stubborn and resistive. It obviously creates a gap in the literature if all of a sudden emphasis there is on the importance of healers without any attempt to articulate the basis of their success of efficiency. Generally speaking researchers and medical practitioners have attributed the indigenous healers' success to cultural factors. Yet their role and responsibility seems to be political in nature.

Hence there is still a need to point to the direction which research and debate with regard to the use and relevance of indigenous healing systems should take. To add to our knowledge of this an attempt will be made to analyze the life history of an Umthandazi. It is important to note that to refer to Umthandazi as a prophet may create an error in our thinking. A more direct translation of the word umthandazi would be a woman of prayer or alternatively a man of prayer. On the other hand one would expect a prophet's emphasis to be on prophesying. However, for lack of a better English word, the words "umthandazi" and "prophet" will be used interchangeably.

My task is to present a case study of an Umthandazi, who in relation to the theme of this symposium forms a part of "indigenous healing systems." To achieve my goal, an attempt has been made to articulate the Umthandazi's personality dynamics. Admittedly there is at the present moment no standardized personality tests for Black people. Hence, the results have been interpreted with great caution. The findings of this paper are severely limited because there is no single case analysis that can resolve such a complex task.[1]

CASE LIFE HISTORY

Tam, a pseudonym, is a 58 year old Zulu woman. She has been told that her mother died on the fifth day after her birth. Tam was then left with her father who had four other wives. Tam was

---

[1] I would like to express my gratitude to the University of Illinois for selecting me for the University of Illinois South African Faculty Fellowship (September-December 1986). This paper was greatly revised during my visit at the University. The thoughts expressed in this paper are, however, mine not those of the University of Illinois.

brought up by her grandmother on the maternal side and sees herself as a person who never had a family life. She maintains that she had limited contact with her father and feels that she had a lonely and sad childhood. Tam feels that there are many children today in a position similar to hers who need support. She strongly feels that it is a function of an Umthandazi to attend to the needs of the deprived and psychosocially disadvantaged individuals or groups.

HETEROSEXUAL RELATIONSHIPS

Tam feels that most of her youth was spent on household activities and farming with very little contact with her peers. Her grandmother is said to have been extremely religious. She maintains that because of her grandmother's religious conviction she was not given permission to attend various cultural observances because they were seen as ungodly. This created serious intra-psychic conflicts and dissonance. Tam saw this as a form of deprivation which led to a serious developmental crisis in her life in relation to her "calling." She believes that had she had a chance to have a complete cultural religious experience, she would have been in close contact with not only God, but also to her ancestors.

At the age of 17 years she decided to rebel against her grandmother's introjected religious teachings which were those of the ama-Nazarites by falling in love with a man of another religion. But, that relationship did not materialize because the man's parents did not approve. Tam feels guilty about the rejection saying it was a form of punishment because she broke the norms of Shembe's teaching. Since she could not bear the shame of being rejected by her boyfriend's people, she decided to leave her hometown to work in a nearby city.

WORK HISTORY

At the age of 28 years, she got a job as a baby-sitter. Tam maintains that she had a serious language problem and could not communicate in English. Therefore, a major conflict developed at that time when her employers threatened to expel her because she could not engage in play activities with the White child. So they looked for an alternative baby-sitter who could communicate and play with the child adequately. Tam recalls that a few days before a new girl came, she had a dream. Shembe, a great leader and prophet, appeared in a dream. He asked her whether she was aware that she would be expelled. He went on to tell her that it was because of the language problem that she was going to be faced with a crisis. While she was still surprised, Shembe took a blackboard and taught her basic English words like sugar, tea, toys, etc. To her great surprise on the following day, she could communicate in English and as a result she secured her job. She remained in that job for the next six years. Tam sees Shembe as a savior who rescued her during a critical moment in her life. Such support, at the time she was faced with an existential crisis, forms an important part of her calling.

MARITAL LIFE

Tam got married at the age of 28 years to a man who was not of Shembe's religion. She stayed with her husband for one year before he died in a car accident. After the death of her husband, Tam left her in-laws to stay on her own. Tam seems to have strong guilt feelings about the death of her husband; she sees that incidence as a curse on her because she was not a Nazarite.

HISTORY OF RELIGIOUS ACTIVITIES

Tam maintains that central to all her religious convictions is her call by God. She feels that because of her special calling to leadership within the independent churches, her life has been full of trials and temptations. Although her family believed in Shembe's teachings, she did not feel committed to any one religion. She admits, however, that because she had no one in her life she felt supported emotionally within the church. She sees her life to have been peculiar and full of difficulties. Tam believes that she had a special calling by God, through the prophet Shembe, in one special dream:

> Shembe appeared in a dream. He looked as though he was seated on a judgment seat and there were all black churches, and there was not even a single White person. Shembe then said to her, "My child, my child, the gift I give you is not only the words, but a child."

Tam points out that in search for fulfilment of the promised gift of a child, she has taken leadership within the church on a number of occasions. In 1963, Tam started her own small congregation in her employer's garage. Almost all the domestic workers in the region participated actively. She maintains that her congregation was dismantled when she changed her job. Within her congregation the emphasis was on brotherhood, and they did not label the congregation by any one name. Her major task, as she sees it, was to draw in as many people as possible, to pray for them. Tam maintains that she also had power to command the demons in the name of Jesus.

In 1970, Tam started a revival meeting at a new employer's place. Members were encouraged to be supportive to one another, to pray for each other, and to carry each other's burdens. She maintains that although the revival group is still functioning, her spiritual energies have been distributed to other areas of life. She joined a Zionist church in 1977 after she had a serious illness. Tam maintains that she emerged as a leading prophet within a year. Her congregation grew so big in such a way that she needed other junior prophets to assist her.

Tam says that she often dreamed of Shembe and his followers calling her. She clearly remembers one significant dream, which pushed her to make a decision:

> Tam, Tam you need people to stay with, you need people
> to talk to, to live with. The power of God within you
> is often blocked by your own insecurities. Shembe is
> the only person who can rescue you in this predicament.
> To work effectively, you need a holy place.

In view of what Shembe had done for her, she decided to go and tell Isaiah Shembe's successor, Johannes Galilee Shembe, about her dream. The advice she got from him was that in order to succeed in her leadership role, she needed to be at the right place, with the right people. As a result, she joined the ama-Nazarites. In this religious group she has no special role but she feels loved and accepted by the brethren. Tam feels that although at the present moment she is not officially designated as a prophet, her role is likely to emerge clearly. What she has is a gift rather than an acquired attribute. She is already gaining popularity amongst a wide circle of members. Following Shembe's request, made known in a dream, Tam has been offered accommodation in Shembe's religious community. She believes that this community represents the promised heavenly atmosphere on earth. She lives with people who have similar life experiences, no accommodation of their own, no children and no family.

MEDICINES
Tam points out that she is at the present moment on Bio-plus; a nerve tonic. She has been on this tonic for more than five years. She takes the tonic to treat the chronic pain

in her body, feet, and backache, etc. Tam acknowledges that other members of her religion would not accept her if they realize that she takes medicine.

TAM'S DESCRIPTION OF HER HEALING PROCESS

Tam maintains that she treats all sorts of ailments whether they are physical or psychological. She commands ailments using charismatic healing methods such as speech, and the laying on of hands. She sees God to be the major source of inspiration behind her success. She cautiously mentioned that one cannot ignore the influence of her ancestors as well. Tam maintains that at any time of the day she can heal a person. She can relate a number of cases where she was called in the middle of the night to treat very ill people. Tam maintains that in some instances when she touches a sick person she can tell whether that person is likely to be healed or not. On special occasions she asks her sick people to bring along Vaseline, water, or salt. She then puts the substance in front of her, prays, and gives it back to the sick to use. She needs to use such substances particularly when people lack faith. She attributes her successes to her faith, respect, and love for people and believes she can enter a person's inner world. Tam maintains that one's congregation plays a crucial role in any healing situation. Sinful members do not facilitate the working of the "spirit" and they can actually block healing from taking place. She refers to this problem as part of her reason for having changed congregations so many times. She sees white gowns as important in any healing situation because they represent holiness. Tam also represents holiness and attributes her success in healing to something in her which has built up over many years. This is a gift from God and her ancestors.

PERSONALITY ASSESSMENT

A formal psychological examination was undertaken not as a diagnostic exercise but with a view of enhancing further understanding of Tam's psycho-dynamics. A brief comment on the test results will facilitate the discussion.

(i) From Eysenck's Personality Questionnaire the following emerged:

	P	E	N	L
Score	8	15	9	14
Normal	5	17	18	12
Age Norms	4	16	17	14

P - Slightly up
N - Very low

Low N means - to be calm, even tempered
            - respond emotionally, slowly and weakly
            - controlled and unworried

High P means - tough mindedness
            - lack of empathy
            - somewhat hostile and aggressive
            - not sensitive to other people

On the basis of both this test and the interview data, Tam was found to be a calm, even tempered and controlled sort of person. She was emotionally responsive and extremely sensitive to other peoples' experiences. She also portrays tendencies of being hostile and aggressive.

(ii) Klopfer and Davidson's system of scoring the Rorschach
was followed. From the Rorschach personality test the
following emerged:

Intellect:
Average intellectual capacity.
Ambition:
Far too high aspirations which might lead to
frustration. W:M is 4:1
Relationships with others:
Tam's early childhood experiences predispose her to
have poor interpersonal relationships with others. She
tends to rely on inner resources for comfort and
stimulus. There is evidence of a lack of stimulation
from her environment.
Ego functioning:
Her ego functioning seems to be adequate. There are
elements of rigidity and being constricted.

(iii) Lee's (1969) system for Zulu Speaking Africans was
followed in scoring: The T.A.T. responses.

Feelings about the self:
Feelings of insecurity emerged and seemed to be related
to specific life experiences.
Anticipation of the worst to happen.
Fantasies:
Indications of repressed sexual fantasies.
Defenses:
Bio-plus, a nerve tonic is taken on a daily basis.
Repression of insecurity feelings.

Needs:

Tam has got a need for love, support and encouragement. She has a strong need for autonomy and independence, hence a tendency to initiate various religious groups.

CONCLUSION

It is evident that indigenous healers have an indispensable role to play in the field of health care, particularly in the South African context where to a great extent people's experiences are determined by the color of their skin. The majority of people from the lower socio-economic segment often have limited contact with Western healers. On the basis of Tam's explanation of the types of cases she treats, it is obvious that the majority would benefit from Western treatment methods as well. It is therefore logical to say, because of the absolute absence of the Western healers in many communities, which in terms of the Group Areas Act are kept exclusively for "non-Whites," indigenous healers are not preferred but are the only choice. In a case where Tam says people wake her in the middle of the night if a child or old person is sick, it is usually because she is the only healer in a community serving thousands of people without a single general practitioner, not to mention a mental health specialist.

Tam and many other indigenous healers need to be commended for strength and stability in their successful search for the meaningful sense of being, to be authentic, against dehumanizing life experiences.

Problems for South African psychology are well summarized in the findings of the World Health Organization (1981; 1983) report that states medical and psychiatric care provided for Blacks is grossly inferior to that provided for Whites. Apartheid was found to be having a destructive impact on Blacks, their families, their institutions and their mental health. In short, the racial distribution of health services revealed quantitative racial differences in health policy and practice.

In summary, I must redefine my perspective of indigenous healing systems in our context. At this point in history psychology has a responsibility to account for its relevance and loyalty to humanity especially in the South African context. It is therefore my strong conviction that research into the role of indigenous healers needs to adopt a broader paradigm that will incorporate not only cultural aspects but factors affecting the whole man. It is important for researchers to analyze indigenous healers' texts so as to understand the leaders and their followers' message. One can safely but precautiously speculate on the basis of Tam's life history that indigenous healers and their followers are in search for a community with loyalties and trustworthiness, for a society that gives its members feelings of security, and for a society that enhances growth amongst its people. If research on indigenous healers, in this country, remains descriptive then psychologists are either active or passive supporters of the system. The so-called neutral stand taken by researchers in this area denies the psychological implications of social contradictions. It inevitably distorts the reality of the effects of life under Apartheid, that refers to problems in the society arising from domination, exploitation, discrimination and the effects of prolonged detention and interrogation without a trial. In short, the role of indigenous healing systems should not obscure or blind the health hazards of the ideology of this country. Logically, the role of an indigenous healer in a South African context will remain ambiguous until the moral and political issues are clarified.

PRIESTS BEFORE HEALERS - AN APPRAISAL OF THE
ISANGOMA OR ISANUSI IN NGUNI SOCIETY
by
J.A. Griffiths, R.W.S. Cheetham

As has been suggested,[1] modern Western medicine has proved largely effective in providing explanations of sickness and the curative processes based on observable and tangible aetiological factors. However, this approach may have frustrated attempts to gain a comprehensive understanding and, to a certain degree, the assessment of sickness or curative phenomena in African cultures. The basis for these difficulties is felt to be the discrepancy between the conceptual models of sickness and health employed by Western and African cultures. Whereas the former has a pure "individual/disease" orientation, the latter is holistic in its approach, combining biological, social, religious and magical factors in an explanation of sickness and health.

Working with this holistic approach and having an overall world-view consonant with the culture of people of Nguni origin are what have been called "traditional healers," such as the iSangoma or iSanusi. The ministrations of these healers appear to have proved significantly effective in alleviating both physical and emotional disturbances, and in the authors' view they continue to represent a major therapeutic resource within African society despite the increasing availability of treatment based on the Western model of sickness and disease. Even when Black patients recognize the value and efficiency of Western therapy this is often but a partial acceptance, and many, as has been observed by the authors when in clinical practice at King Edward VIII Hospital in Durban, attend the iSangoma subsequent to hospital treatment in order to "complete" their cure.

---

[1]Cheetham, R.W.S., Griffiths, J.A., "Sickness and medicine--an African paradigm." South African Medical Journal, 62, (pp.954-56), 1982.

This pattern of behavior, together with continuing self-referral to the iSangoma as a treatment resource, would suggest that the iSangoma is perceived by Blacks as being in possession of powers of as great (if not greater) magnitude as those of the Western doctors, or of uniquely different powers essential to the achievement of complete remission. It has been suggested by Gluckman[2] that the concept of witchcraft explains "why" the illness or incident occurred and why a particular individual should contract a disease, whereas modern Western medicine would explain "how" the condition developed. Thus, Western medicine might not explain the total situation for or answer all the questions of a Black patient regarding the sickness phenomenon, while the iSangoma continues to provide the assurance and explanation essential to the conceptual framework of illness prevalent in his culture. In her description of the difficulties of the Western trained therapist in dealing with a Xhosa patient, Bührmann[3] emphasizes the problems resulting from the doctor's failure to understand the particular anxieties and fears of the patient--and it is assurance regarding these factors that the iSangoma provides. Kiernan[4] suggests that the explanation and assurance which the iSangoma provides the patient with is, however, rarely of a revelatory nature involving new information or facts, but is rather confirmation of the

[2]Gluckman, M. The Logic of African Science and Witchcraft. (Rhodes Livingstone Papers, No.1), Rhodes-Livingstone Institute for Social Research, Lusaka, 1944.

[3]Bührmann, M. "Western psychiatry and the Xhosa patient." South African Medical Journal, 51, (pp.464-66), 1977.

[4]Kiernan, J.P. "Is the witchdoctor medically competent?" South African Medical Journal. 53, (pp.1072-73), 1978.

suspicions, ideas and beliefs already held by the patient as part of his own explanation of his illness.

SOCIAL RELATIONSHIPS

Kiernan[4] goes further, however, to suggest that "diviners are specialists in social relations ..." (p.1072). Indeed, the iSangoma is largely responsible for social cohesion within the clan. This she achieves through the direction of systematized rituals and ceremonies and the observation of taboos. From this position of authority she frequently becomes aware of disturbed relationships within the home or within the clan. She will often attribute certain symptoms to socially disruptive influences of which she, and sometimes the patient, is aware. Similarly, the prescription which she might then make would be directed at resolving the social conflict in question.

From the foregoing it may be seen that the iSangoma's influence derives not only from the healing function but also from her dominant, instrumental, social role within the community and her proved powers of divination. Therefore, her expertise and skills would appear to lie in the fields of not only the treatment of physical and, particularly, psychological disturbances but also the comprehensive understanding and awareness of ecological, sociological and economic variables operating within the community.

ROLES OF THE ISANGOMA/ISANUSI

The iSangoma fulfils a number of roles: (i) as healer, either through divination or provision of muti; (ii) as the center of social integration and cohesion; (iii) as seer or diviner; (iv) as the protector of the people, their possessions and their environment, particularly against lightning; and, most importantly (?) as the religious head of the society and mediator between the ancestors (amadlosi) and their descendants, either for love and protection or propitiation for omission of required rites or for contravention of the social code.

It can be seen that the duties, functions and roles of the iSangoma are extensive. In much of the current literature relating to the "traditional healer," the emphasis is, however, laid upon her role as healer and the procedures and methods she adopts in this context. This emphasis is in keeping with the present technological, mechanistic, chemotherapeutic and laboratory-based orientation of Western medicine. Even ukutwasa, the act whereby the iSangoma is "called" to her vocation by the ancestors and which heralds a period of novitiation for her, is being examined in this way by current researchers. This examination is often conducted without general acknowledgement of or reference to the fact that within the culture ukutwasa is essentially regarded as a spiritual or religious experience, a gift from those amadlosi who protect yet judge their descendants. Ukutwasa is closely associated with the individual's propensity for divination. It is in terms of these divinatory powers acquired through the medium of communication with the ancestors rather than a direct healing function that the core of the iSangoma' extensive role in the community is to be found.

The ancestors inform her in all matters on which she is consulted, including those relating to sickness and distress. It is of note that divination usually occurs in some state of altered consciousness. States of altered consciousness may be induced by trance, the use of snuff, self-hypnosis, and other manoeuvres. Some of the iSangoma describe dream states akin to hypnotic states. Whitlock[5] considers that all these states of altered consciousness can be considered as falling into the realm of parapsychology and extrasensory perception. He also quotes Ehrenwald's suggestion that altered states of consciousness are more favorable to this state of communication than fully awake alertness, and Frank's contrast between the religio-magical and the scientific aspects of psychotherapy.

Belief in the ancestors, their "immortality" and their continuing communication with their descendents is fundamental to the Nguni culture and, indeed, represents the principal "religious" component of these societies, albeit a mediatory one. To quote Soga:[6] "The Xhosa worships the Supreme Being, Tixo, through the ancestral spirits ... (p.150), ... and very largely through the aegis of superstition ... (this) may help to explain their loss of true inward meaning of religious worship in its highest form ..." (p.154). The ancestors (amadlozi--Zulu, iminyanya--Xhosa) are primarily concerned with the welfare of their descendants. The dead person, isithunsi or shadow, is synonymous with the soul,[7] and it is only after a period of mourning and the necessary sacrificial procedures that the deceased becomes idlosi, or an ancestor, and has judicial powers over the descendants.

---

[5]Whitlock, F.A. "The psychiatry and psychopathology of paranormal phenomena." Australian and New Zealand Journal of Psychiatry, 12, (pp.11-19), 1978.

[6]Soga, J.H. The Ama-Xhosa: Life and Customs. Lovedale Press and Kegan Paul, Trench & Truber, Lovedale and London, 1931.

[7]Ngubane, H. Body and Mind in Zulu Medicine. Academic Press, London, 1977.

It is postulated that these powers of benevolent protection or judgment in all matters pertaining to the people can be likened in principle to those of the supreme being worshipped in present-day monotheistic religions. Although these beliefs may not be the highest form of worship, they do possess religious and spiritual connotations. It is therefore conceivable that, at least unconsciously, the Nguni people must regard the iSangoma or iSanusi in the same light of reverence as the Western and Eastern world regards the priest who ministers in the name of God. This is exemplified in the high moral standards, integrity and dedication demanded of the iSangoma, the fact that there is one specific idlosi who advises and guides her throughout her life, and the fact that should she "lose" her idlosi her powers of divination and healing would fail.

Among the Nguni healing cannot therefore be viewed only along conventional Western mechanistic lines; it is a far more extensive concept, and it is in this respect that the major challenge lies. Western medicine has become divorced from religion, the doctor caring for the body, the minister for the soul, the psychiatrist for the mind and the politician for the community and the ecology, whereas all of these aspects remain integral to the role and purview of the iSangoma. For example, that religion is of major significance continues to play a major role in healing among the Nguni people. In a pilot study of non-psychiatric patients in the medical, surgical and gynaecological wards of a general hospital, a large proportion of both urban and rural patients expressed the desire for a religious or traditional approach to their illness (R.W.S. Cheetham--personal communication). This emphasizes the importance that Nguni people accord to religion in the healing process.

The iSangoma is therefore pivotal to the religious life of the community and this, as has been suggested earlier, is probably her most important role and the greatest source of her influence. She is "priest" before "healer," "healer" because she is "priest" and social psychiatrist, sociologist, ecologist, parapsychologist and an intelligent and highly perceptive member of the community. Soga[6] quoting Taylor, compares her to the scriptural high priest who "was at the head of all religious affairs, and was the ordinary judge of all difficulties that belong thereto, and even to the general justice and judgement of the Jewish nation" (p.155). It is for this reason that the term "traditional healer" is a misnomer, and why even that of "priest/diviner" fails to signify the comprehensive function, influence and status of the iSangoma or iSanusi among the Nguni people. Furthermore, it may be suggested that future research into the activities of the iSangoma needs to take into consideration more than her "healing" powers and procedures, as currently emphasized, for these are quite clearly fully integrated into her overall function.[8]

---

[8]This paper is reprinted, with permission from South African Medical Journal, Vol. 62, December 11th 1982.

THE TRADITIONAL HEALER/DIVINER AS PSYCHOTHERAPIST
by
R.W.S. Cheetham, J.A. Griffiths

The traditional healer has his origins in the shaman, an inspirational type of "medicine man" open to possession by spirits and acting as a medium through which such spirits might communicate with men. From the very outset, the traditional healer is also directed by the spirit world of the ancestors. His powers arise out of this contact with the spirits--he is expected to have supernatural powers and to use them for healing purposes. In the sphere of social dynamics he mixes freely within the community but very much in the capacity of an arbiter and decision-maker. He is very conscious of social order and group cohesion, and particularly family harmony and group dependency. He operates within a specific social pattern and assesses problems in terms of the social acceptability of the symptoms. His access to the ancestors also gives him a priestly role, and he has the status of a priest in terms of his awareness of the will of the ancestors and the necessity for their propitiation. He addresses himself to the individual but almost invariably does this in terms of the group: indeed, the family is usually present at "consultations." Furthermore, he is consulted on the cause and alleviation of natural disasters or change, such as drought. He therefore takes the combined role of healer, social coordinator, priest and ecologist.

The reader may wish to compare the following outline of the traditional healer's training to that of the "Western" psychotherapist. The training or development of these healers usually begins with a "calling" or state of ukutwasa, which often takes the form of an early-morning dream-state involving the appearance of an ancestor who directs the individual to the home of an established traditional healer. There are other specific signs associated with this state which are later identified by the traditional healer as part of the "calling." Few have any

308

earlier intention of becoming a traditional healer. The
"calling" is generally accompanied by a sense of fear, if only
because one of the constraints placed upon the individual who has
been called is the belief that failure to proceed with training
might lead to either madness or death. The period of training
involves the novice living with a traditional healer for an
extensive period of apprenticeship with formal tuition in
techniques and practices. The final component is a period of
probation during which the novice must demonstrate his powers of
divination, often through the discovery of hidden objects. Only
then does the traditional healer license the novice to practice.

The essence of his practice is the divination of causative
factors, and this is believed to occur via states of spirit
possession induced by trance, toxins or other forms of
excitation. Spirit possession generally refers to communication
with the ancestors who provide the answers and the important
explanations of not only "how" but also "why." In many instances
the prescribed remedy or solution is also recommended by the
ancestors. The traditional healer's approach to patients is
largely directive, and the explanations of illness employed (and,
more importantly, accepted within the culture) are varied and
applicable to disturbances of the emotions and behavior as much
as to physical complaints.

In order to examine the traditional healer's role as
psychotherapist, it is useful to discuss the psychotherapeutic
process in terms of its components and themes and the effects or
outcomes of such activities. Fuller Torrey[1] has suggested that

---

[1]Fuller Torrey, E. The Mind Game: Witchdoctors and
Psychiatrists. Emerson Hall, New York, 1972.

the components of psychotherapy are universal. They comprise: (i) a shared world-view--this includes a common language and probably, for most effective results, the vernacular; (ii) the particular personal qualities of the therapist which make the professional relationship acceptable to the client; (iii) the aura of the therapeutic setting, linked to the status and qualities of the therapist; and (iv) particular techniques of therapy.

Some attempt can be made to examine the practices of both the traditional healer and the Western psychotherapist in the light of Fuller Torrey's suggestions. Certainly a common world-view is generally shared by the patient and his traditional healer or his psychotherapist. The qualities of the therapist and the setting of the exchange are significant in both cases, and factors such as regalia, proven powers of divination, legal or professional registration, degree certificates, furnishings and social status are apposite here. Similarly, the procedural regimen of divination/diagnosis, communication/explanation and prescription is common to both sets of circumstances. There may, of course, be some major differences in the choice of technique.

Among others, Frank[2] has pointed out that despite superficial differences psychotherapies practiced all over the world have common underlying themes. These are: (i) an intense, emotionally charged confiding relationship with a helping person; (ii) a rationale of myth which includes an explanation of the cause of the person's distress which is compatible with the

---

[2]Frank, J.D. "Common features of Psychotherapy." Australian and New Zealand Journal of Psychiatry, 6, (pp.30-46), 1972.

cultural world-view shared by the client and therapist--the provision of a conceptual scheme for what seems to the patient to be a group of nonsensical symptoms brings powerful reassurance, and it is the function of this scheme, rather than its detailed content, which is of significance; (iii) the offering of new information concerning the nature and sources of the client's problems and alternative ways of dealing with them; (iv) the strengthening of the client's expectations of help through the personal qualities of the therapist, enhanced by his status in society and the setting in which he works; (v) the provision of success experiences which further heighten the client's hopes and enhance his sense of mastery, interpersonal competence or capabilities; and (vi) the facilitation of emotional arousal as a prerequisite of attitudinal and behavioral change.

In terms of Frank's criteria above, again parallels may be drawn between the traditional healer and the Western psychotherapist. In both cases the confiding relationship is open, frank and respectful. Ancestral influences, ritual observance, mythology and folklore, psycho-analytical and other models of psycho-pathology provide the appropriate rationale and conceptual schemata for an acceptable explanation of the causes of his symptoms and distress and a means of providing reassurance. Interpretations made within a particular world-view represent the main source of new information. The patient's expectations of help are raised by the status, proven ability and qualifications of the traditional healer and psychotherapist alike; in both cases "success experiences" are largely provided through the relief of anxiety, and emotional arousal through transference, suggestion or regression tends to be facilitated in both settings.

Wittkower and Warnes[3] have suggested some effects of psychotherapy which, in various combinations, they consider to be the universal outcomes of such activity. These include the rationalization of fears of unknown origin, projection, displacement, penance, and undoing. This intriguing list of "ego defense mechanisms" may be seen to have some plausibility as a proposed set of outcomes of the activities of the traditional healer and the psychotherapist, i.e., rationalization involving the invocation of familiars, sorcery or the id-superego conflict; projection onto ancestors, deities or id impulses; displacement onto witchcraft or parental deprivation; penance by ritual slaughter, fees or the relinquishing of defenses; and undoing through ritual observance, appointment regimens or the talking through of problems.

The easiest answer to the question of whether the traditional healer is a psychotherapist lies in the fact that he tends to be as effective in alleviating psychological and behavioral disturbances as any other "psychotherapist." Nevertheless, while universal features of psychotherapy may be seen to be applicable to the function of the traditional healer, and while much of his activity is clearly psychotherapeutic, it is dangerous to minimize some of the very dramatic differences between the traditional healer and his Western counterpart.

Not the least of these differences is the apparent disparity between the total roles assumed by the two, particularly in view of the Black concept of "medicine," which may be seen to embrace

---

[3]Wittkower, E.D., Warnes, H. "Cultural aspects of psycho-therapy." American Journal of Psychotherapy, 14, (pp.566-73), 1974.

much more than the healing function. Indeed, the traditional healer is much more than a psychotherapist. Not only does he treat physical illness, he also assumes the religious, social and ecological roles mentioned earlier. The Western psychotherapist might well be regarded as a priest in the temple in which Freud, Rogers, Wolpe or Minuchin represent the oracle, but the integral social role enjoyed by the traditional healer appears to have eluded him as yet.

We should perhaps address ourselves to the question of what to do in a situation in which both agencies are available to the client. A number of authors[4,5] have proposed means of integrating the two facilities. It is to be hoped that by promoting and upholding the principle that explanation and treatment should be consonant with the culture and world-view of the client, such integration may occur in a manner which will maximize the effectiveness of therapeutic endeavor.[6]

---

[4]Lambo,T.A. "Patterns of patient care in developing African countries: the Nigerian village program." In: David,H.O.(ed.) International Trends in Mental Health, McGraw-Hill, (pp.147-53), 1966.

[5]Bolman, W.M. "Cross-cultural psychotherapy." American Journal of Psychiatry, 124, (pp.1237-40), 1968.

[6]This paper is reprinted, with permission from South African Medical Journal, Vol.62, December 11, 1982.

THE ISANGOMA, A PSYCHOTHERAPIST:
A SCHEMATIC PRESENTATION

"MEDICINE"

Emphasis on Ancestors

Healing   Family Life   Social Dynamics   Religion

ISANGOMA

Origins in	Shamanism
Focus on	Medicine
Extension to	Healing
	Social dynamics
	Religion
Emphasis on	Ancestors
	(AMADLOSI)
Application to	Individual
	Collective
	Ecological

DEVELOPMENT OF AN ISANGOMA

A.	Calling	(UKUTWASA)
B.	Novitiate	+/- 2-4 years
C.	Probation	N.B. Divination
D.	Practice	Definitive source within world view

FUNCTION OF THE ISANGOMA

A.	DIVINATION	seek causes
		trance toxin excitement
B.	COMMUNICATION	explain how/why
		amadlosi
C.	PRESCRIPTION	recommended action
		ritual "muti"
		procedure

COMPONENTS OF PSYCHOTHERAPY (after Torrey 1972)

A. Shared world view
B. Personal qualities of therapist
C. Aura of therapeutic setting
D. Particular techniques of therapy

THEMES OF PSYCHOTHERAPY (after Frank 1972)

A. Confiding relationships
B. Rational of myth: conceptual scheme
C. Provision of new information
D. Strengthening expectations of help
E. Provision of success experiences
F. Facilitation of emotional arousal

ISANGOMA THERAPIST

A. Confiding relationship	open, frank respectful	open, frank respectful
B. Rationale/ scheme	AMADLOSI RITUAL MUTI	ID Ego-superego Appointments Regime
C. New information	Detail of world-view	Interpretation
D. Expectations of help	Divination/ Social status	Empathy/Statue/ Registration

E.	Success experiences	Relief of anxiety	Relief of anxiety
F.	Emotional arousal	Transference	Transference Regression

INSANGOMA THERAPIST

A.	World view	Culturally Determined/ Novitiate	Culturally Determined/ Training analysis
B.	Therapist qualities	Probation/ Divination	Reputation/ "Empathy"
C.	Aura of Therapy	Regalia/ Social status	Registration/ Social status
D.	Techniques	Divination Communication Prescription	Divination Communication Prescription

HEALERS MODERN AND TRADITIONAL

by

M.V. Gumede

321

INTRODUCTION

For 335 years life in South Africa has been characterized by separateness. This has received different names at different times e.g., Baas-skap, color bar, segregation, white trusteeship, apartheid, consortium, etc. As a result we have missed observing crucial changes. My father was a Kaffir; I was a native; my children were Bantu; my first granddaughter was a plural; my second granddaughter was nearly an African, but some said call them Black, lest they think they are also Afrikaners. We all know my first grandson is a South African as we now all have a common citizenship.

Ladies and Gentlemen, this conference was an epoch-making occasion--when modern doctors and traditional healers get together to share views on the art of healing. In the final analysis we all have the same objective, namely, healing our patients:

To Cure	-	Sometimes
To Relieve	-	Often
But, To Comfort	-	Always

For arranging this meeting the chairman deserves a loud pat on the back.

My function is merely to summarize some issues deserving careful study and future research. I will kick off by sketching the differences between:

1. Indigenous, African izinyanga	1. Western, imported, medical practitioners
2. In existence 4500 BC Kush/ Ethiopia	2. Fathered by Hipocrates

3. Irrational	3. Rational
4. Empirical	4. Scientific
5. Surgical procedures: crude primitive, unscientific	5. Surgical procedures: scientific planned based on gross and morbid anatomy
6. Training is from father to son or from Master healer to Trainee (Udibi), Apprentice, Journeyman. Training takes a lifetime	6. Training is available to anyone who has the necessary requirements. The training takes a minimum of 7 years
7. Disease is believed to be unnatural--man made through the agency of spirits	7. The germ theory postulates disease follows a breach of the laws of nature
8. Diagnosis means who caused the illness	8. Diagnosis means what caused the illness
9. Holistic treatment	9. Treatment is individualistic
10. There are some 120,000 inyangas excluding sangomas, etc.	
11. Inyanga treats the patient within his environment physical, spiritual, emotional--his past and present	11. The modern doctor treats the the disease--destroys the offending organism, patient will be well
12. Rules of Ethics were high enforced by any statutory but by a high code of conduct	12. Code of conduct laid down and enforced by the medical council
13. Stress is laid on (a) the troubled, viz., patient	13. Stress is laid on a) the trouble, viz., the disease

| (b) the soil, viz., the environment--physical and cosmic | b) the seed, viz., the germ and the disease |
| 14. The idiom of approach is social,political,economic moral, religious and even recreational | 14. The language of modern medicine is aetiology, symptomatology, diagnosis epidemiology,endemiology, preventive curative, prognosis, rehabilitation |

African society has shifted from the old extended family when three or four generations were found living together in one kraal to the nuclear family of father, mother and child. The old third and fourth generations resisted and applied brakes to halt too rapid change. The nuclear family is prone to rapid changes. The Zulu like any other Black South African has been subject to wide diffusion of culture and has adopted many ways of the newcomers from the East and the West. Thus rural and urban Zulus only exist in the statute books.

There is an excellent transport service. A Zulu has breakfast at Mahlabathini, boards a combi in the morning to shop at the Hypermarket by the sea, take sanother combi back home to have supper at Mahlabathini. There is thus little difference between urban and rural.

Youth is, at all times, prone to rapid change. Be it remembered: 45% of Black South Africans are 15 years and under. 66% of Black South Africans are 25 years and under.

But compare this with Europe where 15% of the population of the Federal Republic of Germany is 15 years and under. The result is a confused process of acculturation which sets the scene for rapid change--no urban, no rural Zulu.

The Zulu is a polygamist who lives in an exogamous patrilineal society. Inheritance is determined by the laws of premogeniture. The Zulu needs plenty of daughters to recoup his eleven cattle he paid as lobolo for his wife. His wives must give him an heir to perpetuate the name of his family. All these factors lay strong demands on the Zulu's procreation machinery. A large brood enhances his prestige in this and the next world. He must have strong medicine to give him sexual prowess and maintain fertility. The inyanga has a wide range of aphrodisiacs.

The Zulu has always lived with a high perinatal mortality. All authorities confirm that the African perinatal mortality is three times that for Whites.

Year	Place	Mortality per 1000	Authority
1982	Kwazulu	22-93	Pat Garde
1983	KEH	83	Prof.Philpott
1983	Dududu/Zg	147	J.V.Larson
1983	Valley of 1000 Hills	113	Friedman
1984	Northern Natal	119	Darryl Hackland
1986	KEH	55	Sam Ross

By comparison perinatal mortality for Whites in 1982 showed 14-21 per 1999. Thus the African needs strong medicine to replenish supplies in his reproduction factory. He is in all things full of verve and virility. Watch him at his Zulu Ngoma dance!

What do African Patients expect from Western Doctors

Patients are the same the whole world over. All are ill as is. They seek and welcome help from any source. They go to a healer, modern or traditional, expecting to be helped to get rid of their illness--real or imaginary. The process is the same everywhere. Patients expect their doctor to listen to their woes, examine them, arrive at some diagnosis, tell them the diagnosis, viz., to answer the simple question: "Doctor, what do I suffer from?"

Thereafter outline the course of treatment, medical, surgical, or referral to specialist or hospital and why this is necessary for the patients well being.

This is what all of us, you and I, expect of him when we go to the doctor as patients or when we send our loved ones to him. So do Zulu patients.

What they do not expect is
a) To be made to sit on old tomato boxes while they wait for the doctor.
b) To be pushed through a sausage-like machine process with emphasis on the number of patients seen.
c) To see an impatient doctor in a foul mood when he sees them but all sweet reasonableness when he sees patients other than them.
d) To be examined with a stethoscope fully dressed auscultating the forehead, the knee and the toe.

Nor do they expect this from a traditional healer either.

To put the record straight: What they expect is just consultation in a relaxed atmosphere, a good bedside manner which inspires confidence, reassurance of cure, or offers emotional support when a cure is not possible.

This is the traditional healer's trump card. He may even work in his patient's house at night and sleep there. Imagine the confidence inspired in both patient and relatives by the presence of this very gifted son of the gods! When the traditional healer wins the confidence of his patient half the battle is won as both patient and relatives have been placed in a frame of mind psychologically receptive to treatment and conducive to recovery.

If it be accepted in the medical community as in the financial community that the customer is always right, our patients do not agree with us that the traditional healer has no role to play in our health care delivery services. We need to review our attitude toward the traditional healer as a health resource.

Here is some interesting food for thought

1. Over 50% of babies born in the Black community are born outside the hospital and the clinic. TBA's and traditional healers are providing this invaluable service at no cost to government.

2. 80% of all Black patients visit the traditional healer before they visit the doctor, the clinic or the hospital.

3. Of the 20% of unbooked maternity patients at King Edward VIII Hospital, 60% had been attending a traditional healer in Sam Ross' series.

4. The cost of being alive is rising and will soon be a luxury.
    Even medical aid schemes are so expensive. 70% of White
    workers benefit from medical aid. 36% to 26% of Indian and
    Colored workers; and only 4% of the Black work force can pay
    medical aid.

5. Modern medicine is now high tech. Technology is expensive
    and not easy to come by. It takes:
    4 years to train a health inspector
    4 years to train a medical technologist
    4 years to train a pharmacist
    6 years to train a dentist
    6 years to train today's professional nurse i.e.,
    RN, RM. CHN et DPN
    7 years to train a medical practitioner
    The traditional healer is a ready-made, easily available
    health resource within the community at risk--and at no
    expense to the Government. The community health nurses at
    Phungashe Clinic are already engaged in dialogue with the
    traditional healers on management of TB.

    In conclusion, illnesses can be divided into three groups:

    1. Those which are entirely mental.
    2. Those which are physical but tend to limit themselves.
    3. Those which are physical but do not tend to burn
        themselves out.
    80% of all illnesses belong to the first two groups.

    The function of the healer (modern or traditional) is to
    pick out from his patients the 10% to 20% who would die without
    appropriate treatment. Wherefore both the modern and the

traditional healer have an equal chance of success because all of us are given the power and the right to treat our patients--but only He, the giver of all things, does the healing.

HEALING: XHOSA PERSPECTIVE

by

F.S. Edwards

When working with a prophet-healer, Mr. Robert Ntshobodi, who is the archbishop of the Apostolic Holy Church in Zion, I was struck by his frequent references to consciousness in relation to his work. "All sickness is in consciousness," he says. This paper is based on an exploration of this aspect of the Zionist prophet-healer's self-understanding and experience.[1]

The material comes from a Xhosa Zionist community, the Apostolic Holy Church in Zion (AHCZ), in Grahamstown, headed by Mr. Ntshobodi, and served also by five or six other prophet-healers trained by him. Mr. Ntshobodi himself I have known since 1975--a radiant person, conveying a deep sense of presence, awareness, energy and vitality. The paper attempts to trace particularly the connections Mr. Ntshobodi himself makes between consciousness and his understanding of what he is doing when he is healing, and a parallel will be adduced in the work of a seemingly very different category of "prophet healer."

Consciousness is best defined as the process of being aware. We know that consciousness is pluridimensional; we experience different levels of awareness. Mr. Ntshobodi speaks of different kinds of consciousness. Isazela esiphilileyo is what he calls "living consciousness." This kind of consciousness, he says, "is always together with the Spirit of God" and it is, or should be, the normal awareness of the Christian. He explains, "In living consciousness, isazela esiphilileyo, one prays and one is connected with God. When one sins one breaks off this living

[1]The research on which this paper is based was supported by a grant from Rhodes University.

consciousness. When one confesses his sins his living
consciousness revives."

Closely associated with this "living consciousness" is
isazela sengququko. Sometimes Mr. Ntshobodi uses isazela
sengququko as synonymous with isazela esiphilileyo but it also
appears to be more like what in English we would call
"conscience." For instance, he explains that "isazela sengququko
keeps you in the church and keeps you doing right things. You
see something and want to steal. The isazela sengququko tells
you not to do it." Conscience, syneidesis in Greek, literally
"knowing together with," may be understood as an accessing of the
collective unconscious of the group or church or culture, as well
as simply internalizing consciously expressed cultural
determinants. It is also regarded as "knowing together with
God." Thus Mr. Ntshobodi can say, "Isazela sengququko works hand
in hand with the Spirit of God." This consciousness is
understood as given when a person is converted and it is the
consciousness of faith, the result of being connected with the
Spirit of God.

In contrast to this "living consciousness" Mr. Ntshobodi
speaks of isazela esifileyo which is "dead consciousness leading
to condemnation." Such a consciousness produces "bad works." As
biblical backing for this, he quotes Revelation 3:1 verbatim and
incorrectly as, "You say you are alive but you are dead." "If my
consciousness is dead," he says, "I can never convert or heal a
single person." Because it is in isazela esiphilileyo that one
is connected with God, as he puts it, it is in this state of
consciousness that Mr. Ntshobodi prophesies and heals. He uses
this term for the altered consciousness which is evoked and
cultivated in connection with prophecy and healing particularly

during the healing services which we will look at in a later section of the paper.

Consciousness and healing are connected in the holistic understanding of reality that Mr. Ntshobodi holds, as part of his typically African world-view. He recognizes that all levels of reality, including the superempirical, are in dynamic mutual interrelationship. The well-being and vital energy of individual persons and of the community depend on balanced and harmonious relations within and between these levels; sickness and misfortune are the result of disharmony. So an individual must be in harmony with herself, with her family and community, with the natural world, the world of ancestral spirits, and with God, uThixo. When Mr. Ntshobodi prophesies, or "prophets" as he calls it, and when he heals, he is working with these multiple interconnections. His paradigm of healing involves the identification and removal of the cause of disharmony and the restoration of order and wholeness. This is why he understands himself as a prophet-healer, prophecy and healing being both inseparable parts of one process.

Consciousness, as awareness, pervades all the levels of the human person and is in turn affected by them. In Mr. Ntshobodi's definition, he says, "A person is consciousness, (isazela)" and he goes on, "It is consciousness (isazela) that moves the body, because the body is controlled by consciousness." Speaking of diagnosis and of healing, he explains the connection with consciousness, saying, "The sickness of a person is in his consciousness. All the diseases that trouble him are in his consciousness."

There are three ways in which this group of Zionists understand sickness as being in consciousness. Firstly there is the obvious sense in which the patient is aware of his sickness, consciousness being the process of awareness. Secondly, the sickness, or aspects of the sickness or misfortune, or whatever the affliction is, may be at a level of consciousness of which the patient himself is not fully or directly aware. Mr. Ntshobodi works particularly with these levels in prophesying diagnostically.

Thirdly, it is from consciousness that, in many cases, sickness concretises in the body and misfortunes actualize in life events. "Sickness is always in consciousness," he explains and of misfortune he says, "Misfortune is in the consciousness but not in the body. The body may get sick but not necessarily." It is therefore at the level of consciousness, his own consciousness and that of his patient, that Mr. Ntshobodi understands that he, as it were, moves in, to diagnose and heal the patient. "When consciousness is healed," he says, "the body heals."

In order to prophesy and heal, Mr. Ntshobodi explains that his own consciousness must be "clean and strong." Energetic prayer and frequent fasting are the two main ways he uses to purify his consciousness and maintain clarity, as well as leading a rigorously moral life in close connection with what he regards as the source of holiness, the Spirit of God. For Mr. Ntshobodi having "clean consciousness" means that his own consciousness must not be occupied with personal concerns and troubles. He explains, "I have to pray and keep all my troubles away from me so that I can help the others." He knows that he has to work from a level of consciousness that is deeper than, greater than,

his own personal consciousness and also deeper than the personal
consciousness of his patient. He would not, of course, use the
term "transpersonal" here but it is clear, both from what he says
and from how he works, that what he is doing is transcending his
own personal awareness and working from what in contemporary
psychology is called the transpersonal level of consciousness.
This is the level of, for instance, the spiritual gift, the
charismata, in Christianity, the level of the siddhis in Hinduism
and of the sambhogokaya in Mahayana buddhism. As we shall see,
it is primarily at this level of consciousness that he engaged
therapeutically with the consciousness of his patient, and
clarity and strength of consciousness are the prerequisites of
success. To identify with his own personal consciousness, rather
than with this transpersonal level, would mean that he would be
working on a lower, more limited level of consciousness, separate
from the consciousness of his patient and in that state he would
be unable to diagnose and heal. At the transpersonal level all
people and things are inter-connected and as the ego-boundaries
of the prophet-healer weaken and become transparent, so the
transpersonal level is accessed, and the underlying
inter-relatedness between the healer and the patient and what is
going on in the patient's life, comes into awareness.

For Mr. Ntshobodi, "cleanness of consciousness" means also
that he must not have the sicknesses, pains or troubles of others
in his consciousness, since these obscure his clarity as much as
does his own personal "stuff." This is a serious issue since, as
we shall see, in both diagnosis and healing he frequently takes
upon himself whatever is afflicting the patient. If he is
"strong," as he calls it, the transference of the affliction will
be brief. The transferred symptoms will be noted, he will
understand what is going on with the patient and the symptoms

will pass. If, however, what he is accessing in the patient is very powerful and if he himself is not strongly enough established in the transpersonal level, such that he can both contain the transferred symptoms in part of his awareness and also have enough attention or power left over to maintain his own wholeness, then he may be overcome by what he has encountered and he will have to deal with it later in his own person. To take a couple of examples, if the patient presents with a physical problem, say an acute backache, Mr. Ntshobodi says he will feel that backache in exactly the same place, as if, as it were, he is taking the patient's affliction on himself. Or if the patient comes to him in mental confusion or distress the reason for which he does not know, Mr. Ntshobodi will also feel the mental confusion, distress or whatever, taking it into himself, becoming part of it and penetrating further into the patient's deep process in such a way that he is able to identify and articulate the reason for it. But in either case he may be left with the backache or the mental confusion. If this happens, "Then, Sister," he says to me, "I have to go to the desert to pray it away." Going to the desert means going alone to a quiet spot away from the turmoil of the township where he will pray, usually fasting also, until he is free, well, clear and strong. Fasting is an obvious help here. What he has taken from the patient is alien to the integrity of his own body-mind and the physiological correlate of this is toxicity, which is why he feels bad. Fasting accelerates the detoxification of the body; it is also an assault on the ego, which is the focus of personal identity. As egoic identification wakens, the transpersonal level of awareness becomes all the more readily accessible. This is at least one of the main uses made of fasting in all the major religions.

Prophecy and healing are closely related in the Apostolic Holy Church in Zion context. Prophecy is first and foremost diagnosis of sickness and other ills along with the related personal and social or socio-cultural questions: what is causing this to happen to you, why you, why now, is there another person involved as causative agent, the latter being, of course, an important issue where sorcery is suspected, which is quite often. Prophecy also includes accessing information as to how to deal with the sickness, or whatever it is. But even identifying the cause of the sickness may be part of the healing of it. I have elsewhere described prophecy and healing in this community in some detail (Edwards, 1982, 1984), and I am highlighting here only the points in the process which throw light on the state of consciousness of the prophet-healers.

In every case Mr. Ntshobodi prays that the Spirit of God will help him, will tell him what is wrong, and what to do to help and heal the patient. This act of prayer is itself a shift of consciousness. It is moving deliberately into isazela sengququko, accessing the transpersonal level. Prophecy may be what we would call precognitive; it may be in dreams or visions or it may be what Mr. Ntshobodi calls "seeing in the Spirit." He frequently dreams before a patient comes to see him of who is coming and of what is wrong. The dream may be repeated and may need interpretation. Or, while awake he may have what he calls a vision. "I am sitting here in my chair," he says, (this being in a room which does not overlook the road), "and I see a man being brought up the street in a donkey cart ..." and so on. Or, in the healing service itself it may happen that he "sees in the Spirit," as he calls it. This may be almost a literal seeing, but it is seeing which is knowing. It may begin by his seeing a light surrounding a particular person in the congregation. He

338

then prays intensely and knows interiorly, through the Spirit,
what is wrong with the person. He will check it out with the
person, saying to him alone, while the congregation is singing
loudly, so that confidentiality is maintained, "The Spirit says
you are having marriage problems (or whatever), Is this right?"
And the person will say, "Yes."

It may seem strange to the Western mind that the healer has
to "prophecy," to say out, what is wrong with the patient, in
cases where the patient knows perfectly well what is wrong. This
however is precisely what the traditional indigenous healer, the
igqira, will do during a divination session, and his reputation
depends at least in part on his ability to do this successfully.
The Zionist prophet-healer is to his community in many respects
what the igqira is to his, and the same proficiency is expected
of him; he must be able to divine as well as to heal. There is
however an important difference here between the
self-understanding of Mr. Ntshobodi and that of the igqira.
Amagqira, I think without exception, claim to divine the nature
and cause of the affliction by communicating with the ancestral
spirits, izinyanya, both their own and those of the patient. By
contrast, for Mr. Ntshobodi, it is uMoya, the Spirit, or more
precisely uMoya oyiNgcwele, the Holy Spirit, that is the sole
source of this knowledge. I understand that Mr. Ntshobodi is in
this respect rather exceptional among Zionist prophet-healers
most of whom recognize the agency of ancestral spirits either as
well as, or even instead of, the Spirit of God (West, 1975).

A third way of diagnosis is by direct intuition.
"Sometimes," Mr. Ntshobodi says, "I just know what is wrong, but
only if I pray to God to enlighten me." Or, "I know what is
wrong the moment I start praying." Here Mr. Ntshobodi is

experiencing himself as being in harmony with the source of knowledge as well as in touch with the consciousness of his patient.

The other main aspect of "propheting" is to identify the cause of the affliction. On the one hand this may involve several complementary explanations at the physical, emotional and interpersonal levels. Mr. Ntshobodi recognizes physical agencies and effect such as germs, straining of muscles and accidents as causing sickness, but his knowledge of human physiology is vague and limited and his accounts of physiological processes are often highly bizarre by Western standards. He also recognizes the part played by stressful interpersonal relationships in causing illness, this being a glaring example of lack of harmony. On the other hand, he usually parallels his naturalistic diagnosis with an explanation of the cause in superempirical terms. He may refer here to the moral misdemeanors or sins of the patient, in which case God may be cited as having sent the sickness to recall the patient to himself. Alternatively the superempirical cause may be within the realm of sorcery, where another human is thought to have set in motion influences intended to cause sickness, misfortune or even death. In all of this, diagnosis is not simply giving information but is a part of the healing process.

Mr. Ntshobodi practices healing in a variety of situations, but the Wednesday night healing service is the locus par excellence, and it is here that the highest levels of transpersonal consciousness are evoked and shared. The healing service is held in the main room of Mr. Ntshobodi's home from which all the furniture has been removed. Here forty-five to fifty people, men, women and children are tightly crammed. This is Zion, and these people together are the healing community, for although Mr. Ntshobodi is the leader, the other prophet-healers will also be working, and the whole community sees itself as the channel for the healing power of God. The scene is illuminated by two or three flickering oil lamps and there is minimal ventilation, for during the first part of the service, and during the healing as such, the door and the only window are kept tightly closed. This is symbolic of shutting out the outside world, the township, which is the place of personal vicissitudes, social disorders and cultural chaos, (Cf. Kiernan, 1974) in order that the small room may veritably become Zion, the Holy Place where the Spirit is present to his people, where order is restored and wholeness effected. To fully experience this is in itself to undergo a profound change in consciousness.

The service begins with worship which is understood as a yielding to the Spirit whose presence is invoked by praying, clapping, swaying and dancing. Individual confessions contribute to group catharsis as members are able to transcend preoccupation with personal guilt. Next as power of the Spirit is concentrated in a period of simultaneous prayer, each person individually makes herself "strong in the Spirit," as they call it, and thus contributes to the healing potential of the group.

The "hymns" are simple, a line or two of scripture, for instance, or the chorus of a well-known hymn, repeated over and over. This has an effect similar to that of a mantra and is a good example of what is called directional attention-holding and certainly contributes to a shift in consciousness. The rhythm is reinforced by hand-clapping, swaying and dancing, and by the drum, the beat of which comes to be predominant in one's awareness. It has been shown by Neher (1962) that one of the effects of the drum is to induce wave patterns in the brain of around 7-14 cycles/second which is the so-called alpha rhythm associated with the early levels of transpersonal awareness. It is significant that Mr. Ntshobodi recognizes this change of consciousness. He speaks of it in terms of Joel 2:27-29, "You shall know that I am in the midst of Israel" and "I will pour out my Spirit on all flesh; your sons and your daughters will prophecy, your old men shall dreams and your young men shall see visions. Even upon the menservants and maidservants in those days, I will pour out my Spirit." Mr. Ntshobodi also refers to 1 Samuel, 10 which is about Saul among the dervishes, saying explicitly that "dancing causes isazela esiphilileyo." His hands or his whole body vibrate and he may visibly shake. He describes a very intensely concentrated form of awareness, sometimes such that he is unconscious of his surroundings. He also reports that he experiences energy like that of an electric current being transferred from his body through his hands to the patient.

It is at this point that the affliction of the patient may be transferred to Mr. Ntshobodi as described above. This is reminiscent of Isaiah 53 where the servant of the Lord is said to take upon himself our transgressions, and Hindu rishis are known to take upon themselves the ills of their disciples.

Frequently here Mr. Ntshobodi gives the patient specially prayed-for water to drink, or some other remedy, like the bitter-tasting ash of burnt aloe mixed with water--although the Apostolic Holy Church in Zion do not go in for a wide variety of muthi-type remedies. Giving water is particularly important; Mr. Ntshobodi refers to "Jesus having started his way as a living sacrifice in water" (the baptism), and in Genesis we are told that the spirit of God settled on the waters. "So, he says

"whenever we are invoking the Spirit of God, water must be
there."

The patient may now be made to spin or whirl around with
increasing rapidity--which is a very consciousness-altering
process--reminiscent of the sufi dervishes with whom this is one
of the main meditative practices. The healing process is usually
rounded off by what is called "dancing in a circle" (ukugida).
This will usually start with the patient standing still and Mr.
Ntshobodi and other prophet-healers beginning to dance round her.
Then, one by one, other members of the congregation join in until
there may be eight or ten people dancing round the stationary
patient. The word for this "dancing in a circle," ukugida, has
the connotation of offering and sacrifice, and those involved
understand that this dancing is an offering to God of both the
patient and the healing. Explaining why they dance round, Mr.
Ntshobodi says that "when Abraham offered a sacrifice to God he
took some stones and built an altar in a round form." He
explains that while they are going around in the circle they are
surrendering the sick person, and at the same time they are
"finding the consciousness of the person." He says explicitly
that "they connect with the consciousness of the person being
healed." There is other symbolism here too, the circle having
the meaning of wholeness and completion, but I find it
fascinating that these Zionists are aware that, at this high
point in the healing process, they are connecting with the
consciousness of the patient, for this is the level at which the
healing takes place, the level of inter-connectedness in
transpersonal consciousness.

Even more fascinating was the discovery that there is in
Canada a prophet-healer of outwardly quite a different kind who

is pioneering a new paradigm in therapy strikingly similar to that of Mr. Ntshobodi and his colleagues. I am referring to Alvin Mahrer, psychotherapist and Professor at the School of Psychology at the University of Ottawa. I want to conclude this paper by pointing out briefly some of the similarities.

In the usual therapist-patient relationship in Western psychotherapy, therapist and patient experience themselves as existing separately from one another, and the usual therapeutic modalities take place with the presupposition of that separateness and that externality. In contrast to this the new paradigm which Mahrer proposes, and which he practices, involves an intentional merging with the patient and sharing the patient's experiencing. The first principle is letting-be, such that the therapist places himself into "full receptive attentiveness" so complete that he transcends thinking. He is not thinking about the patient or about what to do next. This is very like Mr. Ntshobodi in his receptive yielding in prayer. Mahrer reports that in this state of attentive letting-be a threshold of consciousness is reached where "the virtually complete focusing of his attention disengages the therapist from his ordinary self." He is no longer aware of himself as "a separate, substantive person." In other words, he has attained a transpersonal level of consciousness. I will not go into the details of exactly how he attains this, but it corresponds to the means used by Mr. Ntshobodi and his colleagues to transcend personal identity. Mahrer says that the therapist is now able to enter into "the internal world of the patient ... to merge into the existence of the patient, becoming coterminous with the patient from the inside .... As the therapist loses his own self he merges with the self of the patient" (Mahrer, 1978, p.207). This is precisely what Mr. Ntshobodi does, mutatis mutandis.

344

Mahrer observes that in this state of consciousness the therapist experiences much that may be understood as "precious sharing of the experience of the patient with whom the therapist is merged .... The therapist's bodily sensations, feelings, thoughts, and so on, are resonating sharing of what is occurring in the patient."

Now this is very unusual in normal Western psychotherapy, but it is exactly what Mr. Ntshobodi and his colleagues do regularly. The equivalent in Mahrer of the Zionist's directional attention-holding is the deliberate focusing on one particular aspect of the patient's experience which leads to what Mahrer calls "heightened experiencing" in both therapist and patient (Mahrer, 1978, p.211). The therapist's bodily sensations come in for special attention; Mahrer refers, for instance, to "sudden ache in the temporal region, clutching sensation in the stomach," and so on (p.208). In his paradigm this kind of transference of sensations is part of getting in touch with what he calls the patient's "deeper personality processes" (Mahrer, 1978 p.211) and thereby enabling the patient to relate more fully and adequately to his deeper self, to those processes which include self-understanding, self-acceptance, sense of meaning and all the "therapeutic gains which come from interacting with what is within" (Mahrer, 1978, p.211). Getting deeply into the patient's identity and process, the therapist is able to work in whatever way is appropriate to facilitate healing.

There are, of course, vast cultural differences. Mahrer does not use singing, dancing and drums; Mr. Ntshobodi attributes what he does to the activity of the Spirit, uMoya oyiNgcwele; but both men are working with a healing reality which underlies and cuts across all racial, cultural and geographical boundaries, and with a level of consciousness which is, potentially at least, accessible to us all.

CONCLUSION

INTRODUCTION

Concluding this collection of papers is an older item originally presented at a seminar in Edinburgh by the Reverend F.B. Welbourn, author of such classic works on African Independent Churches as East African Rebels and A Place to Feel at Home. In this paper a number of awkward questions are raised about our understanding of reality and the fundamental differences between Western and African way of thought.

The paper is thus a fitting conclusion to the present collection because it brings the discussion squarely into Western society and forces the reader to realise that what might appear to be an African issue, or series of issues, has in fact, an underlying reality which affects us all. Thus, Welbourn brings us from Africa to Europe and North America forcing us to begin to reflect on fundamental issues which challenge us all as indeed do all the papers in this volume.

HEALING AS A PSYCHOSOMATIC EVENT
by
F.B. Welbourn

I want to start with an example from Dr. Field (1960, p.118). An Akan may know that the most effective treatment for gonnorrhea is readily available in a hospital. But he may first travel hundreds of miles to discover the mystical agent responsible. Another example comes from Professor Evans-Pritchard's Azande (1937, pp.65-8, 508f). If you stub your toe on a tree stump, you apply medicines. If the toe festers, you begin to suspect witchcraft. If you die, witchcraft is proved. Or, again, it was estimated in 1962 that 90% of those admitted to the children's ward at Mulago Hospital in Kampala first reported to the hospital at the instance of a Ganda diviner, who himself dealt with the "mystical agents" he regarded, in many cases I believe, quite honestly, as ultimately responsible.

I do not want to set this up as a universal pattern for Africa. For instance, the Marakwet[1] of Kenya consult a wide variety of herbalists before failure to obtain a cure suggests that they have been ensorcelled; and, so far as I have been able to discover, the two types of diagnosis are alternative. But, at least among the Zande Ganda, and Zulu, all diseases appear to fall in a continuum (Evans-Pritchard 1937, pp.505-10). At one limit treatment is solely in terms of a "mystical cause" which acts at a distance. At the other limit treatment is solely by material medicines taken orally or applied externally to the body.

---

[1] I should like to acknowledge my debt to Mr. B.E. Kipkorir, at present of St. John's College, Cambridge, for any knowledge I have of the Marakwet. This paper was first presented at a seminar on Witchcraft and Healing at the University of Edinburgh in 1969.

but the great majority of diseases require treatment of both types at the same time.

Evans-Pritchard has three diagrams (op.cit. pp.507ff.) illustrating the three types of treatment:

(i) Mystical cause.............Acute illness.....Treatment
     (Sorcery, cats,   (directed
     breach of taboo,etc.)   against
                                                  mystical
                                                  cause and
                                                  disease
                                                  together).

(ii)
     Mystical cause   Disease
     (witchcraft)

                              Illness

     Drugs and other   Oracles
     therapeutic   etc.
     treatment

(iii) Disease....................Illness...........Treatment
                                                   against
                                                   illness

But his descriptions could just as well be illustrated by a single diagram in which the x and y axes of a continuum represent respectively the "mystical cause" and the "disease":

Y

(i) (0, y_1)   Type (i), where the only relevant
                                   treatment is "mystical" is then
                                   plotted as (0, y_1).

     (ii) (x_2,y_2)   Type (ii), where both lines of
                                   treatment are required, is plotted
                                   as (x_2, y_2).

          (iii) (x_3,0)   Type (iii), where the disease is
                                   minor and the mystical factor can
                                   be ignored, is plotted (x_3, 0).

—————————————————————X

But (op.cit. p.488) specific drugs are used in (i); and, although in (iii) the mystical cause may be neglected in practice, it is always present in theory. Diagnosis is in terms not of "x" or "y," nor even of "x + y," but of "xy;" and the weight which is given to each of the complementary factors depends on the character of the disease.[2]

I think it is an important question whether these factors are happily labelled "mystical cause" and "disease." Indeed, Evans-Pritchard's whole discussion of terms seems to illustrate how impossible it is to define terms for a distinction which everybody knows to exist.

Magic in English not only fails to describe the activities of the Magi. It has no corresponding term in Zande culture.

_____

[2]There are points at which I wonder whether Evans-Pritchard is saying that Zande regard the two factors as additive, so that diagnosis would be in terms of "x + y." But they certainly do not regard them as alternative; and I think that my diagram not only includes his three diagrams but represents his overall view.

"Ritual" behavior may have "empirical" consequences. "Mystical" notions" may be used for "commonsense" ends.[3] More immediately, among the Zande, "The 'souls' of the drugs go down into the body of the man and destroy the 'soul' of the disease which is destroying the 'soul' of the organ" (op. cit. p.492). Medicines, disease, the human body are all conceived in "mystical" terms.

The x-axis is as mystical as the y-axis. Moreover, the concept of "soul" is used to explain not only "magic" but any technological gap between action and result, for instance, "the gap between planing (eleusine) and its appearance above ground." The distinction between ritual and empirical actions is not qualitative but lies "in the number of steps in an activity which are, or are not, subject to observation and control" (op. cit. pp. 463f).

The fundamental distinction between the x-and y-axes is surely to be found in Evans-Pritchard's basic definition of the function of witchcraft (op. cit. p.67): "What they explained by witchcraft were the particular conditions in a chain of causation which related an individual to natural happenings in such a way that he sustained injury.[4] The word "natural" is, I think, to be understood at this point as the opposite not of "supernatural" or of "mystical," for disease itself has "soul," but of "social." The symptoms of disease can be observed, its natural cause diagnosed, its prognosis stated, its treatment with specific medicines prescribed--all in terms of well-attested tradition and

---

[3]There are examples of these uses in Horton, 1967, pp. 54, 56 and Turner, 1968, pp.156-97.

[4]In Field's example the question is, "Who sent the illness?"

however wildly wrong, in scientific terms, may be the logic of the aetiology and the therapy. "Natural" causes represent the general character of particular cases, what is impersonal (even if it involves "soul"), what can be abstracted from particular cases in the interests of a general theory of action by direct contact.

On the other hand, belief in witchcraft, which can act at least over limited distances, symbolizes failures in the inter-personal, the social, field (op. cit. pp.99-117). They represent what is unique in particular cases, what each reveals as to the personal relationships of the patient, whatever of unobservable takes place when two people, often enough not in direct physical contact, communicate or fail to communicate. The Zande concept of dual causation therefore insists that, in all particular cases of disease, there is likely to be a social, as well as a natural, factor involved: and that, in some cases, the social factor is dominant. Although Evans-Pritchard is skeptical of the effectiveness of Zande mystical treatment (and, indeed, of most of their medicines), the success of mystical treatment in other cultures is well attested. Horton (1967 pp. 56f.) suggests that, in societies which are ignorant of scientific preventive medicine, the majority of those who survive infancy have acquired a high degree of immunity to common diseases and that, if they are affected by such a disease, the psychological factor in their condition is likely to be dominant. It is precisely by their skilled manipulation of mystical agents as symbols of inter-personal tensions that traditional diviners score such a high rate of success.

II

I have so far, avoided the use of the terms "psychic" and "somatic" because there seems to be, here also, an uncertainty in terminology. "Many trees and plants which are used in magic are employed in technological pursuits" (Evans-Pritchard 1937, p.448). Insofar as there are gaps in those pursuits, they possess "soul." By special treatment they acquire another "soul" which gives them medical potency.[5] Even among the Marakwet, herbs derive their medical reputation not from intrinsic properties but from their designation by Asis, the Supreme Being. Per contra, Zande witchcraft, even if it acts by telepsychic influence, is located in a somatic substance (op. cit. p.21). What Horton describes is not "psychosomatic medicine" in the normal Western connotation of that term. Action along both the x and the y-axis is psychosomatic. Operationally the distinction lies in the belief that one is impersonal and requires physical contact: the other has a personal origin and can act at a distance.

Traditionally, scientific medicine has denied the existence of the y-axis and has refined techniques of observation and control along the x-axis. In so doing, it has developed concepts which are importantly different from those of the Zande:

   (i)   the refinement of observation and control has
         eliminated a large number of "gaps" and given
         hope that there will eventually be none. In
         this sense, it is regarded as strictly
         "somatic" without any "psychic" factor;

---

[5]Zande metapharmacology would have to consider whether the change involved is transubstantiation or consubstantiation.

(ii)   the same development means that scientific medicine is genuinely empirical;

(iii)   as in the case of x-rays, action along the x-axis can be effective at a distance.

Although these may be the scientific concepts, they do not necessarily represent the attitude of Western medical laymen, who, after all, are the majority of those involved in medical treatment. Evans-Pritchard has an interesting passage where he says (op.cit.p.506): "There can be little doubt that when the action of the drug is of a precise and local nature ... the Zande regards its action very much in the same way as a layman in our own society regards similar drugs, not mystically, but also not pharmacologically."[6]   Any general practitioner, who is aware of what he is doing, knows that a great deal of his practice is based not on pharmacology but on magic (in much therapy there are steps which are not subject to observation and control). Controlled experiment has even varied the combination of the factors, active drug/placebo, doctor's belief/disbelief in activity of drug, patient's belief/disbelief; and has shown that the beliefs of both doctor and patient are active agents in successful treatment (Stead, 1963).

Due partly to such evidence, partly to the development of psychoanalysis and similar techniques, there is now recognition

---

[6]It is not wholly irrelevant to instance my neighbor in Gloucestershire whose laundry must always be hung out "to air" even when it gets wetter in the process. This is not mystical, but it is also not scientific.

of a "psychological" factor in disease, which (like the Zande mystical cause) may sometimes be dominant, can sometimes be wholly ignored, but is always potentially present. There is disagreement as to whether this factor is best treated by drugs, by analytical methods which sometimes seem to objectify an unconscious psyche, or face-to-face discussion at the conscious level. But what has come to be called "psycho-somatic medicine" generally regards the two lines of treatment as complementary; and the scientific y-axis can rightly be labelled "psychological." Conceptually it differs from the Zande y-axis at a number of points:

(i)   operationally, it might be said that psychology is still concerned largely with the "gaps." It is possible to observe and control the stimulus and to observe the response. But there is an unknown number of unobservable steps in-between. In Zande medicine, gaps are involved in both axes. At least conceptually, in scientific medicine they are found only along the y-axis; and they are its sole concern;

(ii)   in so far as psychology is an empirical science, it is not possible to distinguish the two axes by labelling the x-axis "empirical." Both scientific axes are, conceptually, empirical, just as both Zande axes are not empirical.

(iii) scientific psychology is concerned with the internal psyche of individuals and (as in the general attitude to ESP) strongly rejects any

suggestion of psychic forces acting at a
distance except through material media. (It
rejects also the concept of psychic forces
existing except <u>in</u> a <u>soma</u>. But, although this
affects its attitude to Ganda medicine, it is
irrelevant to Zande medical concepts).

The continuum of scientific psychosomatic medicine thus
appears to be radically different from that of Zande medicine.
But, while Evans-Pritchard reports (op.cit p.491) that Zande
regarded Zande drugs as being suitable for Zande and European
drugs for Europeans, Field's example and my own suggest a
situation (of which I was widely aware in East Africa) where
European drugs are recognized as superior in treatment along the
x-axis,[7] while traditional methods are still required along the
y-axis. It is even possible to quote well-authenticated cases in
which the latter assumption has been empirically demonstrated.
Are the two continuums more alike than appears on first analysis?

I suggest that the answer lies in the development of social
medicine. Even in the highly individualistic formulations of
Freud, there was always the implication that faults in an
individual psyche were the consequences of infantile faults in
relations with other persons. Now Laing (1961) suggests that
schizophrenia--so long supposed to be somatic in origin--is a
symbol of membership in a maladjusted family. Contemporary
geriatric therapy insists on rehabilitation in the community; and
some psychiatric clinics take case histories of the patient's

---

[7]It would be interesting to know whether Zande now, thirty
years after the publication of Evans-Pritchard's book, takes a
different view of European medicines.

inter-personal relationships, as painstaking as those of any
African diviner.

The psychic factor in psychosomatic medicine is becoming a
matter not of individual psychopathology but of failures in
inter-personal relationships, of the social field. The
insistence of Ganda diviners on keeping y-axis treatment in their
own hands may be interpreted as a symbol of their conviction that
they know more, than Europeans, about Ganda social relationships.
However difficult it may be to define "psychic"--however
operationally suspect it may be of concern simply with the
"gaps"--it is possible to distinguish the x- and y-axes, in the
scientific as in the Zande case, as concerned respectively with
the natural, the general, the impersonal and with the social, the
unique, the personal. The question of whether these are
conceived in ritual or empirical, in mystical or commonsense, in
psychic or somatic, terms is really irrelevant.

III

Or is it? There can be no doubt that the refinement of
observation and control, and of the conceptual techniques which
accompany them, has been wholly beneficial to the art of healing.
The scientific x-axis is pragmatically more effective than the
Zande x-axis; and there is probably a sense in which all of us
regard conclusions based on empirical methods as "true" in a
sense that magic cannot lead to truth. But does it follow that
we have to agree with Evans-Pritchard when he writes, "Witches,
as Azande conceive them, cannot exist" (Evans-Pritchard 193 p.
63), "A witch obviously cannot perform the action attributed to
him" (op. cit p. 387)? Is it necessarily more rational, as
Turner implies (1968, pp.43f), to regard spirits and witches as
symbols for "endopsychic or social drives and forces" than to

reverse the equation? It is difficult to regard an Oedipus complex as any less "mystical" than a paternal ghost.

It is not, I think, possible to ignore the fact that the effectiveness, as therapeutic hypotheses, respectively of the endo-psychic and the exo-psychic, is relative to the culture in which they are used. Elsewhere (Welbourn 1962, p.126) I have suggested that the proper analogy for the difference between the two hypotheses is that between the wave and particle theories of light. They are incompatible. But, for the time being, physics has to work with both, looking for the time when a reconciling hypothesis will emerge. In these terms I can see no rational reason why medical science should not work with both the endo-psychic and the exo-psychic hypotheses. The test should be not a priori but therapeutic--the effectiveness of treatment based on them; and there might be cases in our own society when doctors would find the exo-psychic hypothesis of greater pragmatic value. I am told by psychologists that the statistical evidence for ESP is more impressive than that for a number of orthodox psychological hypotheses. Yet ESP is generally rejected--not, I am convinced, on any rational grounds but on the sacred ground[8] that action at a distance must obey the universe square law.

If, then, ESP is possible at the levels of cognition and feeling, why not at that of the will? Is witchcraft empirically impossible? Turner has an interesting phrase: "social

---

[8]Another example of a priori thinking acquiring a sacred character among scientists is the assumption that UFO's must be interpreted as psychological, never as physical, events (The Times, January 11, 1969, p.5).

364

anthropologists and depth psychologists ... in their professional capacity at least[9] do not concede that spirits and witches have existence." But, if some professionals in their private capacity admit the possibility, they must, precisely as professionals, either "reduce to rational terms" their own private hesitations or recognize that their professional convictions are not as rational as they appear.

The sociological question seems to me to be why some societies hold that witchcraft and curses can be as effective as, say, a spear-thrust, while scientific society[10] holds that, if ill will is to have any effect, it can be only through the response of the victim. It is the victim's worry about the ill will, not the ill will itself, which is the causative agent. It is, of course, possible to say that the scientific belief is true, in exactly the same way as scientific medicines are more effective than Zande medicines. But, while the latter statement is empirically verifiable, the former is metaphysical. It is an assumption, not a conclusion, of contemporary sociological thought. I can see no reason for rejecting--through my blindness no doubt is sociologically conditioned--an alter-native metaphysic which regards the exo-psychic as being as real as the endo-psychic. I say "psychic," rather than "psyche," because I do not think it is consistent with biblical, any more than with contemporary scientific, thought to hypostasise the psyche. But Balint (1968, p.666), in an attempt to illustrate the relation between subject and object in earliest infancy, uses the analogy

---

[9]Italics mine.

[10]I deliberately do not say, "our" society, since, even in urban Bristol, colored people are accused of using the evil eye.

of the water in a fish's gills and mouth. It is, he says, an idle question whether the endo-water is part of the sea or of the fish: "exactly the same hold true about the foetus. Foetus, amniotic fluid, and placenta are such a complicated interpenetrating mix-up of foetus and environment-mother, that its histology and physiology are among the most dreaded questions in medical examinations."

It is possible, without hypostatising, to apply this analogy not only to the relations between a child and its mother, but to the psychic relations between an adult and the whole external universe. Perhaps the endo and exo-psychic hypotheses are not incompatible but "a complicated interpenetrating mix-up." If so, the sociological--perhaps the social-psychological question is why some societies emphasize the exo-psychic and scientific society emphasizes the endo-psychic.

I do not think that this question can be answered simply in terms of "exteriorising" and "interiorising" (Lienhardt, 1961, chap.IV)--of saying "they project, we introject," because at least the Kleinians hold that we all do both all the time. The process is closely analogous to that of the fish and the water. The question is not whether we do one or the other but what is available for introjection and what we select for both intake and output.

An answer in these terms is much more likely. According to Weber: "The great achievement of ... Protestantism was to shatter the fetters of the sib and to establish the community of faith and a common ethical way of life in opposition to the community of blood, even to a large extent in opposition to the family. From the economic point of view it meant basing business

366

confidence upon the ethical qualities of the individual proven in his impersonal vocational work .... Puritanism objectified everything and transformed it into rational enterprise .... The true Christian ... wished to be nothing more than a tool of his God ... he was a useful instrument for rationally transforming and mastering the world" (Weber, 1951:237-48). Persons become instruments and are isolated precisely from the categorical I-Thou relationships (Buber, 1944) of kinship in which they are most closely and continuously aware of the unique and therefore, since the unique is the one aspect of persons and things where there is necessarily a "gap" of the psychic. At the same time, since the world is to be rationally mastered, and since mastery is impossible in the face of "gaps," nature comes to be conceived as gapless, as wholly "somatic."

Both the social and the natural relationships available for introjection are now instrumental. The internal patters to be projected begin to assume the same form. An individual sees himself reflected in an instrumental world and the world reflected in an instrumental self. Introjection and projection reinforce one another until both men and matter are seen primarily as objects to be manipulated by observation and control, that is by the elimination of all "gaps," the denial of the psychic. The technological society can "progress" only by increasing generalization, the mass production of identical units. The social must be interpreted and controlled in terms of a rationalized natural. Sexual intercourse must be observed by the moving camera. Only occasionally is there a breakthrough of the I-Thou experience of earliest infancy--in deep personal relationships or in the recognition that things have a value in themselves.

This slightly emotive paragraph no doubt reveals my private convictions. But Durkheim (1915, pp.427-39) did the same. Professionally, what I think I am trying to say is that non-belief in witchcraft is as much a symbol of inter-personal relations, of the social field, as is witchcraft belief. If Zande emphasize the social at the expense of the natural, it may be that we do the opposite. It may be that a synthesis is possible, in which (perhaps) the social is seen as essentially I-Thou in character and as the necessary condition of a satisfactory relationship between men and nature.[11] I suspect that, in such a synthesis, nature would be experienced as containing a good many more "gaps" (that is, more of the psychic) than is dreamt of in our present philosophy. But what would be the new belief symbols I hesitate to suggest.

IV

Perhaps I should admit that, while the x-y continuum illustrates most clearly the complementary factors in a process of healing, it seems to me to apply equally to the study of a whole society. I want to add a z-axis, which I label "historical." But, for the time being, the x-axis stands for those aspects of society which are most readily amenable to observation and control--social structure and government, technological processes and logistics of all sorts. The y-axis stands for the uniqueness of things, of persons and of events-- in other words, for their "religious" character. If we are

---

[11]Cf. Evans-Pritchard, 1937, p.507: "the disease itself and witchcraft acting with it, not so much as the cause of it as a necessary condition of its occurrence and continued existence in the body of its victim."

studying religion in a unitary society, we are studying not one institution set over against others, but the dimension in which all institutions relate to uniqueness. If we want to study the same thing in our own society, we shall not find it in "religious" groups which scarcely affect the "secular" activities of their members. Nor do I think we need be concerned with phenomenological similarities between "religious" experience, schizophrenia and LSD trips. We shall find it in the "untouchable" (Durkheim, p.213) and often unacknowledged commitments which these activities express.

GLOSSARY

abafundisi	- ministers
abaphansi basifulatele	- ancestral displeasure
abapristi	- priests
abaprofethi	- prophets
abathandazi	- prayer Healers
amadlozi	- ancestors
amandla	- energy
amafufunyana	- spirit possession
amagqira	- diviners
amakhosi	- royal ancestors
Baas-skap	- color bar, segregation, apartheid, etc.
bakuhabule	- pollution
combi	- transportation
dliswata	- poisoned
emijondolo	- shanty towns
ibandla	- band
ichanti	- snake that can change shape at will
ichibi	- pool
idliso	- ground-up mixture--or poison
igqira	- a Xhosa diviner
ihubo	- a ritual song
iigazi elibi	- bad blood
imbovane	- ants
imimoya or imikhondo	- winds/airs or tracks
imimoya emibi	- evil spirits
iminyanya	- Xhosa--ancestors
imikhokha	- unfortunate consequences
impundulu	- lightning bird
indiki	- wandering spirit possession
indlamu	- a spectacular and non-sacred Zulu dance

indlamuihubo — as a magical song,

indlela — Zulu the melody or tune is the "path"

indlu — domestic unit

inhliziyo — heart used metaphorically

inkulu — elder

iNkosi inibusise — may God bless you all

inyanga — traditional herbalist

ilathi — worship--service of thanksgiving

isazela esiphilileyo — living consciousness

isazela esifileyo — dead consciousness leading to condemnation

isazela sengququko — conscience

isidalwa — mental retardation and/or deformed

isigekle — a type of ritual dance

isigodlo — healing homes

isigubudu — harmony

isikhali — staff or weapon

isisindo — weight

isithunsi — dead person--or shadow

isithunywa — messenger

isithuthwane — epilepsy

isiwasho — salt water and ashes

iSangoma or iSanusi — Nguni origin for traditional healers

ixwhale — Xhosa for herbalist

izembatho — forms of clothing

izinyanga — herbalist

izihlabelelo nezingoma — hymns and dance hymns

izikhali — weapons

izulu — heaven

khokheli — a Mama, a female leader

lobolo — payment for wife (dowry)

mamlambo — snake that changes into a young girl

mongameli	- main healer
moya	- wind
Muntu	- corporate personality
muthi	- traditional medicine shop and/or religious or ritual ceremony
muti	- medicine
Ngoma	- Zulu dance
palaza	- vomit
pneumata ta aktharta	- unclean spirits
Qongqothwane	- beetle
thikoloshe	- small mischievous homonculus
ubuthakathi	- poison (i.e., bewitched poison)
Udibi	- trainee
ufufunyane izizwe	- alien spirit possession
ufuzo	- familial and Genetic disorders
uhlanya	- schizophrenia (Madness)
ukubethela	- to fortify--ritual to prevent attacks
ukudlula	- disregard of cultural norms
ukudla kwendlebe	- harmonious music--food for the ear
ukufa kwabantu	- African cosmological diseases
ukugida	- dancing in a circle
ukuhlambuluka hlamba	- to clean or to clear
ukukhonsa	- congregational type of worship
ukukhonza	- congregational type of worship
ukusina	- a ritual, sacred dance
uku-sindiswa	- salvation
ukuthwasa	- ancestral spirit possession
ukusina	- sacred dance
ukusina okwejwayelekile	- the ordinary or common dance
ukuthelelana amanzi	- to pour water for each other
umego	- environmental hazards
umeqo	- stepping over harmful concoction

umhayizo/uvalo/iqondo	- sorcery
Umkhosi Omkhulu	- first-fruit ceremonies such as eating with the ancestors
umkhuhlane	- ailments
umkuhlane	- natural illness
umnyama	- pollution
umnyezane	- willow tree, or tree
umoya	- spirit or wind
umoya uyigwala	- cowardly (spirit)
umoya oyingcwele	- Holy Spirit
umprofethi	- healers i.e., medical doctors
umthandazi	- Zionist faith healer
Umvelingqangi	- God
umvusilelo	- revival service
uNozala	- begetter
un-shumayeli	- Preacher
uThixo	- God
zombi	- a resurrected corpse used by witches to do their bidding

BIBLIOGRAPHY

Ademuwagun, Z.A. African Therapeutic Systems. Crossroads,
    U.S.A. 1979.

Adler, D. "The Traditional Healers in Soweto." Pace Magazine,
    (pp.18-20), November, 1982.

Augustin, G. (ed.). Baptism in the New Testament. Chapman,
    London, 1964.

Balint, M. The Basic Fault. Tavistock, 1968.

Balz, H. Where the Faith has to Live. Part I, "Living
    Together." Heilbronn-Böckingen, 1984.

Barth, M. Die Taufe--eine Sakrament? Zürich, 1951.

Becken, H.J. "Healing in the African Independent Churches."
    Credo, XVII (2), (p.14-21), 1971.

_____ Theologie der Heilung: Das heilen in den
    Afrikanischen Unabhangigen Kirdren in Süd-Afrika.
    Missionshandlung, Hermannsburg, 1972

Bedard, W.M. The Symbolism of the Baptismal Font in Early
    Christian Thought. Washington, 1951.

Berglund, A.I. Zulu Thought-Pattterns and Symbolism.
    David Phillips, Cape Town. 1976.

Best, E. "Spirit-Baptism." Novum Testamentum, (pp.236-43),
    1960.

Blacking, J. "Political and Musical Freedom in the Music of Some
    Black South African Churches." From The Structure of Folk
    Models. ASA Monograph 20, Academic Press (pp.35-62), London,
    1981

Bloch, M. "Symbols, Song, Dance and Features of Articulation:
    Is Religion an Extreme Form of Traditional Authority?"
    Archives Europeennes de Sociologie, XV:1 (pp.55-81), 1974.

Buber, M. I and Thou. T. & T. Clark, 1944.

Bucher, H. Spirits and Power. Oxford, Cape Town, 1980

374

Bourdillon, M.F.C. The Shona Peoples: An Ethnography of
Contemporary Shona. Mambo Press: Gwelo. 1976.

Bührmann, M.V. "Inthlombe and Xhentsa: A Xhosa
Healing Ritual." Journal Analytical Psychology, 26, 1981.
_____ "Some Psychological Factors in Particular Crimes
of Violence in the Black man." South African Journal of
Criminal Law and Criminology, November, 1983, 7:1,
(pp.252-258), 1983.
_____ "Community Health and Traditional Healers."
Psychotherapeia, 30, pp.15-18, November, 1983.
_____ "Cultural Psychiatry." Journal of the South
African Institute of Psychotherapy, 36, (pp.7-12), 1985.
_____ "Xhosa Diviners as Psychotherapists."
Psychotherapeia, 31, (pp.17-20), 1977.
_____ "Western Psychiatry and the Xhosa patient."
South African Medical Journal, Vol.51, 1977.

Bromberg, W. The Mind of Man. 27, Harper, New York, 1937.

Bryant, A.I. Zulu Medicine and Medicine Men. Struik, Cape
Town, 1966.

Callaway, H. The Religious System of the Ama Zulu. Africana
Collectanea, Vol. XXV, C. Struick (Pty) Ltd., Cape Town,
1970.

Carrington, P. The Primitive Christian Catechism. Oxford,
1940.

Chavunduko, G. Traditional Healers and the Shona Patient.
Mambo Press, Gwelo. 1978.

Cheetham, R.W.S. "Conflicts in a Rural African Patient Treated
in an Urban Setting." Medicine, 30, (pp.1563-66), 1975

Cheetham, R.W.S. and Griffiths, J.A. "The Traditional
Healer/Diviner as Psychotherapist." South African Medical
Journal, 62, (pp.957-58), 1978.

_____ "Cross Cultural Psychiatry and the Concept of Mental Illness." South African Medical Journal, 58, (pp.320-25), 1976.

_____ "Concepts of Mental Illness Among the Rural Xhosa People in South Africa." Australian and New Zealand Journal of Psychiatry, 10, (pp.39-45), 1974.

_____ "Changing Patterns in Psychiatry in Africa." South African Medical Journal, 50, (pp.320-325), 1976.

_____ "Patients Before Healers: An Appraisal of the Isangoma in Society." South African Medical Journal, 58, (pp.959-60), 1980.

_____ "Sickness and Medicine an African Paradigm." South African Medical Journal, 62, (pp.877-79), 1982.

Chilivumbo, A.B. "Social Basis of Illness: A Search for Therapeutic Meaning." Grollig, F.X. and Haley, H.B. (eds.) Medical Anthropology, Mouton Publishers, The Hague, 1976.

Chonco, M. " The African Traditional Healers in Z.A." In Ademugan, J. Alloade, E. Harrison, and D. Warren (eds.) African Therapeutic Systems, (pp.21-32), Crossroads, U.S.A., 1979.

Colson, E. "Spirit Possession Among the Tonga of Zambia." In Beattie, J. and Middleton, J. (eds.) Spirit Mediumship and Society in Africa. Routledge and Kegan Paul, London. 1969.

Crehan, J.H. Early Christian Baptism and the Creed, London, 1950.

Cullmann, O. The Taufelehre der Neue Testament, Basel, 1948.

Daneel, M.L. Zionism and Faith-Healing in Rhodesia (Zimbabwe). Mouton, The Hague, 1970.

Dickson, K. Theology in Africa. Darton, Longman and Todd, London, 1984.

_____ Die Religion in Geschichte und Gegenwart. (pp.626-659). Tübingen, 1962.

Dix, G. The Theology of Confirmation in Relation to Baptism. London, 1946.

Dube, J.L. U Shembe. (In Zulu), Shuter and Shooter, Pietermaritzburg, 1936.

Durkheim, E. Elementary Forms of the Religious Life. Allen and Unwin, 1915.

Du Toit, B.M. "The Isangoma: An Adaptive Agent Among the Urban Zulu." Anthropological Quarterly, 2 (pp.51-65), 1971.

_____ and Abdalla, I.H. African Healing Strategies. Trado-Medic Books, New York, 1985.

Dzobo, N.K. "The Sociological Situation in Ghana Regarding Health and Healing." The Ghana Bulletin of Theology, 3(2), (p.6-7), 1967.

Edgerton, R.B.A. "A Traditional African Psychiatrist." Southwestern Journal of Anthropology, 27, (pp.3-29), 1971.

Edwards, F.S. "Healing and Transculturation in Xhosa Zionist Practice." Culture, Medicine and Psychiatry: (An International Journal of Cross-Cultural Research, 7, 1983.

_____ "Amafufunyana Spirit Possession: A Report on Some Current Developments." Religion in Africa, 5, No. 2, 1984.

Edwards, S.D. Some Indigenous South African Views on Illness and Healing. University of Zululand Publication, Series B No.49, 1985.

_____, Cheetham, R.W.S., Majozi, E., Lasich, A.J. "Zulu Culture-bound Psychiatric Syndromes." South African Journal Hospital Medical, 8, (pp.82-86), 1982.

_____ et al, "Traditional Zulu Theories of Illness in Psychiatric Patients." Journal of Social Psychology, 121, (pp.213-21), 1983.

Egan, G. The Skilled Helper. A Model for Systematic Helping and Interpersonal Relating. Brook/Cole, California, 1975.

Eiselen, W.M. "Christianity and the Religious Life of the Bantu." In Schapera, I. (ed.), Western Civilization and the Natives of South Africa. Oxford University Press, London, 1967.

Enklaar, I. Die scheiding der sacramenten op het zendingsveld. Amsterdam, 1947.

Evans Pritchard, E.D. Nuer Religion. Oxford University Press, New York, 1956.

_____ Witchcraft, Oracles and Magic Among the Azande. Clarendon Press, 1937.

Eysenck, H.J., Eysenck, S.B.G. The Eysenck Personality Questionnaire. Hodder & Stoughton, London, 1978.

Farrand, D. An Analysis of Indigenous Healing in Sub-urban Johannesburg. Unpublished Masters Thesis, University of the Witwatersrand. 1980.

_____ "Traditional Healing Practices and the Role of the 'Umprofethi'in the African Independent Church Movement." Proceedings of a Symposium on the Religious Movements in Southern Africa. University of Zululand Publication. 1985.

Fernandez, J.W. "The Precincts of the Prophet." Journal of religion in Africa, V (1), (pp.32-53), 1973.

Field, M.J. Search for Security. Northwestern University Press, Evanston, 1960.

Firth, R. Symbols: Public and Private. O.U.P., London. 1969.

Fleming, W.F. The New Testament Doctrine of Baptism. London, 1948.

Frank, J.D. "Therapeutic Factors in Psychotherapy." American Journal of Psychotherapy, 25, (pp.350-61), 1963.

378

Froise, M. (Ed.) South African Christian Handbook: 1986/87.
World Vision of Southern Africa, Florida, 1986.

_____ "Common Features of Psychotherapy." Australian
and New Zealand Journal of Psychiatry, 6 (pp.34-38), 1972.

Garfield, S.L. and Bergin, A.E. Handbook of Psychotherapy and
Behavior Change: an Empirical Analysis. (2nd edition)
Wiley, New York, 1978.

Gensichen, H.W. Das Taufe Problem in der Mission. Heidelberg,
1951.

Gilbert, A. and Gugler, J. Critics Poverty and Development:
Urbanization in the Third World. O.U.P., London, 1982.

Gilmore, A. (ed.) "Christian Baptism." London, 1959.

Green, E.C., and Makhulu, C. "Traditional Healers in
Swaziland: Toward Improved Co-operation between the
Traditional and Modern Health Sectors." Journal of Social
Science and Medicine. 18, (pp.1071-79), 1984.

Glick, L.B. "Medicine as an Ethnographic Category: the Gimi of
the New Guinea Highlands." Ethnology, 6(1), (pp.31-56),
1967.

Goba, B. "Corporate Personality: Ancient Israel and Africa." In
Moore, B. (ed.), Black Theology: the South African Voice.
C. Hurst & Company, London, 1973.

Gumede, M.V. "African Concepts of Sickness and Bodily
Suffering." Credo XII (3), (pp.7-15), 1965.

_____ "Traditional Zulu Practices and Obstetric
Medicine." South African Medical Journal, 4, (pp.823-824),
May 1978.

Gurman, A.S. "Rating Therapeutic Warmth and Genuiness by
Untrained Judges." Psychological Reports, 28, (pp.711-714),
1971.

Hammond-Tooke, W.D. "Worldview: A System of Beliefs." In
Hammond-Tooke, W.D. (ed.) The Bantu-speaking Peoples of
Southern Africa. Routledge and Kegan Paul, London. 1974.

_____ The Bantu-Speaking Peoples of Southern Africa. Routledge and Kegan Paul, 2nd edition, 1974.

_____ "In Search of the Lineage: the Cape Nguni Case." Man 19, (pp.77-93), 1984.

_____ "Who Worships Whom: Agnates and Ancestors Among Nguni." African Studies, 44, (pp.47-64), 1985

_____ "African World-view and its Relevance for Psychiatry." Psychologica African, 16, (pp.25-32), 1975.

Hanekom, C. Krisis en Kultus - Geloofsopvattinge en seremonies binne ñ Swart Kerk. Academica, Cape Town, 1975.

Hardman, O. A History of Christian Worship. S.C.M. London, 1948.

Harrison, F. "Music and Cult: The Functions of Music in Social and Religious Systems." Perspectives in Musicology, edited by Barry S. Brook, et al, W.W. Norton & Company, Inc. (pp.307-34), New York, 1975.

Hodgson, J. "The Faith Healer of Cancele: Some Problems in Analysing Religious Experience Among Black people." Religion in Southern Africa, 4(1), (pp.13-29), 1983.

Hoernlé, A.W. "Magic and Medicine." In Schapera, I. (ed.), The Bantu-speaking Tribes of South Africa, Routledge & Kegan Paul, Ltd., London, 1937.

Holdstock, T.L. "Indigenous Healing in South Africa: A Neglected Potential." South African Journal of Psychology, 9, (pp. 118-124), 1979.

Horton, R. "On the Rationality of Conversion." Africa, 45, (pp.219-35; 373-98). 1975.

_____ "African Traditional Thought and Western Science." I, Africa, 37.1, (pp.50-71), 1967.

Hunter, M. Reaction to Conquest. O.U.P., London. 1936.

HSRC, Religion, Intergroup Relations and Social Change in South Africa. Human Sciences Research Council, Pretoria, 1985.

380

Idowu, E.G. "Religion, Magic and Medicine--with Special
Reference to Africa." Orita 1(1), (pp.62-77), 1967.

Jeremias, J. "Die Kinder-Taufe in der ersten 4 Jahrhunderten."
Stuttgart, 1958.

Jung, C.G. Flying Saucers: A Modern Myth, Collected
Works. Vol. 10. Princeton University Press, Princeton.
1978.

_____ Wandlungen und symbole der Libido. Basel, 1912.

_____ Die Beziehungen zwischen dem Ich und Unbewusten.
Basel, 1928.

_____ Seelenprobleme der Gegenwart. Zurich, 1931.

_____ Psychology and Religion: West and East. Vol. II,
Collective Works, London, 1958. Translation of Psychologie
und Religion, Basel, 1937.

_____ Symbols of Transformation. Vol. 5, Collective
Works, London, 1959.

Junod, H.A. The Life of a South African Tribe. Macmillan,
London. 1927.

Kagame, A. La Philosophie Bantu. Revandaise de l'Etre,
Brussels, 1956.

Kiernan, J.P. "The 'Problem of Evil' in the Context of
Ancestral Intervention in the Affairs of the Living in
Africa." Man 17, (pp.287-301), 1982.

_____ "Where the Zionists Draw a Line: A Study of
Religious Exclusiveness in an African Township." African
Studies, 33(2), (pp.79-90), 1974.

_____ Ibid, pp.86-96

_____ "Prophet and Preacher: An Essential Partnership in
the Work of Zion." Man, N.S. 11, (pp.356-66), 1976.

_____ "The Work of Zion: An Analysis of an African
Zionist Ritual." Africa, 46, (pp.340-56), 1976.

_____ "Saltwater and Ashes: Instruments of Curing Among Zulu Zionists." Journal of Religion in Africa, IX (1), (pp.27-32), 1978.

_____ "The Weapons of Zion." Journal of Religion in Africa, X (1), (pp.13-21), 1979.

_____ "Zionist Communion." Journal of Religion in Africa, II, (pp.124-36), 1980

_____ "The Role of the Adversary in Zulu Zionist Churches." Unpublished, 1985.

Kiev, A. "Prescientific Psychiatry." American Handbook of Psychiatry, (Vol.3), Wiley, New York, 1959.

Kleinman, A. "Depression, Somatization and the New Cross-Cultural Psychiatry." Social Science and Medicine. 11, (p.3-10), 1977.

Klopfer, B., Davidson, H. The Rorschach Technique: An Introductory Manual. Harcourt Brace Jovanovich Inc., New York, 1962.

Krige, J.D. and Krige, E.J. The Realm of a Rain-Queen. O.U.P., London. 1943.

Kruger, D. The Changing Reality of Modern Man. Essays in Honour of J.H. van den Berg. Juta and Company, Cape Town. 1984.

_____ "The Africanization of the White South African." African Insight, 13,27. (pp.117-124), 1983.

_____ The Changing Reality of Modern Man. Essays in Honour of J.H. van den Berg. Juta & Co., Cape Town; Duquesne University Press, Pittsburgh; G.F. Callenbach, B.V. Mijkerk, 1984.

Lagerwerf, L. "Witchcraft, Sorcery and Spirit Possession." Exchange, 41, (pp.1-62), September 14, 1985.

Lampe, G.W.H. The Seal of the Spirit. London, 1951.

Laing, R.D. The Self and Others. Tavistock, 1961.

382

Lee, S.G. "Spirit Possession Among the Zulu." In
    Beattie, J. and Middleton, J. (eds.) Spirit Mediumship and
    Society in Africa. Routledge, London. 1969.
    _____ "Spirit Possession Among the Zulu." In Lewis, I.M.
    Ecstatic Religion. Penguin, Harmondsworth, 1971.
    _____ Manual of a Thematic Apperception Test for African
    Subjects. University of Natal, Pietermaritzburg, 1953.
Lierhardt, G. Divinity and Experience: The Religion of the
    Dinka. Clarendon Press, 1961.
Little, K. West African Urbanization - A Study of Voluntary
    Associations in Social Change. Cambridge University Press,
    Cambridge, 1965.
Mankazana, E.M. "A Case for the Traditional Healer in South
    Africa." South African Medical Journal, 2, (pp.1003-1007),
    1979.
Marsh, H.G. The Origin and Significance of the New Testament
    Baptism. Manchester University Press, Manchester, 1941.
Marwick, M. (ed.) Witchcraft and Sorcery. Penguin Books,
    London, 1972.
Mahrer, A. "The Therapist-Patient Relationship: Conceptual
    Analysis and a Proposal for a Paradigm Shift."
    Psychotherapy: Theory, Reserach and Practice, 15 No.3, 1978.
Mbiti, J. S. The Prayers of African Religion. Camelot Press
    Ltd. Southampton, 1975.
    _____ African Religions and Philosophy. Anchor Books,
    Heinemann and New York, 1969.
    _____ African Religion and Philosophy. Longman, London,
    1970.
    _____ "Our Stand Towards African Traditional Religion."
    Journal for Christian Writers in Africa, I(1), (pp.9-21),
    1973.

_____ Introduction to African Religion. Heinemann, London, 1975

Masamba ma Mpolo. "Kindoki as diagnosis and therapy." in Africa Theological Journal, 13 3, (pp.149-67), 1984.

Milingo, E. The World In Between: Christian Healing and the Struggle for Spiritual Survival. Edited by M. Macmillan, C. Hurst, 1984.

Mkhize, H. Traditional Healing Methods and Western Psychotherapies. Unpublished, MA thesis, University of Natal, Pietermaritzburg, 1981.

Mkhwanazi, I.S. An Investigation of the Therapeutic Methods of Zulu Diviners. MA thesis, University of South Africa, 1986.

Msomi, V.V. "Illness and Health in Zulu Thinking." Credo, XVIII (2), (pp.10-13), 1971.

Mthethwa, B.N. "Music and Dance in Zulu Christian Worship: Meaning of Religious Dances in the Shembe Church." Bulletin of the International Council for Traditional Music, (UK Chapter), 1985

Mutwa, C. "The Rate of the Medicine Man in Black Society." The Leech, 44(2), (pp.78-81), 1974.

Neher, A. "A Physiological Explanation of Unusual Behavior in Ceremonies Involving Drums." Human Biology, 34 No.2, 1962.

NICSSM. Ninth International Conference on the Social Sciences and Medicine. Section M, discussion group, Finland, 1985.

Nitscheke, H. Jungendgottesdienste. Gutersloh, 1976.

Ngubane, H. Body and Mind in Zulu Medicine. An Ethnography of Health and Disease in Nguwa Thought Patterns and Practice. Academic Press, London, 1977.

Norman, Ed. Christianity in the Southern Hemisphere--The Churches in Latin America and South Africa. Oxford University Press, USA, 1981.

Nxumalo, J.A. "Pastoral Ministry and African World-view." in Journal of Theology for Southern Africa, 28 (pp.27-36), 1979.

Oosthuizen, C.G. Post -Christianity: A Theological and Anthropological Study. Hurs, London, 1968.

_____ The Theology of a South African Messiah: An Analysis of the Hymnal of "The Church of the Nazarites." (Oekumenische Studiën 8), E.J. Brill, Leiden, 1967.

_____ Causes for Religious Independentism in Africa. Fort Hare University Press, 1968.

_____ "The Role of the Prayer-Healer (Umthandazi/Umprofeti) in the African Indigenous Churches." Sociological survey material.

_____ "Oosterse Mistiek in die Weste: Teorie en Praktyk," 1985.

_____ Baptism in the Context of the African Indigenous/Independent Churches (A.I.C.). 1986. Publications of the University of Zululand. Publications Series F:

Otoo, S. "The Need for Christian Healing Ministry." The Ghana Bulletin of Theology, 3(2), (pp.20-23), 1967.

Pauw, B.A. "African Christians and Their Ancestors." In Hayward, V.E.W. (ed.) African Independent Church Movements, I.M.C. Research Papers, No.11, Edinburgh House, London, 1963.

_____ "The Influence of Christianity." In Hammond-Tooke, W.D. (ed.) The Bantu-speaking Peoples of Southern Africa, 1974.

Rappaport, H., and Rapparport, M. "The Integration of Scientific and Traditional Medicine: A Proposed Model." American Psychologist, 36, (pp.774-781), 1981.

Rogers, C.R. "The Necessary and Sufficient Conditions of Therapeutic Personality Change." Journal of Consulting Psychiatry, 21, (pp.95-103), 1957.

Tarcliff, E.C. Liturgical Studies. S.C.M. London, 1976.

Thorpe, M.R. Psychodiagnostics in a Xhosa Zionist Church. MA thesis (unpublished), Rhodes University, Grahastown, 1982.

Turner, V.W. The Drums of Affliction. Oxford University Press, 1968.

Roberts, E.L. Shembe, the Man and His Work. MA thesis (unpublished), University of the Witwatersrand, Johannesburg, 1936.

Schmidt, H. and Power, D. "Liturgy and Cultural Religious Traditions" New York, 1977.

Schoffeleers, M.N. "Christ as the Medicine Man and the Medicine Man as Christ: A Tentative History of African Christological Thought." In Man and Life. 1-2, (pp.11-28), Calcutta 8, 1982.

Schweitzer, R.D. Categories of Experience Amongst the Xhosa. MA thesis (unpublished), Rhodes University, Grahamstown, 1975.

Shanz, J.P. "The Sacraments of Life and Worship." Milwaukee, 1966.

Shembe, J.G. (ed.) Izihlabelelo zama Nazaretha. Universal Printing Works, Durban, 1940.

Sibisi (Ngubane), H. "Spirit Possession and Zulu Cosmology." Whisson, M.G. and West, M. (eds.) Religion and Social Change in Southern Africa, David Phillip, Cape Town, 1975.

Sills, D.L. (ed.) International Encyclopedia of the Social Sciences. Vol. 6, (pp.330-336), Cromwell Collier and Macmillan Inc., 1968.

Sokhela, N.W. Personal Communication.

South African Medical Journal, Editorial: "Doctors and
　　Healers." S.A.M.J. 61,1. 1982.

Soyinka, W. Myth, Literature and the African World. Cambridge
　　University Press, London, 1976.

Stayt, H.A. Bantu Prophets in South Africa. O.U.P., London
　　1961.

Stead, M.H. "The Influence of Doctors' Attitudes on the
　　Patient's Response to Anti-Depressant Medication." Journal
　　of Nervous and Mental Disease. 136, (pp.555-66), 1963.

Stenzel, A. "Die Taufe: Eine genetische Erkläring der
　　Taufeliturgie." Hamburg, 1958.

Sundkler, B.G.M. Bantu Prophets in South Africa. Universal
　　Printing Works, Durban, 1961

　　　　　　　　　　Bantu Prophets in South Africa. (Second
　　edition), Oxford University Press, London, 1961.

　　　　　　　　　　Zulu Zion and Some Swazi Zionists. Oxford
　　University Press, 1976

Taylor, J.V. The Primal Vision: Christian Presence Amid Africa
　　Religion. SCM Press Ltd., London, 1963.

Tempels, P. Bantu Philosophy. Présence Africaine, 1959.

The New Bible Dictionary. IVP, London, 1962.

Thorpe, M.R. Psycho-Diagnostics in a Xhosa Zionist Church.
　　MA thesis (unpublished), Rhodes University, Grahamstown,
　　1982.

Toffler, A. The Third Wave. Pan Books, London, 1980.

Torrance, T. "The Origins of Baptism." Scottish Journal of
　　Theology, II, (pp.158-71), 1958.

Tracey, H. Lalela Zulu: 100 Zulu Lyrics. African Music Society,
　　Johannesburg, 1948.

Tshabalala, M.Z.H. Shembe's Hymnbook Reconsidered: Its Sources
　　and Significance. MA thesis (unpublished), University of
　　Aberdeen, Aberdeen, 1983

Tutu, D. "African Ideas of Salvation." Ministry, 10(1), (pp.119-23), 1970.

Vicedom, G.F. Die Taufe unter den Heiden. Hamburg, 1960.

Vicedom, M. Rites and Relationships: Rites of Passage and Contemporary Anthropology. Sage Publications, London, 1976.

Vilakazi, A.L., et al., Shembe: The Revitalization of African Society. Skotaville Publishers, Johannesburg, 1986.

_____ Zulu Transformations. University of Natal Press, Pietermartizburg, 1962.

Watts, H.L. "Some Reactions to Illness of Urban Black and Indian Families in Durban." South African Medical Journal, 57, (pp.589-91), 1980.

Weber, M. The Religion of China. Free Press, Glencoe, 1951.

Wegman, H.A.J. Geschichte der Liturgie im Westen und Osten. Regensburg, 1959.

Weidinger, G. and N. (ed.) Neu formen der Jungend Liturgie. Marburg, 1981.

Welbourn, F.B. "An Empirical Approach to Ghosts." First Congress of Africanists, Accra, 1962.

Weman, H. African Music and the Church in Africa. translated by Eric Sharpe, A.B. Lundequistska, Uppsala, 1960.

Wessels, W.H. "Culture-Bound Syndromes in South Africa." Proceedings of the Fourth National South Africa Congress of Psychiatry, Durban, 1985.

_____ "Symptomatology of Schizophrenia in the Bantu." Psychotherapeia, 2, (pp.5-7), 1976.

_____ "Histeriese psigose." Psychotherapeia, 29, (pp.22-25), 1983.

_____ "The Traditional healer and Psychiatry." Australia, New Zealand, Journal Psychiatry, 19, (pp.282-286), 1985(a).

388

_____ "Understanding Culture-Specific Syndromes in South Africa--the Western Dilemma." Modern Medicine of South Africa, 10 (9), (pp.51-63), 1985(b).

_____ "Cultural Psychiatry: Theory and Practice." South African Journal Continuing Medical Education, 3 (12), (pp.23-26), 1985(c).

West, Martin, Bishops & Prophets in a Black City. David Phillip, Cape Town, 1975.

_____ "The Shades Come to Town." In Whisson, M.G. and West, M.E., (eds.) Religion and Social Change in Southern Africa, David Philip, Cape Town, 1975.

Williams, C.S. Ritual Healing and Holistic Medicine Among Zulu Zionists. The American University, Ph.D. thesis (unpublished) Washington, 1982.

World Health Organization (WHO), Part I Apartheid and Health. Report of an International Conference Held at Brazzaville, People's Republic of the Congo, November 16-20, 198.

_____ Part II The Health Implications of Racial Discimination and Social Inequality: An Analytic Report to the Conference, Geneva, 1983.

Willoughby, W.C. The Soul of the Bantu, SCM, London, 1928.

Young, T.C. How Far Can African Ceremonial be Incorporated in the Christian System in Africa? Vol. VIII, (pp.210-17), 1935.

CONTRIBUTORS

Dr. H. Jurgen Becken
>
> Secretary for Africa; Association for Churches and
> Missions in South West Germany

Dr. M.V. Buhrmann
>
> Psychiatrist,
> Cape Town

Professor R.W.S. Cheetham (Emeritus)
>
> Former Head of Department of Psychiatry, Medical School,
> University of Natal

Mr. D. Dube
>
> Director, Enumenical Lay Centre,
> Edendale, Pietermaritzburg

Dr. F.S. Edwards
>
> Senior Lecturer, Faculty of Divinity,
> Rhodes University, Grahamstown

Professor S.D. Edwards
>
> Head, Department of Psychology,
> University of Zululand

Dr. J.A. Griffiths
>
> Practising Psychiatrist

Dr. M.V. Gumede
>
> Practising in African Township,
> Inanda, near Durban

Professor W.D. Hammond-Tooke
>
> Head, Department of Anthropology,
> University of Witwatersand

Professor Irving Hexham
>
> Department of Religious Studies,
> University of Calgary, Alberta, Canada

Ms. H.B. Mkhize

       Senior Lecturer, Department of Psychology,

       University of Zululand.

Ms. I. Mkhwanazi

       Principal, Nurses College,

       King Edward Hospital, Durban

Ms. M.B. Motala

       Post graduate Student, Department of Psychology,

       University of Durban, Westville.

Mr. B.N. Mthethwa

       Department of Music,

       University of Natal

Mr. L.M. Nene

       Senior Lecturer, Social Psychologist,

       University of Zululand

Professor G.C. Oosthuizen

       Director, Research Unit for the Study of New Religions

       and Independent/Indigeneous Churches (Sponsored by Human

       Sciences Research Council and University of Zululand)

Professor Karla Poewe

       Department of Anthroplogy,

       University of Calgary, Alberta, Canada

Professor W.H. Wessels

       Head, Department of Psychiatry,

       University of Natal Medical School, Durban

Dr. F.B. Welbourn (1912-1986) former Professor of Religious

       Studies at Makepere University, Uganda, and the

       University of Bristol

Index of Names

Abdalla, 23

Aquinas, 162

Asmus, 55

Associated Health Service Professions Act (No.63 or
    1982), 20

Balint, 364

Barth, 142

Becken, 117, 118, 133, 134, 191, 227

Bergin, 275

Berglund, 53

Buber, 366

Bucer, 173

Bucher, 54

Bolman, 312

Bourdillon, 54, 56

Bromberg, 93

Bührmann, 11, 25, 32, 276, 283, 298

Calvin, 159, 162, 173, 174

Callaway, 246

Carstairs, 265

Carkhuff, 271

392

Chavunduko, 23

Cheetham, 21, 259, 268, 269, 276, 295, 297, 302, 305

Chilivumbo, 217

Chrysostom, 186

Colson, 54

Daneel, 135

Davidson, 291

Dickson, 118

Dlomo, 232

Dowie, 175

Dube, 69, 109

Durkheim, 367, 368

Dzobo, 112

Edgerton, 198

Edwards, 11, 13, 17, 95, 191, 207, 216, 220, 260, 283, 337

Ehrenwald, 301

Eiselen, 197

Evans-Pritchard, 30, 63, 130, 353, 354, 356, 357, 358, 359, 361, 362, 367

Eysenck, 290

Farrand, 20, 22, 37, 41

Fernandez, 119

Field, 353, 356, 361

Firth, 55

Frank, 269, 276, 277, 309, 310, 316

Freud, 144, 145, 312, 361

Friedman, 324

Froise, 5

Garde, 324

Garfield, 275

Gelfand, 268

Glick, 113, 116, 119

Gluchman, 298

Green, 23

Griffiths, 21, 259, 268, 269, 276,295, 297, 305

Goba, 130, 131

Gumede, 112, 113, 260, 319

Hackland, 324

Hammond-Tooke, 11, 43, 47, 48, 53, 56, 77, 270

Hanekom, 196

Hodgson, 119, 122

Hoernlé, 113

Holdstock, 21

Horton, 46, 58, 356, 357

HSRC, 5

Hunter, 52

Indowa, 117

Joseph, 237

Jung, 33, 142, 143, 144, 145

Junod, 54, 56

Kiernan, 49, 63, 78, 119, 120, 121, 122, 123, 124,
    125, 126, 127, 128, 129, 130, 198, 202, 214, 298,
    299, 340

Kieve, 195

Kipkorir, 353

Klopfer, 291

Krige, 52, 55, 56

Kruger, 16, 221, 283

Lagerwerf, 80

Laing, 361

Lambo, 312

Larson, 324

Lee, 55, 89, 291

Lewis, 57

Lienhardt, 365

Little, 203

Luther, 159, 162, 164, 172, 173, 192

Luthuli, 233

Mahrer, 343, 344

Makhula, 23

Masamba, 80

Mbiti, 28, 30, 112, 132

Mdletshe, 238

Minuchin, 312

Mkhwanazi, 259, 261

Mkhize, 259, 264, 269, 281, 283

Mlandu, 235

Motala, 191, 193

Mpofana, 234

Msomi, 112

Mtsdhali, 184

Mthethwa, 191, 241

Nadel, 116

Neher, 340

Nene, 184

Nene, 11, 35

Ndebele, 197

Niebuhr, 60,

Ngrobo, 234

Ngubane, 56, 95, 112, 113, 114, 119, 125, 209, 212,
    219, 269, 283, 301

Norman, 195

Ntshobodi, 331, 332, 333, 334, 335, 336, 337, 338, 339,
    340, 341, 342, 343, 344

Nyambose, (alias Mtethwa) 235

Ogot, 237

Oosthuizen, 6, 7, 45, 69, 71, 134, 137, 209, 231

Otoo, 112

Paisley, 60

Pauw, 45, 59

Peale, 188

Philpott, 324

Rappaport, 21

Rogers, 312

Ross, 324, 326

Schlosser, 82

Schweitzer, 213, 217

Shembe, 192, 232, 234, 235, 236, 237, 243, 246, 248,
    249, 250, 251, 252, 255, 286, 287, 288
Sibisi, 212
Soga, 301, 303
Sokhela, 22
Stayt, 55, 56
Stead, 359
Sundkler, 45, 55, 56, 62, 82, 84, 99, 119, 121, 195,
    196, 202

Taylor, 131, 303
Tempels, 131
Thomas, 195
Tile, 139
Toffler, 16
Toit du, 23
Torrey, 268, 275, 276, 308, 309, 316
Truax, 271
Turner, 362, 364
Tutu, 135

Vicedom, 114
Vilakazi, 84, 115, 120

Warnes, 279, 311
Watts, 283

Weber, 365, 366

Welbourn, 237, 349, 363

Wessels, 21, 69, 91, 95, 100

West, 31, 32, 45, 82, 85, 87, 209, 263, 338

Whisson, 209, 215

Whitlock, 301

Williams, 122, 123, 123, 130, 133, 134, 135

Willoughby, 119, 135

Wittkower, 279, 311

Wolpe, 312

Zwingli, 162, 173

Index of Subjects

Adult baptism, 157, 169, 177

African: attitudes to healers, 38; Christians, 45, 46,
59, 65, 255, 256; culture, 264, 297; music, 243;
National Congress 73; population, 73; theology, 46

African Independent Churches, 5, 6, 27, 32, 62, 73, 75,
76, 77, 80, 81, 139, 140, 142, 145, 152, 159, 162,
168, 172, 174, 175, 177, 179, 180, 187, 229, 238,
263; causes for, 32, 33, 77

Africanized Christianity, iii

Akan, 353,

Allegory, 142

Altered states of consciousness, 301, 342

ama-Nazarites, See Nazareth Baptist Church

Amamzimtoti, 122

America, 231

Ancestor cult, 47

Ancestors, 27, 29, 30, 32, 49, 50, 51, 54, 55, 56n.,
64, 80, 81, 82, 83, 84, 85, 88, 95, 98, 102, 131,
146, 185, 209, 263, 264, 269, 289, 300, 301, 307

Ancestors, communication by, 48

Ancestors of clans, 29, 30, 47

Ancestors of river and forest, 29, 30

Ancestor worship: veneration, reverence, 27, 29

Anglicans, 5, 59

Anointing, 160, 167

Anthropology, 11, 51

Ants, used in muti, 211

Anxiety disorder, 98, 101

Apartheid, 65, 293, 321

Apostolic Churches, 73; Constitutions, 173; Faith
    Mission, 59; Full Gospel Church of Zion; 180; Holy
    Church in Zion, 214, 331, 337

Asceticism, 254

Ash: white ash, ash and water, 85, 86, 171, 173

Assistance: moral and material, 203

Associated Health Services Professions Act, 20

Azande/Zande, 30, 353, 356, 357, 359, 361, 364

Babies, sick, 183

Baboons, 56n.,

Backsliders, 180

Balance: harmony, idea of, 122, 135, 143, 146

Bantu Christian Church in Zion, 181; languages, 53

Baptism. See also Adult Baptism and Infant Baptism, 59,
    77, 141, 145, 147, 148, 154, 157, 160, 162, 167,

Baptism (continued)

187, 234, 341; by immersion, 166, 181; by

tri-immersion, 155, 165; fire, 160; house, 174; in

Zionist context, 141, 142; of the Holy Spirit, 59;

spirit, 160

Baptismal clothes, 161

Beaches, 77

Bible, 79, 80, 172

Biblical commands, 255

Bio-plus nerve tonic, 288

Bishops: archbishops, etc., 146, 151

Black Messiah, 235

Blessing: consecration, "payment", 170, 252

Bloemfontein, 184

Blood, 115, 211; of Christ, 163

Bophuthatswana, 21

Buddhism, 335

Cause of illness etc., - as a "who" question, 116, 265,

339, 357

Calvary, 152

Calvinism, 60

Canada, 343

Candles, 146, 160, 173, 182

Cannibalism, 53

Cape Nguni, 47, 51, 55

Catharsis, 199, 246

Catholic, 60; Apostolic Church, 59

Chaos, 140, 218, 219, 340

Charisma, charismatic, 45, 73, 151

Charms, 120

Catechism, instruction in, 157, 176

Chicago, 175

Chickens, use of, 130, 185

Childbirth, 174

Children, 155, 287

Christians, 11, 45, 59, 61, 80, 83, 141, 238, 248, 331

Christianity, 30, 32, 45, 50, 59, 61, 75, 89, 178, 186,
    246, 249, 335

Christology, 152

Church, 73, 159, 289; statistics, 5, 73-74

Circle, significance of, 146, 175, 182, 183, 186, 341

Clans, 29, 48, 129

Clothing, clothes, 123, 161, 167, 252

Cognition, 45, 50, 179

Collective consciousness/unconscious, 143, 144, 145;
    responsibility, 134

Colors, 123, 176, 182, 267

Community, 126, 128, 131, 134, 178, 293

Consecration. See Blessing

Consciousness, 331, 333, 334, 335, 342

Concern for the person, 133, 135

Confession, 158, 199, 254

Congregational church, 5, 122

Consultations with diviners, 307

Control, of life, 218, 219

Conversion reports, 234

Cooperation between traditional healers and modern
    medical practitioners, 22, 312

Coping procedures, 266

Cords, sacred, 86, 123, 215

Corporate personality, 79, 130

Corpus christianum, 157

Cosmic rhythms, 114

Cosmology, 47, 58, 73, 76, 77, 88, 119, 140, 268, 270,
    276

Council of Associated Health Professionals, 21

Creation myths, 58

Crosses, 145, 153

Crossroads, 231

Cults of affliction, 57

Culture, 255, 270, 340, 344, 345; specific syndromes,
    105, 222

Cultural values, 276

404

Dance, dancing, 147, 167, 173, 183, 186, 230, 245, 247,
248, 249, 251, 255, 256, 340

Dead, death, 143, 253, 201, 308

Decent groups, 47, 64, 65

Deformity, 97

Democracy, 152, 174

Demons. See Devils

Deprivation, 285

Depression, 102, 103, 211

Depth psychology, 32, 144

Devils, demons, etc., 47, 146

Diagnosis, symptomology, 18, 98, 116, 210, 211, 216,
224-225, 268, 309, 310, 335, 337, 356,

Diagrams and Tables, 16, 17, 18, 19, 38-41, 64, 94-108,
180-187, 224-225, 272-274, 279, 290-291, 315-317,
321-323, 354-355, 360

Dice, 55

Disease. See Illness

Dislocation, 65

Divination, 55, 84, 263, 265, 309, 338

Diviners, 40, 62, 82, 83, 85, 86, 87, 94, 108, 119,
263, 266, 267, 299, 303, 342, 353; professionals,
264; training of, 308; paraphernalia, 277;
difference between them and Prophets, 94-95, 263;
compared to therapists, 279, 315-317, 321-323;
different roles of, 299, 210

Doctrine, 46

Domestic servants, 184, 199, 286

Donatist, 160

Dreams, 32, 85, 119, 143, 234, 287, 288, 307, 341

Drums, drumming, 57, 167, 253, 256, 341

Dualism, 150

Durban, 133, 141, 184, 229, 297

Dutch Reformed Church, 5

Dynamic, aspect of African beliefs, 165, 177, 180, 233

Early Church, primitive Church/Christianity, 74, 75,
    80, 142, 148, 149, 150, 153, 155, 157, 164, 168

Easter, 147, 150

Eastern Cape, 209; mysticism/religion, 144, 201

Eastern Orthodox Church-Greek Orthodox Church, 60, 161,
    167, 169

Ebuhleni, 231

Ecstatic religion, 57

Ecumenical, 183

Emotions, emotional, 46, 143, 199, 201, 244, 277, 297,
    309, 310

Empathy, 266, 271

Empirical consequences, 356

Envy, 53, 255

Epilepsy, 97

406

Eschaton, eschatology, 149, 150

Esikhawini Township, 16

Essenes, 150

ESP (Extra Sensory Perception), 363

Established Churches. See Mainline Churches

Ethiopian Churches, 73

Europe, Europeans, 30, 47, 174, 219, 231, 361, 362

Evangelicals, 59, 60

Evil, problem of, 53; spirits, 76, 77, 96, 127, 146,
    167, 169, 181, 183, 186, 210, 221

Existential situation, crisis, 145, 286

Exorcism, 57, 79, 167, 169, 171, 173, 176, 182

Expectations, of patients, 325

Faith, 164, 167, 199, 253, 331; healer/healing, 17, 18,
    22, 23, 33, 37, 94, 101, 102, 108, 236, 237, 263,
    277

False prophets, 75

Family, 179, 203, 307, 323, 361

Fasting, 148, 169, 187, 334, 336

Fear, 308, 311

Federal Republic of Germany, 323

Female revolt, 58

Feminist subculture, 57

First Fruits Ceremony, Zulu, 147

Flags, 145, 175, 186, 230

Fluid retention, 103

Forgiveness, 232, 233, 254

Ganda, 353, 362

Gastro-intestinal tract disorder, 102

Genealogy, 47, 56

Glasgow Missionary Society, 59

Glossolalia, 89

Gloucestershire, 359

Gnostics, gnosticism, 152, 157, 159, 160, 162

God, 58, 59, 61, 75, 162, 169, 197, 230, 245, 246, 247,
    248, 252, 253, 254, 263, 286, 289, 332, 339; the
    Father, 60, 61, 238

Gods, 33

Grace, 162

Grahamstown, 331

Graves, 210

Great Umkhosi, 140

Greek, documents, 166; Orthodoxy, see Eastern Orthodox
    Church

Group, therapy/support, 87, 199, 270, 289

Guilt, 153, 162, 220, 285

Hair, of diviner and prophet, 86

Harare, 231

Harmony. See Balance

Healers, 210, 270, 299, 303

Healing: cures, iii, 27, 31, 74, 75, 76, 88, 116-119,
   126, 128, 129, 133, 134, 135, 156, 179, 198, 209,
   230, 236-239, 246, 253, 297, 302, 333, 357, 341;
   context, 15, 75-80, 293; ministry, 73; services,
   129-130, 215, 339; and salvation, 111, 116, 117

Health, 29, 111-116, 135, 146; education, 23

Herbalists, 40, 75, 211

Heretics, 162

Hinduism, 335, 341

Hlabisa District, 234

Holism, holistic, wholeness, 28, 75, 79, 112, 130-133,
   134, 216, 229, 232, 236, 297, 333

Holy: communion, 166, 179, 185; family, 61; Spirit,
   iii, 11, 32, 45, 53, 54, 58-63, 83, 107, 123, 125,
   146, 147, 149, 161, 163, 164, 167, 174, 181, 182,
   216; stick, rod, staff or staves, 85, 146, 174,
   182, 186, 229; water, 107

Hostels, 184

Homesteads, 50, 264

Human Sciences Research Council of South Africa (HSRC),
   7

Hymns, 126, 143, 249, 251, 340

Hypnotic, 301

Hysteria, 100, 106, 221

Hysterical psychosis, 100

Identity, 123, 143, 222, 321

Illegitimate children, 220

Illness, 45, 57, 73, 75, 76, 78, 85, 87, 88, 95, 104,
    112, 114, 115, 117, 128, 130, 131, 134, 174, 183,
    235, 236, 238, 239, 253, 254, 265, 266, 300, 325,
    331, 334, 335, 354, 367n.,

Indians, 219, 237; languages, 56

Indigenous healing. See Traditional Healing

Indigestion, 102

Individual/ism, 57, 134, 143, 204, 209, 222, 300, 361

Infant baptism, 155-156, 164, 177, 179, 182. See also
    Baptism

Initiations, 150, 164, 180

Intellectual. See Rational

Interpersonal relationships, 217, 357, 367

Insecurity, 115, 120, 132, 220

Integration of traditional healing and modern medicine,
    19, 297, 312, 353, 368. See also Cooperation

Israel, 150

I-Thou, 366

Izingayi trees, 234

Jesuits, 54

Jesus Christ, 60, 74, 80, 82, 132, 141, 150, 151, 153,
    156, 158, 159 163, 164, 234, 341

Jewish, 173

Johannesburg, 170n., 184

John the Baptist, 141, 148, 149, 150, 154

Jordan, river, 141

Judaism, 151

Justification, 151

Kampala, 353

Karanga, 56

Kenya, 353

Kgaga, 48, 54, 56

Khoi, 59

Kimbangu Church, 160

King Edward VIII Hospital, Durban, 297

Kinship, 50, 129, 133

Kiss of peace, 161, 168

Kleptomania, 104

Kwa-Dlangezwa, 16

Kwa-Mashu, 185

Kwa-Zulu, 17

Labelling, of illness, 266, 267

Lady Frere, 220

Language, 286, 309

Laying on of hands, 154, 160, 167, 289

Leaders, 55, 57, 84, 166

Leadership, 287

Legalism, 151, 179

Lesotho, 184

Libations, 49

Life, 143; histories, 263, 284, 289

Lineages, 47, 129

Liturgy, 168, 169, 171, 173

Literacy, 247

Living dead. See Ancestors

Lobedu, 54

London Missionary Society, 59

Louis Trichardt, 170n.,

Love potions, 100, 221

Lower Umfolozi, 17

LSD trips, 368

Luck, 58

Lutherans, 5, 59

Madness, 307

Magic, 33, 93, 95, 164, 178, 359, 362

Mainline, established or historic, Christians/Churches, 45, 54, 59, 80, 82, 155, 159, 179, 184, 185, 187, 213, 249, 255

Malawi, 88

Marginality, 63

Marakwet, 353

Marriage, problems, 88, 107, 286, 324

Mary, cult of worship, 60

Massaging, 216

Medical aid, 327

Medicine. See also Muti, 353, 356; dangerous, 114

Mediums, 55, 56n.,

Mental health team, 283; mental confusions, 336

Messengers, mystical, 120

Metanoia, 149

Metaphor, 50, 60, 61

Methodists, 5, 59, 163, 184

Middle Ages, 170, 186

Milk and honey, 161, 168

Minister, 129

Mission Churches, 31, 76, 178, 179; situation, 176, 180; studies, 231, 237

Missionaries, 45, 58, 59, 75, 77, 231

Misfortune, 51

Modern medicine 15, 16, 21

Modernization, 23, 78

Money, 187

Montanism, 152

Morality, 50

Moravians, 59

Mortality rates, 324

Mother/s, 174

Mozambique, 54, 56, 88

Mulago Hospital, Kampala, 353

Music. See African music, 243, 256

Muti, 17, 97, 99, 100, 101, 106, 115, 120, 176, 185, 299

Myths, 121, 148, 309, 310

Mystical: attacks, 125; cause, 353, 354, 356, 359; forces, 113, 115, 116, 131, 353

Mysterious noises, 115

Mystery cults, 160, 186

Natal, 54; Medical School, 6

Nativistic movements, 45

Nazareth Baptist Church, 246-255, 285, 288; head of, 231, 253; succession struggle, 231; testimonies, 231, 234

Nazareth Church. See Nazareth Baptist Church

Ndau, 54, 56

NERMIC, See "Research Unit ..."

New Holy Church in Zion of South Africa, The, 165

New Testament, 118, 153, 210, 213, 216

Ngoya, 16, 56

Nguni, 31, 49, 50, 55, 56, 59, 297, 301

Nominalists, 162

North Eastern Transvaal, 209

Obsessive Compulsive Disorder - 104

Oil. See Anointing

Old Testament, 171

Orange Free State, 184

Order of Ethiopia, 213

Ordination, ordained, 163

Orthodox Christianity. See Mainline Churches

Paradox, 151

Paradigm, 343, 344

Paralysis of legs, 103

Peace, 143, 161

Pedi, 54

Pentecostals, 60, 163

Pentecostalism, 144

Personal/ality, 204, 217, 290

Personality assessment, 290-291

Phenomenology, 15, 148, 275

Phungashe Clinic, 327

Pietists, 163, 174

Placebo, 359

Pollution, 114

Polygamy, 324

Protection, 269

Positive thinking, 188

Possession, 54, 55, 57, 64, 75, 210; by ancestors, 210;
    by airplanes, 56; ceremonial, 210; cults, 55,
    64; mass outbreaks of, 210; shamanistic, 210

Power, 61, 62, 125, 164, 170n., 181, 266,

Powerlessness, 62

Prayer/praying, 127, 166, 237, 252, 340, 343; healer,
    73, 74, 75, 85, 89

Preaching, 126

Presbyterians, 59

Pretoria, 184

Priest, 15, 23, 34

Primitive Church. See Early Church

Prophecy, 74, 84, 185, 337; as diagnosis, 337

Prophet/s, prophet-healers, 73, 74, 78, 80-82, 83, 85,
    87, 89 94, 95, 100, 106, 108, 119, 185, 210, 214,
    249, 250, 284, 287, 331, 333, 338, 340, 342, 343;
    life history of, 85, 284-289

Prostitution, 115

Protestant, 177, 179

Protection, 299, 302

Protecting objects. See Weapons

Psychiatrists, 303

Psychoanalysis, 359

Psychological, 289

Psychology, 187, 195, 218, 292, 293, 299, 360

Psychologists, 17

Psychiatric value, 139

Psychic, 358, 366

Psychosis, 98, 100, 219

Psychosomatic illness, 57, 87, 102, 325, 358, 360, 361

Psychotherapist, 275, 310, 343

Psychotherapy, 266, 307, 309, 310

Purification rites, 32, 81, 157

Puritanism, 366

Questions: "how" and "why" in explaining disease, 298

Qumran, 149, 150

Race, 151, 196, 211, 345

Rand area, 81

Rational/intellectual, 143, 202, 363, 364, 367

Rebirth, 146-148, 158, 163

Recruitment, 57

Reformation, 168

Reformed Church of Africa, 184

Rejection of alcohol, etc., 73

Religion, 27, 32, 46, 55; in Africa, 209n.,

Religious convictions, 286; exclusiveness of Zionists, 127; experience, 255, 300; groups, 368

Revival meetings, 165, 287

Research Unit for the Study of New Religious Movements and Indigenous Churches (NERMIC), 7

Research methods and areas identified, 23, 24, 200, 284

Revelation Apostolic Church, The, 170n.,

Rhodes University, 331n.,

Rite of passage, 146, 148, 177, 179

Ritual/s, 30, 33, 45, 49, 55n., 64, 76, 78, 79, 82, 106, 114, 135, 164, 168, 170, 245, 246, 251, 265, 268, 277, 310, 362

Robes. See Uniforms

Roman Catholics, 5, 59, 161, 167, 170, 171, 173, 184, 185

Roman religion, pagan, 171, 173

Rhythm and harmony, 243, 340

Sabbath, 250

Sacrament, 142, 154, 161, 164, 177, 187, 239

Sacrifices, 30, 47, 51, 55n., 130, 164, 171, 269, 342

Sashes, 127

Salt, 170, 171, 172

418

Salvation, 233; Army, 163

Saint John Apostolic Faith Mission, 168

Saint John's College, Cambridge, 353

Saint Matthew's Apostolic Church of Christ, 181;
    Mission, 219

Sanctification, 151

Satan, 150

Scapegoat mentality, 79

Schizophrenia, 96, 105

Scientific, 143, 358, 364

Scholasticism, scholastics, 160, 162

Schools, of leaders, 57

Sea of Galilee, 141

Sea, water, 85, 155

Secular, 63

Secularization, 174

Self-understanding, 344

Sense of order. See Control of life

Sex, 33, 285, 366,

Shades, 50

Shaman, 210, 307

Shave cult, 54, 56n.,

Shona, 54

Shoulders, 182

Sickness. See Illness

Sign of the Cross, 168

Sin, 75, 148, 149, 151, 153, 158, 168, 233, 235, 254,

Singing, 85, 147, 167, 184, 230, 245, 249

Social change, 54, 321; relationships, 75, 78, 299,
    357; order, 307; structure, 367

Socioeconomic level, 292

Sociology, 364, 365

Somatic, 358, 361

Sorcerers, 29, 78

Sorcery, 51, 73, 75, 76, 100, 101, 114, 120, 217, 220,
    221, 339

Sotho/s, 487, 55, 184

South Africa, i, ii, 5, 21, 62, 63, 73, 88, 177, 181,
    187, 205, 229, 292, 293

South African National Congress of Psychiatrists, 6;
    Medical and Dental Council, 20, 21; Medical
    Journal, 20

South Sotho, 55, 211

Soweto, 81

Speaking in other tongues, 56

Spectators, at a dance, 252

Spells, 121

Spirit mediumship, 55; possession, 55, 56n., 75, 76,
    80, 98, 209-222, 224-225, 307; epidemic of, 220;
    different types, 210;

Spirit/s, 28, 46, 52, 53, 56n., 64, 80, 31, 99, 173,
    211, 214, 307, 364; of affliction, 54-58

Spirit of God, 331, 332, 334, 337

State Church, 157

Statistics, 18, 39, 271-274, 323, 326

Strengthening, 125, 310

Stress, 222

Stuttgart, 231

Supernatural, 15, 75, 118, 119

Suffering, 32, 45

Sufi, 342

Suggestion, 267

Sunday, 157. See Sabbath,

Supreme Being, 58, 121, 301, 358

Superstition, 80, 164

Survey, research, 17, 18, 37, 81, 93, 199, 271, 278

Suspicion, 217

Swaziland, 21, 23

Symbol/s, 145, 146, 158, 161, 171, 216, 266, 340; of
    transformation, 144

Symbolism, ii, 50, 58, 77, 80, 139, 140, 142, 144, 341

Symptoms, See Diagnosis

Syncratism, 45, 63-65, 178

Synod of Carthage, 156

Taüfbuchlein, 172, 173

Technology, 16, 358, 366

Tension, personal, 244

Thembu Church, 139

Theologians, 27, 46

Theological education, 174

Theology, 46, 58, 60, 174, 209, 234

Therapy, 264, 266, 270, 234

Therapist, 266, 298, 343, 344

Therapeutic, 363

Thixo, 59

Thorns, 234

Thrashing, to drive out evil spirits, 167, 170, 181

Thunderstorms and dance, 252

Time, 141

Tonal music, 244

Tongues, 143, 211

Townships, 115, 181

Traditional African society, 6, 75, 82, 178, 248, 323

Traditional beliefs, 31, 37, 54, 58, 59, 62, 75, 87,
     88, 96, 111, 117 119, 250, 267; customs, 96, 97,
     141, 252; healing practices, medicine, etc., 7, 11,
     15, 21, 76, 82, 83, 84, 85, 111, 116, 185, 209,
     213, 268, 283, 292, 307, 312, 342, 357; healers,
     17, 94, 263, 297, 300, 303, 307, 326, 357;

Traditional beliefs (continued)

    healers/persecuted, 283; /differences in Western

    medicine, 321-323

Traditionalists, 250

Trance, 50, 57, 211

Transcendence, 141

Transcultural psychology, 22

Transkei, 220

Transpersonal consciousness, 335

Transvaal, 54

Treatment methods, 19, 81, 116, 127, 213

Tribalism/de-tribalism, 195, 196

Trinity, 53, 59, 60, 62, 154, 158, 159

Trust, 127

Tsonga, 47, 54, 56

Tswanas, 184

Unconscious, 144

Uniforms, 123, 166, 174, 186, 216

University of: Durban-Westville, 209n; Ottawa, 343;

    Zululand, 7, 11, 16; Department of Psychology,

    (Zululand) 17, 37

Urban areas, 87, 115, 120, 128, 131, 132, 195, 323

Urbanization, 23, 195, 323

Vaseline, 289

Venda, 48, 54

Venereal disease, 101

Vestments, 86

Violence, in Black Townships, 182

Visions, 247

Vomiting, 107, 170, 216

Watch-night services, 148, 167

Wandlungen und Symbole der Libido, 144

Water, 121, 122, 124, 165, 167, 168, 170, 181, 182,
    341, 365

Weapons, 79, 84, 121, 124, 127

Western churches, 197; medicine, doctors, psychology,
    76, 93, 104, 107, 219, 269, 283, 292, 297, 302,
    309, 312, 359; music, 243; observers, 235; thought,
    28, 37, 229, 338

White people, 56n.,

Witch, beliefs, 51-54, 53, 58

Witches, 29, 45, 52, 62, 64, 78, 362, 364

Witchcraft, 58, 75, 76, 79, 96, 120, 298, 308, 353,
    356, 357, 358, 367

White ash. See Ash

Wholeness. See Holistic

Women, role of, 128-129

World Health Organization (WHO), 20

Church, visible and invisible, 112

Worldview, 46, 65, 75, 76, 87, 89, 113, 263, 276, 309, 310

Worship, 27, 198, 245, 247, 248, 250, 302, 340

Xhosa, 184, 211, 298, 301, 331

Zande. See Azande

Zambia, 54

Zaire, 160

Zimbabwe, 21, 23, 54, 88, 231

Zion, 111, 128, 132

Zion Christian Church (ZCC), 6, 196-203; Zion City, Illinois, 73

Zionist/s, 45, 46, 57, 62, 63, 73, 74, 78, 82, 84, 85, 111, 115, 116, 120, 122, 125, 126, 127, 162, 166, 167, 170, 173, 201, 205, 209, 213, 214, 287, 331, 334; congregations, 57, 59, 62, 64, 88, 118, 128, 166, 202; healer, 119-123; healing, 117-119, 123-125, 127; homesteads, 125; services, 202, 250

Zombi, 52

Zulu, 54, 56, 62, 84, 184, 212, 213, 219, 243, 245, 252, 255, 323; law, 20; music 243

Zululand, 212, 229

Index of African Terms

abafundisis/abapristi, 37

abaphansi, 93

abaprofethi/abathandazi, 37, 38

abaphansi basifulatele, 98, 102

Abapostoli, 73

amakhosi, 147

amandla, 181

amandiki, 55

amandawe, 55

amadlozi, 53, 55, 300, 301

amafufunyana, 209-222

amaggira, 209, 213

amathongo, 53

amaTopi, 73

amaZion, 73

anngiphelele, 124n.,

badimo, 53

basifulatele, 93

dithuri, 53

dithongwa, 53

gobela, 57

ibandla, 128

ichanti, 51, 52

ichibi, 122

igondo, 98

idliso, 93, 98, 102, 211

ihubo, 248

iigazi elibi, 115

imikhondo, 113

imikhokkha, 129

imimoya emibi, 167

iminyanya, 300

imioya, 113

impundulu, 51

indiki, 55, 56, 98, 100

idliso, 216, 221

idlosi, 302

indlela, 249

inkulu, 47

inhliziyo, 120

insila, 123

inthlombe, 32

inyanga, 17, 18, 93, 102, 105, 106

iqondo, 94, 101

iSangoma, 17, 18, 55, 93, 105, 185, 263-268, 270-271,
   275, 276. 277, 279, 297-300, 302, 303, 323

isidalwa, 93, 95, 97

isigekle, 248, 249, 255

isigubudu, 244

isikhali, 124

isithunsi, 300

isithunywa, 120

isithutwane, 93, 94, 97-98

isiwasho, 121, 122, 170

ixwhele, 211

izangoma/izinyanga, 37, 40, 321, 322, 324

Izanzela, 333

Izazela esiphilileyo, 331, 332

Izazela sengququko, 332, 337

izembatho, 121

izigodlo, 133

izihlabelelo nezingoma, 249

izikhali, 121

izilwane, 53

izizwe, 93, 98, 99, 100

izulu, 52, 121

khokeli, 182

lelopa, 56

428

manlambo, 51

masabe, 54

mashave, 56

Modimo, 59

mokhoma, 57

mongameli, 216

moya, 53, 185

Muntu, 130

muthi (or muti), 17, 97, 98, 100, 101, 102, 128

palaza, 170, 182

Qamata, 59

thwasa, 31

thikoloshe, 51, 52

Thixo, 59

tshilombo, 56

ubuthakathi, 84

ufufunyane, 93, 98, 99, 100

ufuka kwabantu, 98, 105

ufuzo, 95

uhlanya, 93, 95, 96-97, 124

umhayizo, 100

umkhuhlane, 113

ukubethela, 125

ukubuyisa, 50

ukufa kwabantu, 95, 96, 113

ukugida, 216

ukuhlambuluka, 124n., 126

ukuhlane, 95

ukubethela, 115

ukukhonza, 247, 248

ukusina, 247, 248, 249, 250, 251, 253, 254, 255

ukosina okwejwayelekile, 249

ukuthelenlana amanzi, 121, 121n.,

ukuthwasa, 81, 98, 307

umbelini, 31

umeqo, 93, 98, 103

umhayizo, 93, 98

Umkhosi Omkhulu, 147

umkuhlane, 95, 104

umnyama, 93, 98, 102

umnyezane, 123

umpundulu, 52

umpropheti, 93

umthandazi, 15, 17, 18, 22, 93

umoya, 119, 121, 123, 126, 127, 128, 132

umoya oyingcwele, 181

uMvelingqangi, 84

umvusilelo, 160, 165

Unkulunkulu, 59

uNozala, 124

uvalo, 98

xhanntsa, 32 - Being, 58

Index of Biblical References

Acts 8:36, 8:16, 19:1-7; 154

1 Chronicles 15:29, 247n.

2 Chronicles 13:5, 171, 172

Colossians 152, 2:12,153; 4:6, 172

1 Corinthians 1, 1:13, 15; 6:11, 151; 7:7, 151;
    12:4ff, 151; 13:8-12, 74

2 Corinthians 1:21ff, 152

Ecclesiastes 3:4, 247n.

Ephesians 152

Exodus 7:9-12, 86; 15:20, 247n.

Ezekiel 47:11, 172

Genesis 341

Hebrews 9:10, 149; 10:22, 154

Isaiah, 53, 341

Jeremiah 31:13, 247n.,

John 3:5, 156; 3:23, 149; 5:22ff, 158; 9:7, 158

432

Joel 2:27-29, 341

Judges 13:5, 86

2 Kings 2:19ff, 171, 172

Lamentations 5:15, 247n.,

Leviticus 2:13, 172

Luke 8:26, 29, 210; 12:50, 149

Mark 1:4, 148; 7:4, 149; 7:34, 169; 9:50, 171, 172;
    10:38, 149

Matthew 3:11, 150; 5:13, 172; 8:28-34, 210; 19:14,
    155; 20:22ff, 149; 28:19, 154

Numbers 18:19, 171, 172

Psalms 149:3, 247n; 150:4, 247n.

Romans 5:5, 161; 6:5, 163; 6:10, 10:9, 151; 12:6ff,
    151

1 Samuel 1:11, 86; 18:6, 247n.

2 Samuel 6:14, 21, 247n.

Titus 1:9, 171; 3:5ff, 163

AFRICAN STUDIES

1. Karla Poewe, **The Namibian Herero: A History of their Psychosocial Disintegration and Survival**

2. Sara Joan Talis, **Oral Histories of Three Secondary School Students in Tanzania**

3. Randolph Stakeman, **The Cultural Politics of Religious Change: A Study of the Sanoyea Kpelle in Liberia**

4. Ayyoub-Awaga Bushara Gafour, **"My Father the Spirit-Priest": Religion and Social Organization in the Amaa Tribe (Southwestern Sudan)**

5. Rosalind I.J. Hackett (ed.), **New Religious Movements in Nigeria**

6. Irving Hexham, **Texts on Zulu Religion: Traditional Zulu Ideas About God**

7. Alexandre Kimenyi, **Kinyarwandi and Kirundi Names: A Semiolinguistic Analysis of Bantu Onomastics**

8. G.C. Oosthuizen, S.D. Edwards, W.H. Wessels, I. Hexham (eds.), **Afro-Christian Religion and Healing in Southern Africa**

9. Karla Poewe, **Religion, Kinship, and Economy in Luapula, Zambia**

10. Mario Azevedo (ed.), **Cameroon and Chad in Historical and Contemporary Perspectives**

11. John Eberegbulam Njoku, **Traditionalism vs. Modernism at Death: Allegorical Tales of Africa**

12. David Hirschmann, **Changing Attitudes of Black South Africans Towards the United States**